# HOW
# DO MORE
## IN LESS TIME

### THE COMPLETE GUIDE TO INCREASING YOUR PRODUCTIVITY AND IMPROVING YOUR BOTTOM LINE

## ALLISON C. SHIELDS AND DANIEL J. SIEGEL

ABA LAW
PRACTICE
DIVISION
The Business of Practicing Law

# Contents

# About the Authors

**Allison C. Shields, Esquire**

Allison is the President of Legal Ease Consulting, Inc., where she provides coaching and consulting services for lawyers and law firms on practice management and business development issues, including productivity, law firm operations, billing, client service, marketing and social media. Her goal is to help improve law firm efficiency so that lawyers can focus on serving their clients.

Allison is a former law firm manager and partner. She is a nationally recognized speaker, presenting workshops and programs in both public and private settings. She is the author of numerous published articles on practice management and business development/marketing issues. She writes the *Legal Ease Blog* (www.legaleaseconsulting.com) and the Simple Steps column for *Law Practice Magazine*, the Law Practice Division's magazine. Her website, Lawyer Meltdown (www.lawyermeltdown.com), provides resources and information for lawyers about managing and building their practices. She is the co-author, with Dennis Kennedy, of *LinkedIn in One Hour for Lawyers* and *Facebook in One Hour for Lawyers*. Allison can be reached at Allison@LegalEaseConsulting.com.

## Daniel J. Siegel, Esquire

Attorney Siegel is the founder and President of Integrated Technology Services, LLC, a practice management consulting firm that teaches lawyers and their staff how to use technology to make their practices more effective and efficient. Dan helps lawyers not only by teaching them how to use a wide range of software, but also by helping them get the most out of the programs they generally take for granted, such as Microsoft Outlook, Microsoft Word and Adobe Acrobat. He is also a nationally-known speaker and author on law, technology, and ethics.

In addition, Mr. Siegel is the principal of the Law Offices of Daniel J. Siegel, LLC, where he applies these time management concepts to workers' compensation and personal injury matters, as well as his role as "silent second chair" to numerous law firms. In the latter role, Mr. Siegel serves as trial and appellate counsel, and also helps lawyers use technology to prepare for trial. Because of his hands-on focus, Mr. Siegel can pinpoint the tools attorneys need in every area of their practices, from mobile technology to case management software to CaseMap and TextMap case analysis software.

A Philadelphia native, and die-hard Philadelphia sports fan, Mr. Siegel is the author of *Android Apps in One Hour for Lawyers*, *The Lawyer's Guide to Case-Map*, and *Checklists for Lawyers*, which are published by the American Bar Association Law Practice Division; *Changing Law Firms: Ethical Guidance for Pennsylvania Law Firms & Attorneys*, published by the Pennsylvania Bar Institute, and *Pennsylvania Workers' Compensation Law—The Basics*. Mr. Siegel can be reached at dan@techlawyergy.com or dan@danieljsiegel.com.

# Acknowledgments

This book, an outgrowth of my program "How to Do 90 Minutes of Work in 60," highlights how even those of us with rudimentary technology skills can use basic technology—like Word, Windows and Outlook—to get more work done more quickly. But this book is also my way of thanking all of the people who have attended that program for about a decade for their positive feedback. I also want to thank my former partner, Ed Chacker, for coming up with the program's name. In addition, this book wouldn't be nearly as helpful without the brilliant contributions of co-author Allison Shields, with whom it has been a joy to work. And finally, thank you to my family, my wife Eileen, and my sons Bradley and Douglas, for letting me play with all of my tech toys so that I could continue to refine the program and have some fun while doing so. The three of you have always encouraged me to do what I love, and it is your love that really makes this book possible.—**Dan Siegel**

Like Dan, for me, this book is an outgrowth of a program which has had many titles over the years, but always focused on productivity strategies that lawyers could employ in their day-to-day work. Putting our two program concepts together has made them both stronger and, we hope, more useful for lawyers in their quest to get more done in less time and focus on their most important priorities. My thanks to Dan for being willing to put these two programs together in one book and for the countless hours spent in making this book come to life. Thanks, too, to the staff at the Law Practice Division and to those who reviewed early drafts of this book for their time spent in helping to make it better. But most of all, thanks to my family, especially Fred Johs and my parents, CaroleAnn and George Singhel, for their patience, love and support always.—**Allison Shields**

# Introduction

Many lawyers work long hours and still feel that they don't have enough time to complete their work, let alone accomplish important tasks like marketing and business development, training, mentoring, or strategic planning. In some ways, they feel trapped, unable to dig out from what seems like a never-ending pile of paper. But then they look around and see other lawyers seemingly handling the same workload and still going home for dinner and having time on the weekend for leisure activities. How do those lawyers do it?

Everyone gets exactly the same twenty-four hours in every day. If you're struggling, the problem often isn't that you don't have enough time; the problem is that you either aren't managing your activities effectively enough to fit within the time you have available or that you aren't using the tools you have as efficiently as possible.

This book helps tackle both sides of the problem.

Managing your activities well means eliminating or minimizing obstacles to productivity. These obstacles may include allowing others' priorities to control your day, failing to accurately estimate how long tasks will take, allowing constant interruptions, using to-do lists inappropriately, planning poorly, or simply not knowing the most efficient way to accomplish what you need to accomplish.

In a recent article in the *Harvard Business Review*, the authors note:

> Some forward-thinking companies have taken a different approach entirely. They expect their leaders to treat time as a scarce resource and to invest it prudently. They bring as much discipline to their time

budgets as to their capital budgets. These organizations have not only lowered their overhead expenses; they have liberated countless hours of previously unproductive time for executives and employees, fueling innovation and accelerating profitable growth.[1]

But despite thinking that time is an important resource, people waste a great deal of it every day in workplaces. Salary.com conducts a "Wasting Time at Work" survey every year. According to the 2014 study, 89 percent of respondents said they waste at least some time at work, compared with 69 percent in 2013.[2] The vast majority (78 percent) waste between thirty minutes and two hours at work daily, and 4 percent waste four or more hours every day.

The Salary.com study, along with other surveys, reveals that going online is the biggest time waster.[3] Other significant time wasters include the following:

- **meetings or conference calls** (especially those in which more time is spent discussing work than actually executing it)
- **coworker distractions**
- **e-mail** (One study by Jive Software revealed that 79 percent of U.S. workers waste time checking e-mail during the day rather than engaging in more productive activities, with 20 percent saying that e-mail was their biggest distraction. It also showed that the average American worker spends 16 percent of a workday checking irrelevant e-mail.[4])

An article from "Inside Tech" at Monster.com identified the top ten worst time wasters at work[5]:

1. Instant messaging
2. Overreliance on e-mail
3. Meandering meetings
4. Short gaps between meetings

1. Michael Mankins, Chris Brahm, and Gregory Caimi, "Your Scarcest Resource," *Harvard Business Review* (May 2014), http://hbr.org/2014/05/your-scarcest-resource/.
2. Aaron Gouveia, "2014 Wasting Time at Work Survey," Salary.com, accessed August 7, 2014, http://www.salary.com/2014-wasting-time-at-work/.
3. "Email and Co-Workers Among the Biggest Distractions at Work, According to Survey by Jive Software," Harris Interactive, March 25, 2013, http://www.harrisinteractive.com/vault/JIVE-Survey-Results-Press-Release-FINAL.pdf; "New Ask.com Study Reveals Workplace Productivity Killers," Ask.com, May 7, 2013, http://about.ask.com/press-releases/new-ask-com-study-reveals-workplace-productivity-killers/.
4. "Email and Co-Workers Among the Biggest Distractions at Work, According to Survey by Jive Software," Harris Interactive, March 25, 2013, http://www.harrisinteractive.com/vault/JIVE-Survey-Results-Press-Release-FINAL.pdf.
5. Tania Khadder, "10 Worst Time Wasters at Work," Monster.com, accessed August 7, 2014, http://insidetech.monster.com/benefits/articles/5667-10-worst-time-wasters-at-work?page=1.

5. Reacting to interruptions

6. Ineffective multi-tasking

7. Disorganized workspace

8. Personal communications

9. Web surfing

10. Cigarette/coffee breaks

But do general workplace studies apply to lawyers and other knowledge workers? A 2011 survey conducted by Webtorials for Fonality showed that knowledge workers at small and midsize businesses spent 50 percent of their workday on necessary yet unproductive tasks, including routine communications and filtering incoming information and correspondence.[6] According to the survey, these knowledge workers spent an estimated 36 percent of their time trying to contact customers, partners, or colleagues, find information, or schedule a meeting. And approximately 14 percent of their time was spent duplicating information (e.g., forwarding e-mails or phone calls to confirm if fax/e-mail/text message was received) and managing unwanted communications (e.g., spam e-mails or unsolicited time-wasting phone calls).

Just imagine if you could turn even a portion of that unproductive time into productive time.

Although technology is supposed to make our lives easier, in some ways it has only added to our "time management" problems. The Jive Software study noted that 19 percent of employed Americans are more overwhelmed by technology today than they were five years ago.

A 2012 article on *Entrepreneur* magazine's website identified five top technology time wasters[7]:

1. E-mail

2. To-do list apps

3. Social media

4. Instant messages

5. Talking on the phone

---

6. "Fonality Survey Finds Knowledge Workers at Small & Mid-Size Firms Spend Half of Workday on Essential, but Unproductive Tasks," Fonality, June 27, 2011, http://www.fonality.com/press-release/fonality-survey-finds-knowledge-workers-small-mid-size-firms-spend-half-workday.

7. Andrew Kardon, "5 Tech Time Wasters and How to Avoid Them," *Entrepreneur*, October 1, 2012, http://www.entrepreneur.com/blog/224526.

## WHAT THIS BOOK WILL COVER

This book addresses many of the time wasters discussed above: interruptions, e-mails, long to-do lists, meetings, and more. At their core, all of these are the result of a combination of two things:

- an inability to *identify the right activities* (reluctance to say no, lack of direction, allowing interruptions—both human and electronic)
- an inability to *perform those activities efficiently* (procrastination, ineffective delegation, lack of organization, inefficient use of technology)

Productivity is about first knowing what to do (ensuring you are focusing on the right things) and then getting those things done in the most efficient way possible.

You can be efficient at organizing the supply closet, but if that task isn't the highest use of your time and energy, your efficiency isn't going to improve your overall productivity. You're being efficient but not effective, because you're not focusing your energy on the right things. There's not much benefit to doing the *wrong things* efficiently.

In Part I of this book, you'll learn strategies for conquering your feelings of being overwhelmed and taking back control of your day. You'll find out how to determine what you should be spending your time on and how to eliminate or delegate the tasks that you shouldn't be doing. You'll discover why deadlines are important and how to use them effectively and why your calendar is one of your most important defenses in the battle to be productive. In short, you'll learn to identify—and focus on—the *right things*.

Once you've determined which tasks are appropriate for you to undertake, you want to ensure that you're working as efficiently as possible to get them done. Toward the end of Part I, you'll learn how to conduct meetings effectively and create systems for increased efficiency. Then in Part II, we'll show you some time-saving technology tips. These sections of the book will show you how to do things the *right way*. Think of them as your guide to efficiency.

The technology time-saving tips focus on many of the programs that lawyers use on a daily basis. As of the writing of this book, most lawyers are using Windows-based programs, even if they're working in a Mac environment.[8] In our

---

8. *TechnoLawyer Demographics 2014*, a research report from the TechnoLawyer website, shows that over 78 percent of its members are still using Windows (http://www.technolawyer.com/tll/demographics.asp).

experience, most lawyers are continuing to use Word, Outlook, and the other programs in the Microsoft Office suite, as well as Adobe Acrobat. As such, our technology tips focus on these programs.

If you can save six minutes per day with these tips (and that is a highly conservative estimate), you will save thirty minutes per week (more than twenty-five hours per year) doing routine, repetitive activities. At $150 per hour, this means that you can recoup more than $3,750 per year in billable time, which can be devoted instead to client service—or, perhaps, to family and other personal priorities.

Let's get started.

# Part I
## DEVELOPING GOOD PRODUCTIVITY HABITS

# Chapter 1

## SET GOALS AND PRIORITIZE

Productivity expert David Allen has observed that productivity boils down to determining how best to deal with all of the things you have to manage and learning how to focus. But first you need to know what to focus on. Too often, lawyers fall into the trap of expending time and energy on the wrong things because they seem urgent or simply because something happens to be in front of them: the telephone rings, the e-mail arrives, or a colleague or staff member knocks on the door. But if those are the wrong things, what are the "right things"?

## SET GOALS

It's hard to decide what the "right things" are when you haven't determined what your goals are. The first step toward becoming more productive is to decide what you need to accomplish; only then can you determine how you are going to get there. Even if you have no control over your firm's goals, you can (and should) set your own short- and long-term business goals.

The central theme of this book is personal productivity, which means we'll be concentrating mostly on individual short-term and microlevel goals and actions to improve your day-to-day efficiency and effectiveness. Long-term and firm-wide goals are also extremely important, but they are not the main focus of this book. It does, however, bear mentioning that all of your short-term goals should align with your long-term, big-picture goals, and preferably with your firm's goals as well.

## Goal-Setting Guidelines

If you're going to bother setting goals at all, they should mean something to you—you're not likely to stay on track with goals you don't think are important. They should be tied to the core values and principles of your practice and the services you provide to your clients.

If you are new to goal setting, begin with something that is attainable but isn't too easy to reach. Taking on too many goals at once, or setting unrealistic goals, will overwhelm you and may slow—or even halt—your progress. Although you don't want to make your goals too easy, you can always add more if you reach them sooner than you expect. Or go home for the day, recharge, and enjoy some time away from work.

Goals need to be realistic and achievable within a specific time frame. They should be measurable so you can see if you are making progress and can identify what else needs to be done to meet them.

Some experts call these "SMART" goals. SMART is an acronym:

**S:** Specific—You should be able to state the goal clearly and concisely; vague statements about "improving" or "increasing" are not enough.

**M:** Measurable—The best goals are those that make it easy to tell whether they've been reached, and if not, how far off you were.

**A:** Actionable/Achievable—Goals only work if you can do something to achieve them; they cannot be dependent on the actions of others, on market forces, or on anything you cannot control.

**R:** Relevant—The relevance component will help to ensure that the goal is tied to something important for you personally or professionally. You can set goals that meet the other criteria, but they won't do much to improve your bottom line, advance your career, or improve your clients' lives. Make sure your goals, if achieved, will make a real difference. Focus on the benefits. The relevance component should answer the question "Why am I doing this?"

**T:** Timed—The element of time is important; a measurable goal is no good if you don't know when to measure or how long it will take to reach the goal. Set deadlines or benchmarks you must meet. Without deadlines or time expectations, it's too easy to put goals on the back burner, as we will see in Chapter 6.

Here are some examples of vague goals and SMART goals:

*Vague goal:* Get more clients.

**SMART goal:** Add three new estate planning clients within the next three months.

*Vague goal:* Improve the firm's website.

**SMART goal:** Update all lawyer bios and practice area pages on the firm's website to reduce legalese and incorporate keywords by October 1.

*Vague goal:* Improve client service.

**SMART goal:** Obtain client feedback on every engagement using the firm's client feedback questionnaire.

In addition to performance-based goals, you may want to set goals that focus more on learning and mastery than on performance, particularly if you are a new lawyer or are taking on new practice areas or initiatives.

Some experts claim that setting goals can actually be harmful, asserting that the process can lead to "unethical behavior, over-focus on one area while neglecting other parts of the business, distorted risk preferences, corrosion of organizational culture, and reduced intrinsic motivation."[9] When goals are set without reference to firm values, culture, ethics, and overall objectives, this can occur. But at the same time, goals are necessary to articulate the direction for a law firm or individual lawyer and to help to measure performance and progress. Even the naysayers concede that incentives and goals are useful.

Done right, goal setting should take into account the firm's and individual lawyer's culture and values. Review of goals and the progress made toward them should always be done with the understanding that there may be competing values or activities that need to be considered.

## Make Goals Concrete

Setting a goal in your mind won't improve your productivity on its own. It is important to write down your goals. Writing down your goals will clarify them, make them more concrete, and reinforce them. You may also want to share your goals with others.

---

9. Sean Silverthorne, "Why Setting Goals Can Do More Harm Than Good," *Forbes*, January 2, 2013, http://www.forbes.com/sites/hbsworkingknowledge/2013/01/02/why-setting-goals-can-do-more-harm-than-good/.

A study performed by Dr. Gail Matthews at Dominican University of California found that participants who wrote down their goals accomplished significantly more than those who did not.[10] Those who sent commitments to a third person accomplished significantly more than those who did not. Results were further improved when participants sent weekly reports about their progress in addition to writing down and sharing their goals.

The study showed that overall, people and businesses that simply write down goals are 50.4 percent more likely to achieve their goals than those that don't. The success rate increases when people have regular progress reports to measure how they are doing against their goals. People are 77.6 percent more likely to achieve their goals when they complete planned progress reports.

Goals mean nothing without execution; they need to be paired with *actions*. Once you have your SMART goals in place, documented and shared, it's time to choose the *right activities* to pursue to reach those goals. Begin by setting priorities to determine what is most important.

## IDENTIFY PRIORITIES

### The Jar of Rocks

There are many different versions of the story of the jar of rocks (just enter "jar of rocks" on Google and you'll come across several text versions, as well as YouTube demonstrations and more), but the elements are all essentially the same:

> A professor stands in front of his class and pulls out a big glass jar, which he proceeds to fill with large rocks. When he can no longer fit any more rocks in the jar, he asks the class if the jar is full. The class responds in the affirmative.

> The professor then brings out a container of pebbles, which he empties into the jar of rocks. The pebbles fill the spaces between the rocks. Again he asks the class if the jar is full. Again the class responds affirmatively.

> Next, the professor empties sand into the jar, which settles between the pebbles. Once more, he asks the class whether the jar is full. Now the class is not so sure.

---

10. Gail Matthews, "Goals Research Summary," Dominican University of California, accessed August 7, 2014, http://www.dominican.edu/academics/ahss/undergraduate-programs-1/psych/faculty/fulltime/gailmatthews/researchsummary2.pdf.

Finally, the professor brings out a pitcher of water, which he pours into the jar until some begins to overflow. This is when he tells the class that the jar is full.

The jar represents your available time, and each item put in the jar represents a task or project that takes up part of your time. The large rocks represent the most important items in your life or practice; they are things you most need to accomplish—and often the things that are most neglected.

The small stuff (pebbles, sand, and water) will manage to find its way in between the larger rocks, but you have to put the large rocks in first, or you'll never get them in. To fit the larger rocks into your day, you first need to identify what they are; you need to define the activities that are of highest value to you so that you can focus on those tasks first. In short, you need to prioritize.

This is a skill that is especially critical for lawyers to learn because they are so often working under deadlines imposed by others, whether by a court, by statute, or by the circumstances of a particular deal or matter. In addition, clients are often anxious or highly emotional—the outcome of their legal matters will likely have a significant impact on their lives, families, or businesses. These circumstances place pressure on lawyers, which often results in a failure to prioritize effectively.

## Purpose + Result = Priority

Prioritizing tasks helps you get out of the "reactive mode" by determining in advance where to focus the majority of your time and energy. Ensuring that each task has a legitimate **purpose** (i.e., it helps to advance your goals or your clients' goals) is one way to prioritize. Another is focusing on the outcome or anticipated **result** of the task rather than on the task itself.

You probably have tasks on your list that are "priorities" that you avoid because you don't like to do them. For example, you may not enjoy creating billing entries or sending out bills, but billing is a priority—you can't get paid without it. Sometimes the tasks you want to avoid can be delegated, but sometimes they can't because you're the only one who can do them. (We'll talk more about delegation in Chapter 4.) When unpalatable tasks cannot be delegated, focusing on the outcome can be all the motivation you need to get them done.

If the task has an important purpose and a high-value result, make it a priority.

## Stephen Covey's "Importance vs. Urgency" Matrix

Readers of Stephen Covey's *The 7 Habits of Highly Effective People* know that "urgent" tasks tend to get done. For example, when you have a scheduled meeting with a client or a hearing date for a motion, somehow the preparation work gets finished on time. Those deadlines create urgency and provide a framework within which to structure your activities.

But the tasks that Stephen Covey calls "important but not urgent" are the ones that often get carried on a never-ending to-do list. (See Figure 1.1 for Covey's matrix of importance vs. urgency.) They usually do not have built-in deadlines. And even though they are the activities that will make the biggest difference to your practice—they'll save you time and money or generate more revenue in the long run—they are often neglected.

**Figure 1.1**   Importance vs. Urgency Matrix

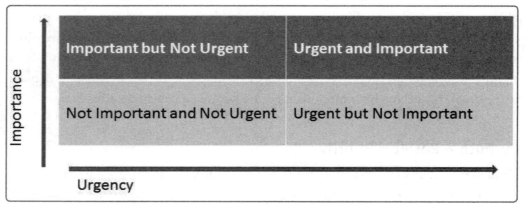

## FOCUS ON THE ACTIVITIES THAT BRING THE HIGHEST RETURN

High-value activities are those that make the biggest impact, often while using the fewest resources. Many times, these are the same "important but not urgent" tasks that are ignored because you're too wrapped up in the day-to-day work of the practice or putting out fires to make them a priority. Other times, you just don't know how to identify which activities are high value.

Here are some questions to help you identify your high-value (and thus priority) activities or tasks:

- What is the purpose of this task?
- How important is this task for my practice or career?

- How important is this task to my client?
- Is this task related to one of my goals? How?
- Is this task directly related to my personal or firm values?
- How will I feel when this task is done?
- What will be the result of this activity emotionally, productively, financially, or organizationally?
- What will the impact of this task be?
- Is the impact short-term or long-term?
- Is this a "need" or a "want"?
- Is this task more or less important than the other things I need to accomplish?
- How will my firm/practice/clients/employees be affected by this task or its outcome?
- Is this activity something I get paid for?
- Am I truly the only one who can perform this task?
- Does this project require my unique skills and expertise?
- Will this activity further my business goals?
- Can this activity help strengthen my relationship with an existing client?
- Will this task help me to gain a larger share of my client's business?
- Is this endeavor likely to introduce me to new prospects?

These questions can help you balance your activities. If the task isn't high value, consider whether it should take precedence over other tasks because of impending deadlines, its age, or the amount of time and energy you have available to devote to it. You may also want to ask yourself whether a task can be delegated to someone else—especially someone who may be able to accomplish it better, cheaper, or faster than you can.

Using this method can help you more easily determine which activities and clients to take on and which to pass by—at least for now. It will help you stay on track and avoid what some call "Bright Shiny Object Syndrome": Rather than being distracted by every new idea or opportunity that comes your way, you can decide quickly and easily what deserves your attention.

## PLANNING

Many law firms have overall strategic plans, which include big-picture goals, and there are many resources available to aid lawyers in creating strategic plans or long-term goals,[11] but productivity often requires focus on the day-to-day or week-to-week activities that must be performed to keep a law firm running, get the work done, and provide excellent service to clients.[12] Unfortunately, too many lawyers fail to plan their days or weeks in advance. Do you have a plan for the day, or do you constantly just react to what comes up—e-mails, telephone calls, or other interruptions? If you're simply reacting, you aren't getting the most important things done, and it isn't likely that you're focusing on the task at hand or that you will reach those larger long-term goals.

Prioritizing and ensuring that you are devoting time and energy to high-value tasks is one way to focus. Another is planning. Before every day, week, or month begins, you should know what you plan to accomplish. When you have a plan, it's much easier to say no to interruptions. If those interruptions aren't actually urgent *and* more important than what you already have planned, don't let them distract you. (We'll talk more about interruptions in Chapter 2 and about creating daily and weekly plans in Chapter 6.)

## THE POWER OF THREE

Don't let your list of priorities and your plan overwhelm you. Lists can be helpful to keep track of tasks that need to be accomplished, but most typical to-do lists are of limited use because they're never-ending. No matter how hard you try, your list gets longer instead of getting shorter—new tasks crop up, unanticipated client problems arise, or a last-minute emergency that "must" be handled today gets in the way. The typical to-do list gets carried over and repeated from one day to the next. Instead of keeping you focused and making you feel productive, to-do lists add to your feelings of being overwhelmed and helpless. They're frustrating, exhausting, and, ultimately, completely unproductive.

---

11. See Thomas C. Grella and Michael L. Hudkins, *The Lawyer's Guide to Strategic Planning: Defining, Setting, and Achieving Your Firm's Goals* (Chicago: American Bar Association, 2004).

12. Another excellent resource for a different kind of planning that is beyond the scope of this book is *Legal Project Management in One Hour for Lawyers* by Pamela H. Woldow and Douglas B. Richardson (ABA Law Practice Division, 2014), which addresses management of client matters, fee predictability, and enhanced client communication.

You can only focus on a limited number of priorities at a time. Instead of focusing on your entire to-do list at once, including your wish list of all the things you would like to accomplish and all the things you have left undone, use the Power of Three to help you prioritize.

The Power of Three can be used for both macrolevel (goal setting, big-picture items) and microlevel (action steps and daily to-do lists) planning. Choose only three big goals for your practice at a time. For each big goal that you set, there will be a lot of objectives to reach and many action steps to perform to get there, so you'll have plenty to do with "only" three goals.

Use the Power of Three to create your daily and weekly plans; identify the three most important tasks that need to be accomplished in a given day and focus on those first. Complete all three of those items before moving on to something else. The resulting sense of accomplishment will motivate you and help to keep you energized in your practice.

By all means, keep a master list that contains other items and your wish list of projects, but use that master list as a "brain dump" to simply capture ideas, not as a daily working list. When an opportunity, project, or task arises, you can evaluate whether or not it's worth your time and effort by asking yourself if it will advance you toward one of your three main goals or if it "trumps" one or more of the three tasks you've already planned for the day or week. If not, put that item on the master list for the future.

## THE POWER OF ONE

Sometimes even accomplishing three tasks in one day is overly ambitious, particularly in a busy law practice. This can happen as a result of a real client crisis or simply because some tasks are so time-consuming or complicated that they overtake everything else. (For example, if you're working on an appellate brief or preparing for a trial, you may be able to focus only on that one task for an entire day or more.)

To avoid feeling helpless or out of control (or becoming discouraged by even a short to-do list that doesn't get done), **ask yourself each day, "What one thing, if I accomplished it today, would make me feel as if my day had been productive?" Focus on that task first.** And keep in mind that one task may be only a small part of a larger activity; for example, completing the statement of facts for your brief or gathering the documents and information you need to prepare a contract. If all else fails, at least you'll leave at the end of the day knowing you accomplished something to keep you moving toward your goals.

## WRAP-UP

The first step to avoiding being overwhelmed (or what Allison calls "lawyer melt-down") and beginning to be more productive is to develop your own goals and prioritize your activities based on those goals. Make sure you put the big rocks in first. Keep your goals and priorities realistic; to create laser focus, use the Power of Three and the Power of One. Use your feelings of accomplishment to motivate you to increase productivity.

## CHAPTER 1 ACTION STEPS

1. Make a list of three main goals you would like to accomplish in your practice in the next six months; use the SMART goal framework.
2. Make a list of the main projects on your current to-do list; use the priority questions on pages 8–9 to determine which you should focus on first.
3. Practice using the Power of Three and the Power of One over the next week to identify the high-value tasks you want to complete each day.

# Chapter 2
## ELIMINATING DISTRACTIONS

As we discussed in Chapter 1, perhaps the biggest enemy of productivity is lack of focus. Despite our intentions, productivity often falls by the wayside because there are too many distractions, interruptions, or outside demands on our time and attention. These distractions make every task take longer to complete. As a result, a key component to taking back control of your practice and becoming more productive is being able to eliminate (or at least limit) many of those distractions.

As you saw in the story about the jar of rocks, if you don't ensure that the large rocks have a place in your day first, the smaller rocks will take up much of the available space and time, and the "large rock" tasks that are important but not urgent won't get done. Interruptions are the sand and the water—do they deserve that much of your time?

## GIVE UP MULTI-TASKING

Our society has become one in which multi-tasking is seen as a good practice; people brag about being "good multi-taskers and wear their attempts to accomplish many different things at once as a badge of honor. Many of those people think that they're being productive or getting a lot done because they're multi-tasking.

In fact, studies have shown that (with few exceptions) the more you multi-task, the less attention and focus you devote to any of the tasks you're trying to accomplish. In other words, when you multi-task, chances are that you're not performing any of those tasks well.

Studies have also shown that multi-tasking wastes time rather than saving it.

"Who Multi-Tasks and Why? Multi-Tasking Ability, Perceived Multi-Tasking Ability, Impulsivity, and Sensation Seeking," a study published in 2013, examined "individual differences in multi-tasking ability by testing participants on multi-tasking activity, perceived multi-tasking ability, impulsivity, and sensation seeking."[13] The findings suggested that people often multi-task not because they are good at it or because it makes them more productive *but because they are simply unable to block out distractions and focus on a single task.*

An earlier study, "Cognitive Control in Media Multitaskers," published in 2009, found that "heavy media multitaskers are more susceptible to interference from irrelevant environmental stimuli and from irrelevant representations in memory."[14]

The study also noted that heavy media multi-taskers performed worse than those who did not multi-task on a task-switching test, likely because of the reduced ability to filter out interference from the irrelevant task set. Thus the authors concluded "that media multitasking, a rapidly growing societal trend, is associated with a distinct approach to fundamental information processing."

Once again, those most likely to multi-task were least able to discern which items most deserved their attention; they were unable to separate relevant from irrelevant stimuli. According to James Watson of the University of Utah, based on a study in 2010, only 2.5 percent of the population (called "supertaskers") can actually process tasks simultaneously.[15] In reality, then, *for over 97 percent of the population, there's no such thing as multi-tasking.*

The truth is that you can't accomplish two things that require you to expend mental energy at once. You can only do one at a time. When you "multi-task," what you're really doing is constantly switching back and forth between two or more tasks. In his book *The Myth of Multitasking*, Dave Crenshaw calls this "switch-tasking." Switch-tasking actually *costs* time.[16]

---

13. David M. Sanbonmatsu, David L. Strayer, Nathan Medeiros-Ward and Jason M. Watson, "Who Multi-Tasks and Why? Multi-Tasking Ability, Perceived Multi-Tasking Ability, Impulsivity, and Sensation Seeking," *PLoS ONE* 8, no. 1 (January 2013): e55402, doi:10.1371/journal.pone.0054402.

14. E. Ophir, C. Nass, and A.D. Wagner, "Cognitive Control in Media Multitaskers," *PNAS* 106, no. 37 (September 2009): 15583–7, doi:10.1073/pnas.0903620106.

15. " 'Supertaskers' That Can Drive and Talk on Phone Rare," Live Science, March 29, 2010, http://www.livescience. com/8186-supertaskers-drive-talk-phone-rare.html.

16. A study in the *Journal of Experimental Psychology: Human Perception and Performance* (Vol. 27, No. 4, August 2001) by researchers Joshua Rubinstein of the Federal Aviation Administration, David Meyer, and Jeffrey Evans of the University of Michigan, involving four experiments that measured the amount of time lost when young adults

If you've ever had the experience of not remembering what you were doing after you've been interrupted, you know that it actually takes more time to get things done when you try to multi-task. In his book *Brain Rules*, John Medina contends that people who are interrupted—and therefore have to switch their attention back and forth—take 50 percent longer to accomplish a task. Essentially, multi-tasking is nothing more than constantly interrupting the flow of work on one task to replace it with another, supporting the theory that this process is really switch-tasking.

Switch-tasking also costs time because it results in more errors. In *Brain Rules*, Medina confirms that those who attempt to multi-task make up to 50 percent more errors. That means those tasks will need to be revisited or repeated. Simply put, fixing mistakes takes time.

Did you get that? *What most people call multi-tasking actually results in a task taking 50 percent longer to complete, and multi-taskers make 50 percent more errors.*

In general, switch-tasking causes as much as a 40 percent drop in overall productivity. Further, one study performed on behalf of Hewlett Packard indicated that switch-tasking can also cause up to a 10 percent drop in IQ.[17] That study showed that workers who constantly allowed e-mail and phone calls to distract them reduced their mental sharpness, similar to losing a night of sleep.[18]

In addition to lessening productivity, switch-tasking damages relationships. In this day and age, with technology all around us—e-mail, text messaging, smartphones, and tablets—creating an expectation that responses will come immediately, chances are that one of the tasks you're trying to accomplish involves communication with someone else. Let's look at a few examples:

- When you are talking on the phone and colleagues enter your office, you wave them in or hold up a finger for them to wait.
- You respond to e-mail while on the phone or with a client in your office.
- You check e-mail during a meeting.

---

repeatedly switched between two tasks, showed that multitasking may actually be less efficient—especially for complicated or unfamiliar tasks—because it takes extra time to shift mental gears every time a person switches between the two tasks, resulting in less efficiency. Moreover, the time lost increased with the complexity and the unfamiliarity of the tasks, as reported by the American Psychological Association's *Monitor on Psychology* (Vol. 32, No. 9, October 2001), http://www.apa.org/monitor/oct01/multitask.aspx.

17. "'Infomania' Worse than Marijuana," BBC News, last modified April 22, 2005, http://news.bbc.co.uk/2/hi/uk_news/4471607.stm.

18. Peter Bregman, "How (and Why) to Stop Multitasking," *HBR Blog Network, Harvard Business Review*, May 20, 2010, http://blogs.hbr.org/2010/05/how-and-why-to-stop-multitaski/.

In each of these instances, you're not fooling anyone; in fact, when you believe, as even we the authors do at times, that you're accomplishing more by multi-tasking, you're doing just the opposite. Think of how many times you answer an e-mail or text message while on the phone—and then think about how many times you go back to the e-mail or text because you "forgot" something. And if you don't set all your e-mail messages to delay sending for a few minutes, you end up writing multiple e-mails to accomplish a result that could have been handled appropriately if you had focused your energies *only* on that task and sent only one e-mail.

Similarly, think of the times you've been on the phone with colleagues and you can tell you've lost their attention; they either stop responding or they ask a question about something that, had they been listening, they would already know the answer to. Chances are, those people were trying to multi-task. How did that make you feel? How do you think your clients feel in that situation?

On some occasions, you *can* do more than one thing at a time—if only one of those things requires mental energy and the other is a rote task requiring limited brain power. Some examples might include folding laundry while watching TV, listening to music while on the treadmill, or putting labels on envelopes while talking on the phone. Crenshaw calls these activities "background tasking"; one task is the main focus while the other occurs in the background and is essentially automatic and doesn't require your direct attention. But those occasions are rare, especially in the business world.

The next time you're tempted to multi-task, keep these statistics in mind. Focusing on only one thing at a time is far more productive than trying to accomplish two things at once.

## INTERRUPTIONS

As you've seen, multi-tasking is nothing more than allowing yourself to be constantly interrupted, and interruptions are enormous time wasters. When you commit to giving up multi-tasking, you'll be faced with a choice when interruptions arise: continue working on your original task or stop, take on the new task and then return to the original task later. Sometimes you don't have a choice—if a true emergency arises and you need to take care of it immediately, for example.

If you *must* be interrupted, make a note about what you are doing and where you are and put that task *away* so that you can fully focus on the new priority. If you are working on a task and something unrelated comes to mind that you need to do or remember, simply make a note and continue working. Process those notes (and your e-mail inbox) at specific times during the day to be sure they don't get lost.

But most interruptions don't represent real emergencies or significant priorities that trump the task you're already working on. In those instances, it's better to avoid the interruption entirely. Resist the urge to permit any and all interruptions:

- You ***don't*** have to answer the telephone just because it's ringing.
- You ***don't*** have to check your e-mail every time you hear the tone that announces a new message.
- You ***don't*** have to entertain everyone who darkens your doorway and asks, "Got a minute?"

Interruptions represent huge productivity losses. In a 2013 article in *The Wall Street Journal*, frequent interruptions are linked to higher rates of exhaustion, stress-induced ailments, and a doubling of error rates.[19] And according to a survey of 252 working adults published recently in the *International Journal of Stress Management*, "[e]mployees who experienced frequent interruptions reported 9% higher rates of exhaustion—almost as big as the 12% increase in fatigue caused by oversize workloads." The study states that interruptions also sparked a 4 percent increase in physical ailments such as migraines or backaches. And we've already seen how constant interruptions can mimic lack of sleep and reduce productivity.

The *Wall Street Journal* article also noted that it can take more than twenty-five minutes, on average, to resume a task after being interrupted, and after resuming complex tasks, it can take an additional fifteen minutes to return to the same focus or concentration as before the original interruption. This was confirmed by a study of Microsoft employees as reported in *The New York Times*, which revealed that it took an average of fifteen minutes for employees to return to full function at complex tasks like writing computer code after checking e-mail.

All of the interruptions discussed above allow the priorities of others to take precedence over your priorities. But many of these interruptions can be avoided if you set some ground rules for how others interact with you.

---

19. "The Biggest Office Interruptions Are . . .," *The Wall Street Journal*, September 10, 2013, http://online.wsj.com/news/articles/SB10001424127887324123004579057212505053076.

## Dealing with Staff or Colleague Interruptions

Not all lawyers have staff, but those who do often find that staff interruptions can be a major cause of loss of productivity. Busy lawyers can be out of the office frequently: in court, meeting with clients, networking, and more. Even when they're in the office, they may be busy with client meetings or calls, making them largely unavailable to staff. Solos or small-firm lawyers who are involved in just about every matter the office handles may experience an even greater number of interruptions.

When you *are* present or "available" (usually when you're alone in your office trying to get work done), you can be bombarded with interruptions simply because your staff doesn't know when you will be available next. As a result, they will take up additional time trying to remember every possible thing they need to speak with you about because they might not have another chance any time soon. Once they have your attention, they may be afraid to let it go because it is so difficult to get your attention in the first place.

You can limit or eliminate these problems with a few simple steps.

First, train staff to hold all questions for a specific time so you can tackle several issues at once rather than dealing with multiple interruptions. Have an assistant screen your calls, or use an answering service when you are doing important client work. Give a definite time when you will return calls and then follow through. Block out "do not disturb" (DND) time and instruct others not to interrupt; close your office door or, if all else fails, leave your office to ensure that important work gets done without interruption. In Dan's office, for example, when Dan needs DND time, he puts a Post-it on the door and turns on the "DND" setting on his phone to alert others that he is not to be interrupted.

Second, give staff a clear time when you'll be available to speak with them, and make sure you are actually available at that time. This will eliminate their urge to grab you every time they see you. Whether you have set office hours or alert your staff to specific times each day when you'll be available, they must know when they can reach you.

Third, schedule recurring meetings with those who are accountable to you or have regular questions for you. For example, you could schedule a meeting with your assistant every day at 4:00 p.m. to resolve any remaining issues from the day and plan for the following day, and have a weekly meeting with your associate to report on progress of ongoing projects.

In short, give your staff clear expectations about your availability. As Dave Crenshaw points out, often it isn't unavailability itself that causes the interruptions—it's the uncertainty about when staff might see you again.

Colleagues are another oft-cited source of interruptions. Even solos can experience these interruptions, particularly if they are working in an office suite or shared office arrangement. Colleagues may stop by for feedback or questions, or they may simply want to take a break and shoot the breeze. This can be incredibly frustrating. Follow the steps we've outlined above to deal with colleagues as well: create a "do not disturb" sign, close your office door, or ask them to make an appointment with you to discuss their issue when you have more time and can focus on their problem. Don't be shy about telling a colleague that you'd love to hear about his or her latest vacation but that you can't do so until you've completed your task; perhaps set a time for coffee, lunch, or a drink with the person instead of chatting during regular work hours.

To further reduce wasted time, remove the chairs from your individual office if you can. While this may not be possible for solos with limited access to a conference room, for many lawyers it is an effective way to limit interruptions in their main work area. Chairs in your office or by your desk serve as an open invitation for people to take a break in your workspace. If people need to ask you questions, they can do it standing up. If you need to have a more in-depth meeting, you can move to a conference room or other space where there are fewer (guess what?) distractions than in your office.

Moving to a conference room for planned meetings, whether with clients or colleagues, can help you mentally shift from work mode to meeting mode, and meeting outside of your office or away from your desk reduces the temptation to glance at e-mail or answer calls during your meeting.

Another reason to consider removing the chairs from your office is that, in Allison's experience, "guest" chairs in lawyer offices often turn into additional horizontal storage spaces for files, papers, or other miscellaneous clutter, rather than serving their intended purpose (See Chapter 3 for more on dealing with clutter in your office.)

When you learn to set expectations and follow through, staff, colleagues, and clients know when they will have access, so they will hold questions. You may even find that when staff can count on your availability, they learn how to resolve some issues on their own.

Keep these same concepts in mind when dealing with others in your office. Respect their time. Ask if you can schedule a time to talk. If you don't want to be interrupted with "quick questions," don't do it to others. Save up questions for those you work with frequently to ask all at once (preferably at a designated time).

When leaving messages for others, let them know when you will be available so they can call back at a time that is convenient for both of you (and avoid playing telephone tag).

## Technology Interruptions

Some of the biggest interruptions are those that result from technology (e-mail, phone calls, text messages, and social media alerts). Just because you have a cell phone doesn't mean you should always be available or that every client needs to have the number. This kind of access doesn't necessarily serve you or your clients. Remember: switch-tasking damages relationships.

Give your full attention—don't look at the computer screen when someone is in your office. Don't try to talk on the phone and check your e-mail at the same time.

In the same way that you schedule time for staff, you can schedule time for technology. Only check e-mail at specified times, using the "do not disturb" feature on your phone, and designate time for social media.

As Richard Branson says, "Manage your mobile, don't let it manage you."

## Your Role in the Interruption Problem

Unfortunately, you'll never eliminate interruptions entirely, but being mindful of interruptions and taking steps to prevent interruptions by others can result in a significant increase in productivity. But lawyers should also not ignore how their own behavior contributes to interruptions or distractions.

On her website (http://theproductivitypro.com/), Laura Stack highlights the problem of "self-sabotage." Stack emphasizes that many distractions are self-imposed, like getting up for a cup of coffee when doing so slows you down and distracts you from your project. She then categorizes types of self-imposed distractions, including "perfectionism," "procrastination," and "negative self-talk."

Perfectionism, she explains, "is based on the admirable desire to do the very best job possible; but when taken to extremes, it can distract you from getting the job done." To overcome perfectionism and avoid the paralysis that can result, she suggests that "once you've made a decision to do something, get started and work through the details as they arise." (We'll talk more about overcoming perfectionism and "analysis paralysis" in Chapter 5.)

We're all familiar with procrastination. Stack suggests that when procrastination rears its head, you need to force yourself to do the work (remember, you won't get paid if it's not done, or, worse, you could commit malpractice if it's late), and "visualize what you need to do, break it down into smaller tasks that are easier to handle, and then buckle down and get it done." (We'll talk more about procrastination and breaking large tasks into smaller "chunks" in Chapter 5.)

Finally, Stack addresses self-sabotage, or negative self-talk, which is probably more common than any of us want to admit. We all go through life constantly thinking about and internally commenting on the situations we encounter. She notes that "self-talk can be self-defeating" and that "[i]f you convince yourself that something's too difficult or that there's no point in trying, you throw roadblocks in the path of productivity." Her solution is for you to challenge your negativity by asking these questions:

- Is the situation really as bad as it seems?
- If so, what's the worst thing that could happen?
- How about the best thing?
- What's most likely to occur?
- How would I perceive this situation if I were in a positive mood?

While Stack concedes that it is difficult to eliminate self-sabotage because many of us are our own worst critics, we "have to be realistic and ruthless about facing down [our] subconscious."[20]

## THE "DON'T-DO" LIST

As we discussed in the previous chapter, a long to-do list leads to discouragement and feeling overwhelmed. You're so preoccupied with how much needs to get done that you rush from one thing to the next, to the next. And while you're

---

20. Laura Stack, "Dealing with Distractions and Interruptions: Strategies for Staying Focused on Important Tasks" (copyright 2011), on Laura Stack's website, accessed August 8, 2014, http://www.theproductivitypro.com/FeaturedArticles/article00144.htm.

busy doing the first thing on your list, ten other things crop up, or you're think-ing about what you need to do next before you complete the task at hand.

**What you really need is a don't-do list.**

What's a don't-do list? It's a list of the things you shouldn't be doing, the things that could be delegated to someone else or outsourced. The don't-do list also includes all of the things you completely let go—things that can be eliminated entirely (or for a specified time period).

Creating a don't-do list doesn't necessarily mean that you need to take time to write an actual list, but it is a conceptual reminder that you need to first identify habits, behaviors, and tasks that are time wasters or reduce your productivity and then constantly reevaluate what you're doing and how you're doing it to make sure that the tasks you undertake are serving you, your firm, and your cli-ents. If you need a physical reminder to stop engaging in those behaviors or taking on those tasks, by all means make a list and refer to it.

## Narrow Your Options

Law school trains lawyers to spot issues, but this issue-spotting behavior isn't necessarily the most efficient way to run a law practice. In fact, it often leads to "analysis paralysis"—every issue must be at least considered, if not addressed, and this hampers lawyers by creating too many distractions.

Have you ever been to a restaurant with a huge menu and found it so over-whelming that you ended up just ordering a burger because there were too many choices? The same thing happens with an overwhelming to-do list; it is so mas-sive that it's easier to do the familiar or return to reactive mode, even if the resulting tasks are not priorities. The don't-do list counteracts this by narrowing your options so that you're not overwhelmed by so many choices every time something new arises.

Having a don't-do list lets you identify tasks you don't want to do or that you shouldn't be doing because they distract you and prevent you from accomplish-ing more important tasks; if it's already on the don't-do list, it's easy to immediately recognize it and move on to more productive endeavors.

How do you decide what goes on the don't-do list? Anything that distracts you from the main goals that you want to accomplish belongs on the list. The don't-do list can come into play in a variety of areas in your practice: in the choice of day-to-day activities, your selection of clients or matters, or even which matters you should respond to first.

Take, for example, one of Allison's clients, the managing partner of a four-law-yer firm who felt it was her obligation to open the mail every day so she could be on top of what was going on at the firm. But the time it took for her to open and sort the mail was time away from other more valuable duties. When she finally used her don't-do list and gave the job of opening and sorting the mail to her receptionist, she reclaimed a lot of billable time. Now she can breeze through the already opened, date-stamped, and sorted mail and still keep current.

Your don't-do list may also include certain types of clients. Another lawyer finally fired a client who was difficult from the very first meeting; she finally drew the line when the client began treating her abusively. She's added abusive clients to her don't-do list. Now when she sees one coming, she just says no. She won't add to her stress level by dealing with clients who don't respect her and don't value her work. The money they might bring in just isn't worth it. She is saving herself endless hours of worry and unproductive activity—because dealing with that abusive client was distracting, even when she was working with other clients. (We'll talk more about eliminating clients later in this chapter.)

Think about your strengths and weaknesses when making your don't-do list. If you're a great speaker but a poor writer, perhaps writing articles, motions, and briefs should go on your don't-do list. You can create a "go-to" list, including copywriters, contract lawyers, and others whom you can rely upon to do the work for you, or delegate the task to someone else in the firm with excellent writing skills and, if necessary, simply provide final approval. Then you can focus your energies on trying cases, giving seminars or presentations, or other activities where you can showcase your speaking skills.

Some marketing activities may belong on your don't-do list. Consider the solo lawyer who belongs to so many networking groups that he's at a networking event every day, sometimes two or three a day. That means he's at his office late into the night and every single weekend handling his regular work. As a long-term strategy, this might not be the best for him or his family. Marketing and practice building are very high-value activities for a solo. But they're only valuable if they are strategic—if they're putting the solo in front of potential clients or leads, or if the groups or events are ones which the solo is passionate about.

Saying no is an essential part of your don't-do list. Accepting a request when you're already overburdened is a mistake. If you're unable to devote the time and energy necessary to a project or group, your participation can end up working against you by creating a negative impression. Evaluate which groups or activities will be the most beneficial to you (or to the people or causes you're supporting). Limit your participation to the most valuable events or organizations. You can get more value for less time, energy, and stress. If the things already on your to-do list are more important or more valuable, these "invitations" belong on the don't-do list.

Although lawyers need to be responsive and accessible to clients, a good don't-do list might include particular days or times when you're "off-limits." Allowing constant interruptions of family or leisure time—including taking work calls at home or on your cell phone—robs you of much-needed recharging and rest, and, as we've already seen, it is a disservice to clients, who are only getting part of your attention. The same goes for interruptions of important business or client-related activities. It's rare that clients have a real emergency that can't wait an hour or two for you to finish preparing your motion *in limine* or complete a meal with your family.

Your don't-do list may also highlight where you need to set boundaries with clients and others. As we've discussed, technology has added to our daily interruptions; smartphones, e-mail, text messages, instant messaging, and the like have contributed to the idea that lawyers are available to clients 24/7. By allowing those interruptions and responding to clients immediately, regardless of where you are and what you're doing, you reinforce clients' expectations that you're always available. Instead, train your clients to expect responses within a specific period of time or within a particular time frame, but set boundaries and limits in the same way you would set them for staff or colleagues. For example, you may want to explain to clients that your office policy is to return all calls within one business day or that you only respond to e-mail in the late afternoon.

Practice areas can also be items to add to your don't-do list. If your practice focuses on family law and a client brings you a medical malpractice case, or if you're a transactional lawyer who has never seen the inside of a courtroom and a client wants you to try a case, turning down the request or referring it to a colleague who regularly handles such matters is probably the right decision. Compile a list of referral lawyers (to whom you send these cases and who refer cases in your practice areas to you). If you aren't well versed in a particular area of the law, don't have the time or resources to learn, or don't have someone in your firm to help you, you may be asking for more trouble than the case is worth. Having a network of lawyers to whom you can refer cases in other practice areas so you know that clients are well taken care of can assure that you're meeting clients' needs while still remaining true to your own goals.

Identifying your "don't dos" can be an effective tool for managing your time and reducing your stress. Knowing in advance the things you won't do lets you move on quickly, without wasting time analyzing everything that comes to your attention.

The don't-do list also reminds you to ask for help in the areas that aren't your strengths so you can focus your efforts on what you do best and what brings the most value to your clients and to your life. It allows you to let go of the idea that you can do everything and be everything to everyone. It's a shorthand way of cutting through all the clutter of what needs to be done so you can get back to providing great service to your clients.

## ELIMINATE CLIENTS!

Some clients may belong on your don't-do list. All lawyers have horror stories about clients they never should have agreed to represent or matters they should not have agreed to take on.

### The 80-20 Rule

You may be familiar with the 80-20 rule, also known as the Pareto Principle, in which 80 percent of your work comes from 20 percent of your clients. Twenty percent of your clients will cause 80 percent of your problems.

Focusing on your best clients rather than on your worst clients brings a big return. Unfortunately, in reality, the bad clients tend to get more of your time and attention than the good ones.

Take a look at your current client/matter list. Are there some clients that you would rather not work with? Do you cringe when you know a particular client is on the telephone or wants to schedule a meeting with you? Make a list of those clients.

Why are these clients on the list? Are they difficult to deal with? Do they fail to see the value of the work that you do? Are they uncooperative? Do they fail to pay their bills on time? Do they constantly question everything you're doing? Is the work boring or outside of your comfort zone?

Now make a list of those reasons, whether they describe your clients or the particular matters you're handling for those clients.

## Eliminate the Worst Clients

To keep your best clients coming back and referring additional work to you, you must ensure that lower-value clients are not taking the place of higher-value clients. One way to keep focusing on the highest-value clients in your practice is to get rid of the bottom tier of your clients.

Consider firing your "nightmare" clients, such as the ones who don't pay on time or aren't the proper fit for your practice—your practice will benefit, and so will you.

While the idea of firing clients might be a scary one, allowing bad clients to pull your focus from your highest-value clients can be even more detrimental to your practice.

**Bad clients drive out good clients. If your practice is filled with clients who don't value your work, who are price sensitive, or whose work you just don't feel like doing, you won't have room to take on the higher-value clients. And you'll shortchange your existing high-value clients because you'll be focusing on the problem clients.**

You might be afraid that getting rid of clients isn't a prudent financial move. But not all clients are profitable. Consider the damage that bad clients do to your bottom line, your stress level, your focus, and your ability to provide quality work for *all* your clients, whether good or bad.

Bad clients and/or low-value matters (or matters that are a bad fit for you) have the following effects:

- They drain your energy.
- They make it more difficult to concentrate on the matters you're handling for your best clients.
- They prevent you from seeking additional work from your good clients.
- They cause you to turn away business from potentially good clients because you're too busy.
- They sabotage your productivity.
- They increase stress and anxiety.

Is it time for you to get rid of some clients? Perhaps there's another lawyer in your area who needs additional work or who is a better fit for your "bad" client's personality or the type of work that client wants or needs. Now is the time to pull out your go-to list.

Being busy isn't the same as being successful or profitable. Getting rid of bad clients makes room for you to take on additional higher-value clients—and chances are that your higher-value clients will be less price sensitive. You can often make more money with a few high-value clients than you can with a high-volume practice filled with lower-value clients.

But getting rid of less desirable clients is only part of the solution. Once your practice is free of bad clients, you'll want to keep it that way by not taking on problem clients in the first place. You'll need to put some systems in place to help you determine at the outset which clients are good and which are bad so you can send the bad ones packing before they cause trouble.

## Client Selection—Are You Ignoring Your Gut?

Client selection is one of the most important and most overlooked levers for lawyers' success. Much attention is paid to marketing and client acquisition, but much less emphasis is placed on determining whether lawyers are attracting and working with the *right kinds of clients*.

As we have seen, not every client is a good client. In fact, some clients are downright awful. If you can eliminate these clients before they shift your focus away from the good high-value clients who might bring you more business, you'll be ahead of the game.

Intuition (and sometimes fear) gives clues that should not be ignored. Too often, lawyers talk themselves into accepting clients they shouldn't. They disregard the gut feeling and the red flags that are almost always present or make excuses for a client's bad behavior, inability to listen or follow directions, or other warning signs. But if more lawyers heeded their intuition—the feeling that something just doesn't seem "right" with a situation, fewer would be stuck with clients who don't pay—or worse. Ignoring your gut can put you and your practice at a disadvantage. Reconnect with that feeling in the area of client selection.

Lawyers often don't reach out for help until *after* they have already accepted the client and the situation has gotten worse. At that point, they're just trying to find a way to salvage the situation or end the relationship. Frequently, the best thing to do is to get out, and get out fast. But sometimes it's too late and the circumstances (or the court) require you to continue. That's why identifying and avoiding bad clients early is so crucial.

Allison has had countless conversations with lawyers who come to her before entering into an engagement with a potential client. Some red flags have been raised, or they just have a "bad feeling" about the client. Instead of listening to that feeling, they try to talk themselves out of rejecting the client. They don't trust their gut.

## Why Lawyers Take On Bad Clients

Most people who enter the legal profession genuinely want to help others. Sometimes the reason for taking on bad clients and ignoring your gut is simply that you want to help them. Sometimes you think you can convince them to be reasonable. Other times you don't want to reject a client because the client was referred to you by a friend, a colleague, or someone to whom you feel you owe a favor.

Young lawyers, lawyers just starting their own practices, or lawyers facing financial difficulties will sometimes take bad clients because they fear turning away one client will result in a reduction in inquiries or because they simply don't know where their next case will come from, and they fear that they won't have any work to do.

But sometimes taking on a bad client is more harmful to a lawyer's practice than having no client at all. When you take on a client who refuses to pay, is unreasonable, drains your energy for others, or, worse, files a complaint or grievance against you, you're worse off than if you had rejected the work from the beginning.

Dan has what is called the "manure" rule. Manure doesn't smell better the longer it's in your office. Thus, if a client is a bad client, or a case goes from good to bad, it's time to cut your losses. Your gut is often the best judge of bad clients—and remember, there is a difference between bad clients and bad cases, but you need to evaluate both. Don't ignore the gut feeling that signals that a client might not be the right fit for you (or might not be telling you the truth). Take the time to process what you hear, how you feel, and how clients react to you during your initial interactions with them, whether those interactions are by telephone or in person. Does an individual seem more like your best clients or your worst clients? Does something seem "off"? Are you questioning whether you should agree to represent this person?

## Identify Bad Clients Early and Avoid or Disengage from Them

Lawyers who have found themselves in a difficult situation can often recall warning signs or clues that the client would be trouble—often these warnings appeared at the time of the initial consultation or first telephone call. For example, if you and the client have difficulty agreeing on a fee, it's likely that you'll have difficulty agreeing on just about everything else that happens down the road. Lawyers will often admit that they considered not taking a case but talked themselves into it because it was referred by someone they didn't want to disappoint or because they were simply afraid to turn away any work. But operating from a place of fear puts you at a disadvantage from the outset.

The feeling that something is wrong is itself the warning signal—everything else is just a way of explaining the feeling. But you may be so used to second-guessing your intuition that you no longer recognize or trust the feeling.

Look for patterns in past client relationships. How did prior bad client relationships begin? What were the warning signs or red flags? If you look at several of those relationships together, patterns will begin to emerge. The clients may have said similar things at the beginning of the engagement or had a similar (poor) attitude. Each of them may have given you the feeling that you weren't getting the whole story. Or perhaps you felt that you were on the defensive with them, having to justify what you were doing rather than providing advice and guidance. Use these patterns and the following list of warning signs as a guide for the future.

## Ten Bad-Client Warning Signs

If you can recognize the warning signs, you can stop bad clients before they enter your practice.

1. They are overly concerned about the fee, ask about the fee before you discuss their legal problem, won't talk to you about their budget or don't know what it is, or simply cannot agree with you about the fee. (Remember, if clients cannot agree with you about fees, they probably won't agree with you about much else either.)

2. They have tunnel vision about the matter and don't want to listen to new ideas, aren't interested in other options, or can't face reality about their role in creating the situation.

3. They have overexaggerated expectations, particularly for their budget or time limitations.

4. They need everything in a rush.

5. They don't keep the initial appointment, show up late, or fail to call when they say they will (particularly in combination with number 4).

6. They don't listen to or don't understand simple initial instructions.

7. They take a long time to return your retainer agreement or to provide requested documents or materials.

8. They have fired (or have been fired by) several lawyers before you.

9. They don't exhibit an understanding of the issues involved, even after you explain them.

10. They bully or disrespect you or your staff.

## Educate Your Referral Sources

Sometimes it's hard to turn clients away because they've been referred by a friend, colleague, or client that you do not want to disappoint. But if a client is not right for you, it probably is not worth the headache. The disappointment is greater if the attorney-client relationship breaks down, if the client is dissatisfied, or if you are forced to withdraw at a later date.

Some referral sources aren't clear about what you do and whom you want to work with. Others understand that not every client may be the right "fit," but they'd rather have you make that decision. Be open with referral sources about whether you want all referrals or only targeted ones (being a "hub" has its advantages), and make sure they understand that not every client may be right for you but that you appreciate that they thought of you.

Be polite if you need to reject a client. Then contact your referral source, explain that you could not take the client, and say thanks. Offer an alternative or a referral to another lawyer who may be better suited for the client or matter where possible. Use the conversation as an opportunity to educate the referral source about what kinds of clients you're seeking.

Remember that the attorney-client relationship is a two-way street. Sometimes a bad client is created because of the interaction between lawyer and client. If you continually encounter the same warning signs or find that every potential client exhibits some of them, the problem may be with your prescreening or prequalifying procedures or your own inability to communicate properly. Take a good hard look at how you (or your staff) are interacting with potential clients to see where you can improve. Be sure that you are managing expectations properly to help ensure your client interactions are positive.

If you're confident that the problem is not you, listen to your gut, heed the warning signs, and turn away those clients who don't fit into your practice. You'll be glad you did.

## WRAP-UP

Interruptions, whether they come in the form of phone calls, e-mail messages, colleague and staff questions, or other sources, account for much of the time wasted during most lawyers' workdays. If you can learn to limit those distractions, your productivity will improve dramatically. Giving up multi-tasking, setting aside "do not disturb" time, and training colleagues, staff, and clients on how to interact with you more effectively can go a long way toward providing productive work time. Eliminating other kinds of distractions, including unproductive tasks and bad clients, can help you hone your prioritizing skills even further, allowing you to focus on the highest-value tasks and clients.

## CHAPTER 2 ACTION STEPS

1. Create your own list of warning signs or red flags for problem clients. Look at your past client relationships beginning with the first interaction: Were there certain questions, attitudes, or other things all of those bad clients had in common? Did you have the same gut reaction to all of them? Using a list of warning signs can take the emotion out of saying no to a potentially problematic new client.

2. Resolve to limit multi-tasking. When you catch yourself doing it, *stop*! Ask others to point it out to you if they see you doing it.

3. Set rules with employees and colleagues about interrupting you. When you're working on an important project, turn off your e-mail notifications and turn down the ringer on your phone, or ask your assistant to hold your calls. If all else fails, move to a different location to eliminate the interruptions.

4. Set expectations and boundaries with both staff and clients about communication and response time.

# Chapter 3
## ELIMINATING THE CLUTTER OBSTACLE

Organizing and time management go hand in hand. Managing your activities necessarily includes organizing your tasks and your environment. To be productive, you need to manage both well. But many lawyers don't effectively manage their environments, which can lead to additional stress, the feeling of being overwhelmed, a lack of productivity, or potentially even malpractice.

Many (if not all) of the top time wasters are in some way related to clutter of one or more types:

- physical clutter
- mental clutter
- technological clutter
- clutter related to old or outdated priorities
- a cluttered to-do list
- clutter created as a result of rushing from one task to the next

Clutter includes all things unfinished, unused, unresolved, tolerated, or disorganized. Clutter bogs you down, suppresses energy, and disrupts growth. Clutter obscures what is most important.

## THE IMPACT OF CLUTTER

With a busy law practice, it's difficult to keep control of the clutter. If you're like most lawyers, your office is a clutter collector: catalogs, CLE fliers, bar association announcements, periodicals, office supplies, and paperwork just keep piling up.

Instead of being reduced as a result of technology, clutter is multiplied or, at a minimum, electronically duplicated. In addition to all of the above, we have e-mail, social media notifications, and all sorts of other digital detritus to deal with.

Clearing away the clutter means getting rid of anything and everything that is outdated or no longer useful.

Why should we care about clutter in the first place? After all, is it really important to have a clutter-free office when we've got important client work to do?

**Clutter wastes time.** How much time have you spent over the past week looking for files in the office, notes on tiny pieces of paper, documents on your computer, or the business card of the person you met last week at a networking event?

**Clutter wastes money.** If you bill by the hour, anything that wastes time wastes money. But clutter also wastes money because you may purchase duplicates or reinvent the wheel if you can't find what you're looking for. If your e-mail inbox is so cluttered that you miss a new client inquiry or a request from an existing client that could have led to more work, clutter has just detracted from your bottom line, too.

**Clutter creates distractions.** Piles of paper, files, periodicals to be read, and other miscellaneous clutter cause distractions. It's difficult to focus on the task at hand when the "stuff" that represents unfinished projects or work to be done is literally looming over you. The physical reminder of all the other tasks that need to be accomplished can lead to the urge to multi-task.

**Clutter wastes energy.** Physically, you've got to work around or climb over clutter. Mentally, it zaps your energy by overwhelming you. Clutter causes you to postpone making decisions, and the longer an item (or a decision) stays on your to-do list, the more it drains your energy.

**Clutter is scary.** Just look at the piles of paper on your desk or at your e-mail inbox that seems to go on forever. Those piles (paper or electronic) should scare you. After all, you can't possibly know what is in each pile or what deadlines or other "traps" are hidden there. As a result, clutter should not simply scare you; it should also be a red flag that a malpractice claim could lie within. Why? If you don't have good organizing, filing, and naming systems so that you can find files easily, clutter can lead to missed deadlines.

Based on our experience as lawyers and consultants, here are some common causes of missed deadlines:

- The client supplies misinformation about the time and date of underlying events.
- You miscalculate the deadline or expiration of the statute of limitations.
- You apply the incorrect statute.
- You lose interest in the case.
- The file "falls through the cracks."
- No one is specifically assigned to work on the file.
- No one is working on the file.
- You wait until the last moment and then do not have time to complete the task.
- You are unsure how to proceed.

Clutter prevents you from working efficiently by distracting you, covering up important documents or files, and adding to anxiety and stress.

Many lawyers have said that once they moved to a new office, things started opening up in their practice; they started getting the clients they wanted, inquiries increased, and other positive changes occurred—in part because the move forced them to get rid of clutter and set up their new office in a positive way. But even without relocating, you can achieve some of the same results in your existing office.

Mastering some of the skills discussed in this book will help you get rid of clutter, eliminate missed deadlines, and better meet your client commitments.

## ORGANIZATIONAL TYPES

If past attempts at organization have failed, it may be because you haven't taken your personality and your approach to work into account.

Do any of these sound familiar?

- You don't know when good enough is good enough, or you fail to delegate because you think you're the only one that can do a task right. (perfectionist)
- You don't do anything until the very last minute, or tasks never get completed because you just never "get around" to them. (procrastinator)

- You constantly rush from one thing to the next, focusing on the big issues but allowing the details to fall through the cracks. (multi-tasker)
- You keep track of all the details but hold on to everything "just in case" you might need it sometime. (pack rat)[21]

There's nothing necessarily "bad" about any of these types, but you must understand them to stay organized. If you consistently operate in the same manner, there must be some benefit or "payoff" or you wouldn't continue to behave in that way. Perhaps clutter is your excuse for not meeting deadlines. Remove the clutter and you remove the excuse.

Whatever the payoff is, you have to be willing to give it up. For example, if you're a perfectionist, can you give up the idea that you're the only one who can get a task done right and admit that others are competent, too? Can you accept when something is "good enough"? If you're a multi-tasker and being busy and rushing from one thing to the next makes you feel important, you must be willing to let that go and find something else that gives you the same feeling.

If you're a procrastinator, perhaps you work better under pressure or you enjoy the adrenaline rush involved in trying to beat the clock. You may need to give up that rush or find some other way to get it. If you procrastinate when the task is simply unpleasant or outside of your comfort zone, you may need to give up the notion that you should know everything and be willing to find someone who is an expert. And if you're a pack rat, you may need to give up the security blanket of "stuff" and recognize that it is an obstacle to getting your work done.

Once you understand your individual style and the unique challenges it presents, you can address those challenges. The strategies below will help any work style, but they address the specific issues associated with different types. We'll address strategies for each of these types throughout the book, but no matter what your type, you may need to give up the idea that you don't need outside help to get organized.

If you're a perfectionist, you can learn to delegate by starting small and delegating less important or less valuable tasks, particularly those that do not require your expertise (and following the steps to good delegation described in this book). Try delegating tasks you've been avoiding, or try breaking large tasks down into smaller increments—and delegating one small bit at a time. Talk to

---

21. Adapted in part from Office Depot's "Put Your Work Style to Work" organizational plan, http://www.officedepot.com/promo.do?file=/promo/makeover/getorganized.jsp.

your staff and help them to understand how you like things done and why it's important to you. Create checklists or procedures that will help you to follow up and feel comfortable that tasks are being completed. Delegating is a skill that can be learned and perfected over time, as we'll see in Chapter 4.

If you're a multi-tasker, you can benefit from good, solid systems and defined deadlines with reminders to ensure that details don't get lost and those deadlines aren't missed. Rely on your calendar and schedule specific appointments to get the "important, but not urgent" tasks done. (See Chapter 6 for more on using your calendar effectively.) This is especially important for multi-taskers since they are doing too many things at once and usually have difficulty keeping track, only responding to the "urgent." Creating deadlines with consequences will add a sense of urgency where it otherwise might not exist for the procrastinator as well. (See Chapter 6 to learn how to create deadlines.)

If you're a procrastinator, you can also benefit from the "doing the worst first" strategy described in Chapter 5. Procrastinators tend to avoid the most important tasks or tasks that require the most attention. Getting those tasks out of the way will keep them from cluttering up your thinking and pulling focus from the other things you're working on.

If you're a pack rat, you'll need some guidelines to help you determine what you really must keep and what can be tossed. (Pay special attention to the Quick Sort and Purge described in the next section.) In this digital age, most any kind of information can be found on the Internet, and electronic documents, PDFs, scans, and the like can really cut down on the amount of paper you need to retain. (We'll talk more about reducing paper later in this chapter.)

Of course, if you're relying on electronic storage, you'll need to make sure that you've got backups in place and that sensitive client information is encrypted. But even electronic storage doesn't have to be bulky anymore: flash drives can store thousands of cases, briefs, articles, or other information in a pocket-sized format, and cloud-based backup and storage systems are becoming commonplace.

Whether you're organizing paper or electronic documents, a good filing system is essential. And realistically, you will save time whenever you convert paper files to electronic ones and can use your computer instead of getting up from your desk to find something. Your filing system and other procedures and systems must also be easy for everyone in your office to understand to ensure that you maintain your organization. The simpler the better. Don't file things just to get them off your desk; first decide whether you need them. If an item is part of a client's file and needs to be retained, scan it immediately and save it electronically (we'll talk more about working with electronic files later in the book). Electronic storage space is cheap, and the pack rat will be relieved to know that documents and information are quickly and easily accessible through a good electronic filing system with appropriate search functionality.

Although all lawyers need good filing systems, this is especially important for the pack rat since reference materials are only valuable if you can access them easily. In Chapter 8, we'll talk more about filing systems and the need to have an easy-to-understand and consistent file-naming protocol.

## HOW TO GET RID OF THE CLUTTER

The television show *Clean Sweep* on the Learning Channel took two incredibly cluttered rooms in someone's home (you wouldn't believe the *mountains* of stuff that some people have hiding behind closed doors) and transformed them by showing the homeowners how to eliminate clutter and make room for what was really important to them. We'll try to do the same with your office clutter in this chapter.

Perhaps the worst thing we do is save every piece of paper or electronic document. Why do we do it? Because we're accustomed to doing so (and this is even more true for the pack rat). It's not efficient—in fact, it's terribly inefficient. Why? Because it takes time to search for the information you need, and the more information you have to search through (and the less organized it is), the more time it takes to find. And if you have to get up from your desk to go and look for it, you lose even more time.

One solution to paper clutter is converting it to electronic format: scan it, save it with a name you'll remember, and use programs with good search functionality to easily and quickly locate what you need. But remember this is only a partial solution that may lead to electronic clutter. We'll tackle working with electronic documents in Chapter 8, but for now, here is a simple five-step process to get rid of your physical clutter:

### Step 1: Clear Out

The first step in decluttering is to determine what you have. The best way to do that is to clear everything out. When dealing with physical space such as your office, this means taking *everything* out. But if it's just not possible or practical for you to tackle your whole office at once, you can begin decluttering on a smaller scale by focusing on one area (such as one shelf, one desk drawer, or your desktop) at a time. As you go through the decluttering process, remember that one of the enemies of organization is duplication: clutter breeds duplicates because if we don't know what we have or if we can't find it, we tend to collect multiples. If you're not decluttering your entire office at once, you'll have to be even more aware of duplicates.

Once you've gotten everything out, look around. Notice how the space feels when it's empty. (And take advantage of the opportunity to give your office a thorough cleaning. Banish the dust bunnies!)

## Step 2: Quick Sort and Purge

Now your office is empty, but you've got a big pile of "stuff" to deal with. The next step is to sort it out.

Sort into these piles:

- Toss (goes directly in the circular file)
- File in space (for any filing that needs to remain in the space you're working on)
- File elsewhere (includes items to be scanned by others and electronically filed)
- To do (actual client or administrative work to be done or delegated)
- To read
- In space (items such as mementos, books, and office supplies that will stay in the space)
- Elsewhere (anything other than filing that belongs somewhere other than the space you're working on)

The initial sort is done on a "one touch" basis—pick something up and make a snap decision about which pile it belongs in. During this initial sort, don't give yourself too much time to think; go with your gut feeling. You usually won't miss an item if it's gone, especially since you probably didn't even remember having it in the first place.

Your office should only contain paperwork that you're currently working on, supplies and files that you need on a *regular basis*, and a limited number of mementos that are meaningful. The rest is trash or should find another home. Keep only those items in your office that you need to take action on or that you need to refer to when doing your work. This keeps clutter at a minimum and reduces distractions.

While you're sorting, remember David Allen's two-minute rule from *Getting Things Done*: If some action will take less than two minutes to accomplish (like making a quick phone call or entering something on your calendar), you should do it right away while you're going through your sort. If it takes less than two minutes, you're better off getting it out of the way rather than wasting time making a note and coming back to it later.

However, this may not work for you if you're going to try to get your whole office organized at once. In that case, you may want to create a two-minute pile for all of the two-minute items and then tackle that pile as soon as you've completed your sort.

One of the most important parts of the initial sort is the purge—getting rid of what you don't need. This includes everything from old telephone messages and flyers for past CLE programs to periodicals and files that should go to archives or can be destroyed entirely. Eliminate drafts of old documents that are no longer needed and notes or working files that are not part of clients' files.

Purging is important for electronic clutter as well. Don't forget to archive or purge old client files, unneeded documents, and outdated reference materials.

If you're feeling stuck in your practice, you might be surprised at the effect that a good purge can have. Getting rid of the old makes room for the new and frees up your energy.

After this first round of sorting, you'll probably still have more stuff than you really need to keep. That's where Step 3 comes in.

## Step 3: Organize

First, take everything that shouldn't be in your office and put it where it belongs—the file room, your secretary's desk, and so on. Then you'll only be organizing what needs to go back in your space.

But before you put anything back, make absolutely sure that each item belongs in the space. Ask yourself these questions:

- When was the last time I used or referred to this?
- Is this something I need to use or access frequently?

- Is this information I can easily find elsewhere (like the Internet)?
- Does it fit my current practice and my goals for my firm?
- Will it advance what I am seeking to achieve?

The answers to these questions will make it clear whether you need to keep the item.

## CATEGORIZE

Categorizing will help you decide where each item belongs and how much space you should allocate to each category when you are organizing. Create broad categories (too many categories or categories that are too specific or narrow may be difficult to remember and actually make organization more difficult). Some categories you might consider include the following:

- marketing/promotional materials
- client files
- personal files
- personal items (photos, mementos)
- office supplies
- books
- reference materials
- work to be done immediately
- archive
- delegate

As you categorize, you'll find more items that can be removed from your work space (such as items that can be archived or work to be delegated to others). Get those things out of the space as soon as possible.

## GIVE EVERYTHING A HOME

Next, you'll need to create a home for everything that's left. You might consider organizing by these methods:

- proximity (put things that you use together near each other)
- space (put things where you have room for them; use space to your advantage)
- frequency of use (how often you need to access something—the more you need it, the more accessible it should be)

Ensure that the following items are taken care of:

- High-traffic areas are free from congestion. (Don't put boxes or files on the floor!)
- Storage space and necessary materials are accessible.
- Memo boards and important information that are accessed daily can be easily seen.

 **Get Help**

The same tip that works for managing activities works here, too. It can be tough to tackle a project like this on your own, and it can be difficult to be objective about your "stuff." Asking a friend or colleague to help you out can give you a different perspective. You can also do this on the telephone by telling a friend what you want to do. Check in with each other at a predetermined time. Report what you have completed and what you will do in the following hour. Working with a friend also helps improve your productivity by providing accountability. It's embarrassing to tell someone what you intend to do and then have to tell the person you didn't do it.

## Step 4: Schedule

Regardless of your organizational type, your calendar—whether paper or electronic—is one of the best tools you have for organizing your activities *and* organizing your space. We'll talk more about using your calendar in Chapter 6, but for now, schedule time for organizing and clutter-busting your office on a regular basis (see Step 5). This is a vital part of keeping clutter at bay. The weekly fifteen-minute pickup discussed below helps, but you should do a more thorough decluttering every few months. This involves decluttering your space and electronic files as well as getting rid of bad clients, planning for the future, and creating schedules and procedures that work for your office. Make adjustments where necessary.

It won't get done unless you block out the time on your calendar now. Schedule time regularly to sort through your e-mail inbox and get rid of anything you don't need to take action on. Eliminate what you can and print it or save anything that you need to retain to the electronic file and delete the e-mail.

## Step 5: Maintain

To keep up your clutter-free environment, you've got to maintain it regularly. This is the hardest part of conquering clutter. It's easy to fall back into the clutter trap as daily life (and law practice) gets in the way, but don't let that make you give up on organization and clutter-busting.

The periodic review and purge is important for all organizational types, but especially for the pack rat and the multi-tasker. These types tend to hold on to unnecessary items or paperwork either because they are afraid to get rid of things or because they're constantly moving from one task to the next, often not taking the time to evaluate whether items should stay or go.

Schedule time for organizing and clutter-busting your office on a regular basis. Review your schedule and your immediate tasks, along with your goals, priorities, and project lists. Daily maintenance may be too ambitious, but weekly or monthly maintenance is essential. One of the keys to keeping clutter to a minimum is to ensure that everything you keep has a purpose and a "home," or a place where it's always found, so that you don't waste time looking for items (whether it's your stapler or a client's file). Add "clutter maintenance" to your calendar for larger blocks of cleaning and organizing time.

### FIFTEEN-MINUTE PICKUP

Before you leave the office at the end of the week, take fifteen minutes to do a quick pickup of your space: move out files and paperwork that don't belong, get rid of any unnecessary mail or junk flyers, and so on. Take a few minutes to review your calendar and tasks for the following week, and make a plan.

When you use the weekly fifteen-minute pickup strategy, Monday mornings will be much easier. You'll arrive to a neat, organized office and a plan. Rather than spending precious time at the beginning of the week trying to figure out where you left off and what you have to do, you'll be able to get right to work.

## REDUCING FUTURE CLUTTER

Sometimes the best strategy is to start now and work forward rather than trying to deal with the backlog first. The strategies outlined in this section can help you keep clutter from building up in the future and help you maintain your reduced-clutter existence once you've tackled the backlog.

### Cure "I Need to See It" Syndrome

What is "I need to see it" syndrome? It's that habit—common to many lawyers—of keeping files, paperwork, and notes in piles on the desk, floor, or office chairs, or a pile of sticky notes on the computer, as "reminders" to accomplish particular tasks or work on particular files. But those who do this are just kidding themselves.

Clutter piles up because you have become dependent on physical reminders of tasks you need to accomplish; in other words, you are afraid that if you can't see it, you'll forget it, and the task will never get done. But the problem is that once the pile, file, or note stays in one place for too long, it no longer serves as a good reminder. Instead, it becomes part of the furniture—you become so used to seeing it in the same place day after day that you stop noticing it. Its utility as a reminder or a trigger to act disappears over time.

Using the item itself as a reminder actually reduces, rather than increases, your efficiency and effectiveness because it is more difficult to focus on the task at hand with those reminders physically looming over your head; you're literally getting buried under your "to-dos!" And the more of those reminders you have, the more difficult it is to distinguish the truly important from the unimportant.

Often, the pile of files isn't the most urgent or important thing you need to do, but just seeing it there makes you think you need to address it right away. But putting the pile first is like filling the jar with sand and keeping out the big rocks. And as you add piles, they blend into the background and eventually you don't see them anymore, which defeats the purpose of having them there in the first place.

Break the habit by putting good systems in place to ensure that important tasks get done. Instead of using files, paperwork, or notes as physical reminders, use your calendar and your action folders or master project list as the triggers to take action. Schedule an appointment with yourself to do the work. Then put the files away until the appointment date and time arrives.

If a task needs to be done but is not urgent and you can't fit it into your calendar now, schedule a reminder for a specific period of time in the future and put the reminder on your calendar with the name of the file or task and a short description of what you need to do. When the reminder date arrives, you can decide whether the task is important enough to schedule or whether you should push the reminder into the future.

You'll learn more about how to do this in Chapter 6.

If you really can't do without the physical reminder, consider using David Allen's system of folders or lists grouped by category.[22] Instead of keeping a big

---

22. See David Allen's website at http://www.davidco.com/ for this and other aspects of the "Getting Things Done" system.

bulky file in your office, you'll have only an item on your list or one piece of paper in a file folder noting what you need to do. Use a "tickler" system with one folder for each month and folders numbered 1 to 31 representing each day of the month to diary items for follow-up.

## Your Desk

Your desk is *prime* real estate—the most prime real estate in your office. That means anything that's kept on your desk should be something that's used daily. Remove items not related to work. Keep office supplies in drawers or on shelves where they're within reach but not cluttering up your desk. Make use of vertical space: hang shelves or wall pockets or bulletin boards to keep control of those "important" papers that regularly pile up. These methods keep important reference information or reminders in view without interfering with your work.

Don't keep shuffling paper around on your desk. If it needs action, *schedule* it (more about this in Chapter 6).

## Paper

Eliminate paper as soon as possible after it arrives; perhaps nothing can make you more efficient than reducing your reliance on paper. Paper gets lost, coffee gets spilled on it, and all kinds of other things happen. In fact, one study found that workers spent an average of three hours per week searching for paper that had been misfiled, mislabeled, or lost.[23] That's why it is so important to open your mail over the trash and immediately toss anything that you don't need. Scan everything else. And don't let junk mail sit around and clutter up your workspace.[24]

## Business Cards

Lawyers collect business cards whether they want to or not. Cards are exchanged in court, at bar events, when networking, and even at social events. Use your scanner or consider a dedicated card scanner. Scan the information into your

---

23. K.J. McCorry, "The Cost of Managing Paper: A Great Incentive to Go Paperless!" September 16, 2009, Que Publishing, http://www.quepublishing.com/articles/article.aspx?p=1393497.
24. For more tips on eliminating paper, read Sheila M. Blackford and Donna M. Neff's *Paperless in One Hour for Lawyers*, from the ABA Law Practice Division (2014). http://shop.americanbar.org/eBus/Store/ProductDetails.aspx?productId=214238.

contact system and toss all of those business cards! If you're an Evernote user, consider the Premium account, which will let you scan business cards and enter all of the information into your address book and into LinkedIn, making following up and connecting with new acquaintances even easier.

## Periodicals

You've probably got all kinds of periodicals and other materials that you'd like to read but just haven't had time to go through. Newspapers, trade magazines, and other journals multiply quickly. They might contain valuable articles or other information, but if you've got a pile of periodicals three feet high, chances are that you'll never get to it. One way to combat this is to begin where you are; toss the old ones and start anew. Almost every piece of information can be found online more quickly and easily than by wading through a stack of periodicals because you think you might have seen an article somewhere in an issue . . . assuming you remember that you saw the article in the first place.

To keep publications from piling up, skim through the table of contents and pull out only those articles that you want to read. Toss the rest. Keep a "reading" folder in your briefcase for those times when you're waiting in the doctor's office, waiting for your adversary in court, or riding on the train. You may consider having a secretary or assistant prescreen your periodicals and pull articles for you.

We all love paper articles. We were raised on them, and nothing replaces the feeling of reading that nice original publication. But the reality is that we can't schlep all those magazines around. That's why, despite our love of paper, scanning the materials (or converting an online piece) into an electronic document saved to the cloud, which can be read just about anywhere and on any type of electronic device, is much more effective.

If you see an article that you think might be helpful to archive, scan it (desktop scanners scan quickly and can scan both sides of a document at the same time) and save the resulting PDF file on your computer, or save it to a cloud utility like Dropbox in a folder you can open when you're stuck in the airport or the start of your court hearing is delayed for hours. The Fujitsu ScanSnap desktop scanner is a popular model, and it comes with Adobe Acrobat software. You'll feel lighter without all of that paper!

If you find the articles online, use Evernote, Microsoft OneNote, or similar apps that will clip an article and allow you to read it later on your computer, your smartphone, or your tablet. Allison saves scanned articles in a subfolder of her "My Documents" folder, labeled "My Library," or uses Evernote or Microsoft OneNote to save and tag articles.

Dan sorts his articles by topics and even numbers them (starting at 01) so that he knows which articles are most recent; he deletes the material after review. If he needs to save it for the long term, he stores it in Evernote or e-mails it to himself and then stores it in his office's electronic filing system, whichever makes more sense. And it's there if he needs it again.

Evernote (https://evernote.com/) is online archiving and note-taking software with desktop versions for Windows or Mac and apps for iOS, Android, Windows Phone, and Blackberry, in addition to the web-based version. You can create notes directly within Evernote or capture web pages (or e-mails) and then add annotations, tag for easy categorizing, sync across multiple devices, and easily search. The program even lets you search text within a photo.

Diigo (https://www.diigo.com/) is a cloud-based knowledge management program that archives the web pages for the links you save and makes them fully searchable; even if the link is broken or disappears, you'll still have the information you need. Instapaper (http://www.instapaper.com/), Delicious (https://delicious.com/), Reeder (http://reederapp.com/ios/), and Pocket (http://getpocket.com/) are other popular options.

When all of this information is in one central location, it is easy to find when you have downtime.

Although saving items in electronic form can reduce paper clutter and help you keep better track of documents and information, beware of creating electronic clutter. Don't save everything simply because the information is stored electronically. Use the strategies you've learned to eliminate unnecessary electronic files or move them to archives. And don't save everything in your e-mail inbox. Having a thousand items in the inbox is not a badge of honor; it's merely turning that overcrowded inbox on your desk into one on your computer. There are ways to tame this inbox beast, including using rules that we'll discuss in Chapter 10.

## Paper Files

You must have an efficient filing system for both paper and electronic files. The best systems are those that mimic each other; that is, your paper file folders have names that are the same as or similar to your electronic ones. When creating a filing system, the simpler the better. Don't file stuff just to get it off of your desk. Only file what you'll actually need. Statistics show that 80 percent of what you file will never get used or referenced again anyway, so be selective.

To reduce "reference" files, ask yourself these questions:

- Can this information be found elsewhere (such as on the Internet, with a simple Google search)?
- Do I need the whole thing (i.e., just cite vs. whole case)?
- Will it be outdated by the time I need it again?
- Can I scan it and save it electronically?
- How would I find this if I needed it again?

## Paper Filing Systems

There is no one "best way" to maintain your office files. The "best" filing system is the one that is easily understandable by everyone in the office, that is followed consistently, and that makes it easy for you to find the information you need when you need it. Your practice area and jurisdictional rules may impact how you maintain your files and how long you keep them. Many lawyers use Redweld files with internal file folders separated by category, but this method might not work for everyone in every practice area. Some lawyers find it easier to work with binders and dividers instead of files and folders. And sometimes a combination of both works best (for example, using Redwelds with internal folders for litigation files but creating notebook binders specifically for trial). You may want to experiment to find what works the best for you.

Whatever method you choose, you'll want to keep your filing system as simple as possible and keep a master index or database of all of the files in your office and their names and/or numbers. In Chapter 8, we'll talk more about systems and protocols related to documents and files.

Use shelves or file cabinets to keep files neat and organized, or leave the files in the file room. It's far better to walk to the file room or file cabinet than to have files piled all over the floor and furniture in your office. But of course, as we'll explain later on, you save a ton of time if your files are on your computer or office server and you never have to get up from your desk to view a file or anything in the file.

Move closed files to an out-of-the-way or off-site storage area. Don't let them use prime space in your office. Even better, scan them and save them electronically, use cloud or other backup storage solutions, and then dispose of the physical files. Make sure, however, that you return original documents to clients and that you disclose in advance that you intend to dispose of their paper files. If the client wants the hard copy, you can send it on after you convert it to electronic format and eliminate the time and cost in shredding the file.

## Mail (Snail Mail)

Open your mail over the trash and immediately toss anything that you don't need. Don't let junk mail clutter up your workspace. Divide the rest into the following piles:

- **Do** (items that require action)
  - Your highest priority should be items with dates or deadlines, such as hearing notices, trial scheduling orders, and briefing schedules. The best practice is to immediately enter these items into whatever calendars, to-do lists, and case management and other systems your office uses. That way, if someone gets sidetracked, the event or deadline is recorded. Scan the notice and attach it to the calendar or reminder so that you can instantly see it. For hearings, this provides a quick way to confirm where and when the hearing is, without the need to run around searching for the original notice.
  - Next, address any other client-related items and be sure they are noted in the client files.
  - Then *scan everything* that needs to be retained. If you need to keep the paper version because there is a legal requirement to retain it or because it will need to be returned to the client in the future, mark the original to confirm that it has been scanned.
- **Decide**
  - Some mail represents decisions that need to be made that are not related to a client file. These items might include CLE programs, invitations to events, or offers from vendors. These items can also be scanned, particularly if there are dates or deadlines that will impact your decision.
  - It can be helpful to make a note of the event and schedule a specific time on your calendar to make a decision.

- Alternatively, you may want to create a "decide" folder that you review as part of your weekly plan.
- **File** (items that need to be saved in a client's file or for your records but don't require other action) everything or, if you are paperless, place the non-original items in your shredding piles. Make sure, however, that you never shred anything until it is docketed, scanned, and backed up. There's no rush to shred—but remember, don't just throw out items with client or confidential information, which should be securely disposed of (which, in most cases, means shredding).
- **Pay** (bills to be paid)
- **Read** (handle like periodicals above)

In some offices, the scanned items are still given to attorneys (Dan likes that method). This is fine as long as the attorneys know that they can't keep everything on their desks and should dispose of the items once they are reviewed. Don't let your staff or attorneys circumvent the scanning process.

Once the mail has been sorted, your work is not done. Add to-do items to your calendar or task list. Delegate filing and bill paying where necessary or create homes for those items and designate a specific time for those tasks to be performed.

## E-mail

Most lawyers have e-mail clutter. Many have inboxes with thousands of messages in them. Because e-mail is such a major clutter and productivity obstacle, we've dedicated an entire chapter to it later in the book. See Chapter 10 for our e-mail tips.

## Faxes

Consider switching to an e-fax service to cut down on paper (and get your faxes by e-mail even when you're not in the office).

Anything named "e-something," such as e-mail or e-fax, was created and designed to be electronic. Thus, electronic mail (e-mail) is an alternative to paper mail. Similarly, e-faxing was created so that lawyers (and others) could stop wading through piles of paper faxes and instead have faxes delivered to their inboxes as another form of e-mail. By using e-faxes, recipients no longer have to go through every paper fax, including all the junk advertising CLEs, vacation packages, and the like.

Most faxes are junk or don't need to be kept in hard copy. As a result, there is no reason to send or receive faxes in the traditional paper form. Instead, use one of the many services such as RingCentral (www.ringcentral.com) or eFax (www.efax.com) that allow you to send and receive faxes by e-mail. With these services, you e-mail faxes to a specified e-mail address (from a list of approved addresses you specify), and they will be faxed to the recipients (many of whom use the same type of service). When you receive a fax, it will be e-mailed to you at the fax number registered with the service, and then you can (only if necessary) print it. You can save it electronically as well.

E-faxing can help to reduce paper and improve efficiency. First, you don't need to have a dedicated phone line for faxes. Most services will designate one, which eliminates your monthly fee for the fax line. You'll also eliminate long-distance charges for sending faxes because they will now be sent as e-mail attachments. And you'll eliminate the time and expense associated with printing something, faxing it, and then discarding the printed document.

Second, your faxes will be delivered to your e-mail and the e-mail of anyone else in your office who should be receiving them. This means that there are no more piles of paper to wade through, and if the fax isn't for you, just hit Delete.

Third, e-faxing eliminates all fax machine expenses, including paper, toner, and maintenance and repairs. These costs add up, and just like reducing your reliance on paper is good for the environment, so is eliminating your use of paper fax machines.

Fourth, most electronic fax services are inexpensive and require no setup (unless you have a larger firm and want every staff person to have a dedicated fax number).

Fifth, you can send an e-fax from anywhere that you have Internet service (so you can e-mail the fax to the service).

Finally, because the services are online, you can send and receive multiple faxes at once, and the quality is generally better than that of most fax machines. Plus, if you accidentally delete a fax, most services store the faxes and allow you to log in and retrieve them, even months later.

## WRAP-UP

The battle against clutter is an ongoing one, even in this age of electronic media. Lawyers still create, receive, and exchange large amounts of paper, and lawyers who have been practicing for some time may have difficulty letting go of old habits and reducing their reliance on physical files, folders, and documents. But creating good habits around paper and clutter can help reduce anxiety and improve organization and productivity within your office.

## CHAPTER 3 ACTION STEPS

1. Determine your organization style and choose the clutter-busting strategies that will work best for you.

2. Take one area at a time, whether it's a desk drawer, a file cabinet, or your desk itself, and follow the five steps to decluttering.

3. Don't try to tackle everything at once; get in the habit of using the strategies outlined in this chapter to deal with new items coming into your office so that you don't contribute to clutter in the future.

# Chapter 4

## ELIMINATE BY DELEGATION

Managing your activities effectively allows you to enjoy your work more and have time to devote to those things that are important to you—whether they're related to your practice or not. One of the best ways to manage your activities is by learning how to delegate effectively. Just because a task or item on your to-do list is a priority doesn't mean *you* are the only one (or even the best one) who can do it.

As we discussed in Chapter 1, your time is best used by focusing on tasks that are high value: tasks that require your personal touch or your specific expertise. In Chapter 2, we saw how eliminating unnecessary tasks can be effective. In Chapter 3, you got rid of a lot of clutter so that you could create more breathing space within which to work, and by doing so, you may have identified additional tasks or to-do items that need to be completed.

In this chapter, we'll tackle the tasks that cannot be eliminated and don't fit in your schedule, tasks that are priorities but that you can't focus on, and tasks that may not be your strengths. Those tasks can often be delegated to others, either with or without your direct supervision.

Delegation helps you get more accomplished in less time and helps you develop your skills as a manager. By giving work to others, you will also get an outside perspective on what you're doing, and those workers may even be able to make suggestions to improve what you do and how you serve your clients.

Delegation is important for you as a lawyer and for the associates, staff, or others who get the work. Delegating to people allows them to contribute to the firm and to your goals. It lets them grow, gain skills, and feel that they are an important part of your efforts.

## WHY YOU DON'T DELEGATE

Lawyers tend to be perfectionists. Unfortunately, perfectionism can be an enemy of productivity, as we'll see in Chapter 5. It is also an enemy of delegation. Although most lawyers acknowledge that delegating is generally a beneficial strategy, those same lawyers have multiple excuses for why they themselves don't delegate. These excuses include the following:

- They think they do the work better than anyone else and that it will take longer to explain the project and make corrections later than to just do it themselves. (Remember the perfectionist from the previous chapter?)
- They think they have no one to delegate to. (This is often the excuse of the "true solos," who think that since they don't have staff, they can't delegate.)
- They are getting a payoff by not delegating; they like to be seen as the one person who can do it all or who is always on the go.

But here's the truth:

- While it may take longer in the short run to train someone else, if the task is one that truly should be delegated, the overall long-term return on your time is well worth it.
- Delegation is even more important for "true solos" than it is for attorneys with staff. Because solos have to wear so many hats, they need to choose where to focus their limited time and energy even more wisely if they want to be effective.

On the other hand, despite the clear benefits, some persist in their belief that delegation just isn't worth it. Ask yourself what you're gaining by not delegating. Do you secretly like being too busy, bragging about how much work you have to do? Are you proud of how late you stay at the office every night? What is the *real reason* you don't delegate? In most cases, that reason is not more important than improving your bottom line, spending more time with your family, or truly providing excellent service to your clients.

In some cases, lawyers don't delegate because when they've tried in the past, it hasn't worked as well as they'd hoped, or it didn't work right away, so they gave up. But many delegation failures can be easily solved by following a few simple steps.

If you're truly sick and tired of killing yourself, you can learn to delegate effectively.

## WHAT SHOULD YOU DELEGATE?

The first step is deciding what to delegate. Knowing your strengths and weaknesses can help you to make that determination. Anything that you avoid doing, hate doing, or just don't do well is a potential candidate for delegation. If someone else can do it faster, cheaper (without sacrificing quality), better, or more consistently, delegate it. But even if you happen to be great at a particular task, it might not be effective to spend your time on it. If someone else will get it done well enough and it isn't your highest priority or doesn't require your personal touch, delegate it.

These questions will help you determine whether a particular task should be delegated:

- Is this the highest use of my time?
- Is it my strength?
- Is it at the core of what I get paid for?
- Is it one of my highest priorities?
- Does it serve my goals?
- Does it require my individual participation or my personal touch, skills, or expertise?
- Is it something I can teach others to do?
- Is it something that is done repeatedly in my practice?
- Do I enjoy doing it? (If so, why? Is there a higher-value activity that gives the same payoff?)
- Is this a task that goes to the heart of what I do as a lawyer?
- Does it go to the heart of how I bring in business?
- Do I have the requisite expertise to complete this task effectively?
- Will it cost less (for me or the client) if someone else does it?

Use these questions to delegate effectively in the same way you used the priority questions in Chapter 1; learn how to balance what needs to be accomplished and when with how important that work is and whether it requires a specific individual to complete it.

Focus your energy on the tasks that

- further your core values,
- are the most profitable, and/or
- require your personal participation or expertise.

Delegate the rest.

If you're like most lawyers we know, you lament about clients who try to handle their legal matters on their own, often making the situation worse instead of better. Don't be a DIY lawyer! Know when to hire a professional. A professional can be anyone who is specifically trained or has detailed knowledge about a certain project or task that needs to be done. Your training is in law. Know when to hire someone who has training in marketing, or spreadsheets, or bookkeeping, and so on. Focus on what you've been trained to do, and let others focus on what they've been trained to do.

## TO WHOM SHOULD YOU DELEGATE?

Once you've decided which tasks you want to delegate, you need to choose who will do them. One way to do so is to determine the strengths and weaknesses of the available individuals. Some of them may already be working in your office, but you may need to search for others outside your office, particularly for specialized or highly technical tasks.

Solos are often concerned about expense when it comes to delegating, because they don't have available staff, which usually means outsourcing. But delegating to someone else doesn't mean that you have to spend a lot of money. The "cost" of doing something yourself is often higher than the cost of hiring someone else to do it—especially if that person can do it better or faster or if you are freed up to do the tasks that contribute directly to the bottom line.

You don't have to actually hire an employee or make a long-term commitment to start delegating. One advantage of delegating by outsourcing is that it can be a short-term, temporary arrangement with individuals who don't require a lot of supervision or extra benefits.

Many tasks can be delegated to technology. For example, digital dictation services can get your typing done while you sleep, and case management software can automatically track deadlines and tasks.

## WHEN DELEGATION DOESN'T WORK

There are many reasons why delegation may not work. Some of these reasons include the following:

- poor hiring
- choosing the incorrect employee to delegate to
- poor or no training
- lack of incentives or motivation for employee
- employee fear or risk aversion
- unclear job duties or unclear task assignment
- constant criticism of task results and techniques
- unrealistic goals
- unclear objectives
- micromanaging

Some of these reasons are the fault of the delegatee, and some are the fault of the delegator. Even if you have no control over hiring and firing and don't have the opportunity to choose the individual to whom you will be delegating, you *can* work on becoming a better delegator.

### Levels of Authority

Delegation can be done by handing an entire task to someone else, or you can delegate only a portion of a task, project, or activity to others. There are different levels, beginning with only delegating a very small portion of the task—such as information gathering—with most of the responsibility retained by the supervising lawyer, all the way through delegating the whole task, with the lawyer being completely uninvolved and the delegatee having complete authority over the project.

Delegatees must understand how much authority they have to make decisions with respect to the task or project you're giving them. Failing to do so can create confusion and foster mistrust, resentment, and other problems.

One of Allison's clients, the managing lawyer in a midsize law firm, has begun to give additional responsibilities to some of the senior lawyers in the firm, over and above their client and case work. These responsibilities include management tasks such as reviewing and revising client bills, dealing with vendors, and supervising staff. But the managing lawyer was unclear about the level of authority the lawyers had for these tasks, and as a result, he felt that the younger partners were "overstepping" their boundaries, while the younger partners felt that he was micromanaging them, leading to frustration and miscommunication on all levels.

See Figure 4.1 for an example of these delegation levels.

**Figure 4.1** Levels of Delegation Authority

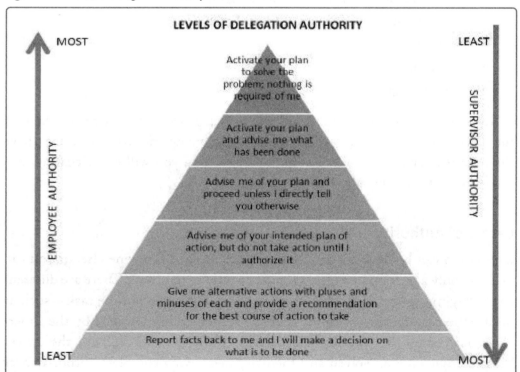

It is important to include as part of your instructions a discussion of the level of authority or responsibility you are expecting your subordinate to undertake.

## FIVE STEPS TO EFFECTIVE DELEGATION

Haphazard delegation—done with little thought or planning, usually on the fly—is bound to fail. To successfully delegate, follow these five steps:

1. Give clear, comprehensive instructions.
2. Ensure that you've been understood.
3. Set a definite deadline and establish priorities.
4. Check in.
5. Evaluate and share the outcome.

### Step 1: Give Clear, Comprehensive Instructions

This is the single most crucial component of effective delegation. It's harder than it sounds and may require some trial and error. What makes this element so difficult is that when you are an expert or have been doing something for a long time, you often assume that others know as much as you do; you forget that what is obvious to you may not be obvious to someone else, especially someone who is new to the task or to your expectations or way of working.

To make delegating easier, try creating checklists or other written instructions, particularly for tasks that will be performed repeatedly, for jobs where turnover is likely, or for tasks that are performed by more than one person. A great resource for checklists is Dan's *Checklists for Lawyers*, published by the ABA Law Practice Division.

Be specific about the scope of the project: how long, how much time, how many, and other details. For example, provide a guideline or estimate of the length of time you anticipate that it should take to complete the task or how many pages the end product should be. If the delegatee finds a task is taking longer than you estimated, the person can check back with you to determine whether to keep going, cut the project short, or go in another direction.

Designate maximum time limits or create "check-in" times. For example, you might specify that a project should take no longer than three hours and that the person must stop and report back when time is up. Alternatively, have a set time limit at which the person must stop working and "check in." For example, ask your delegatee for a progress report after two hours of working on the task before going further.

Communicate why this assignment is important and how it fits into the overall work of the firm:

- How does it affect clients?
- How does it help the firm function?
- How does it fit into the overall strategy of a particular case?

When employees know that their roles are important and how they fit into the work that you do for your clients, they are more "invested" in the project—and more likely to get it right.

## Step 2: Ensure That You Have Been Understood

Miscommunication is inevitable. To an experienced lawyer, a "memo" might mean a short, one-page, bulleted document setting forth the current state of the law. But to a newly minted associate, a "memo" may mean a full-length legal brief complete with case citations.

Encourage questions, even when using written instructions and checklists. Too often delegation fails because employees are afraid to ask questions or to let their boss or supervisor know that they don't understand. Foster an atmosphere of communication; it is better to find out that employees don't understand the assignment *before* they get started than to find out after they've already wasted hours on the wrong task.

Have delegatees repeat back to you their understanding of the project *in their own words*. This process clears up misunderstandings, reduces omissions ("Oops, I forgot to include that step in the instructions"), and creates greater accountability. Don't just ask, "Do you understand?" The answer will invariably be yes, whether they understand or not. Let them tell you what they think you want them to do. This is your opportunity to ensure that your instructions were clear and that you've properly defined both the scope of the project *and* the ultimate goal. Let delegatees tell you their understanding of the project before they begin. This will also increase their buy-in to the project.

There is no negative to having delegatees write down the assignment; in fact, it is a huge positive. Think about the times when a server takes your order, never writes anything down, and then your meal is prepared incorrectly, and you wonder why the server didn't write down what you wanted.

## Step 3: Set Expectations and Priorities

Delegation often fails because expectations are unclear, no deadlines are set for completing the project, delegatees have no idea whether the project is a priority, or delegatees don't understand the expected outcome.

Communicate goals, deadlines, and priorities to employees so that they know when the project must be completed and how important it is in relation to other work they have to do. That way, if they receive another assignment and they're not sure what should be done first, they can ask you or decline the other assignment. If you delegate several projects to the same employee, make sure you establish the priority of each project in relation to the other work you have assigned. Human nature dictates that work that is urgent gets attended to first. If there are no deadlines, there is no urgency.

## Step 4: Establish Benchmarks and Check-Ins

Keep track of project deadlines on your calendar or in your reminder system, but don't wait until the deadline to determine whether your delegatee is on track, particularly if you're new to delegation or to working with this particular employee.

Schedule a check-in meeting with delegatees when you think enough time has passed to have uncovered some questions, but don't wait so long that you can't rein them in if they're completely off track. Even when you encourage questions, some will still be afraid to ask. Establish specific benchmarks or milestones or a definite check-in date. Add the check-in date to your calendar.

When you're first delegating to someone, you'll probably want to be a bit more vigilant, but checking in does not mean micromanaging. You must develop confidence in those you delegate to, particularly professionals, and allow them to do their jobs. Micromanaging will ensure that they never learn and can never progress to higher levels of authority.

The necessity for checking in depends upon the nature of the project and how well you know the delegatee's work. If you've been delegating to someone for a while and that person is meeting your expectations, the need to check in should be reduced drastically, and perhaps eliminated, particularly once you're satisfied that the individual will ask questions if necessary.

## Step 5: Evaluate and Share the Outcome

Completion of the task by the delegatee or return of the work to you isn't the end of the delegation process.

Feedback is an important part of good delegation. A major complaint of lawyers who have to delegate but insist that it doesn't work is that their tasks are never completed properly (perfectionists) and they end up having to do things over. But when these lawyers are asked whether they shared any complaints, disappointments, or deficiencies with the individual to whom the task was given, many say they never bothered. If you can't take the time to teach your employees and let them know where they've gone wrong, you can't expect them to grow and improve.

Give praise for a job well done. Positive feedback can be even more important than negative feedback, particularly for those who are new to a task.[25] Positive feedback fosters loyalty, to both you and your clients, and it helps motivate employees to continue to improve. Let your employees know what you think of their work. Let your employees know what they've done right.

Share the outcome of the overall case or project with those who worked on it. Sharing the outcome signals to your employees that their work is an important part of what you do and that they are an integral part of your success. Bring the process full circle.

Delegation is a two-way street. The delegatee has a task to complete, but the delegator has an obligation to hold the delegatee accountable and to provide feedback. Failure to follow through with accountability causes associates and staff members to lose respect for the process, question the partner's or firm's commitment to them, to their work, and to their clients, and may even result in an employee failing to follow through with future assignments.

Feedback can go both ways. In addition to giving feedback to delegatees, ask for feedback from them so you can continue to improve your delegation skills.

---

25. Ayelet Fishbach, Tal Eyal, and Stacey R. Finkelstein, "How Positive and Negative Feedback Motivate Goal Pursuit," *Social and Personality Psychology Compass* 4, no. 8 (2010): 517–30, http://faculty.chicagobooth.edu/ayelet.fish-bach/research/FEF%20Compass%202010.pdf.

## WRAP-UP

Delegation is an important leadership skill that too few lawyers take the time to master. It will help you leverage your employees and get more done in less time, but it will also empower your employees and help them to grow.

To be an effective delegator, you need to master all five steps to effective delegation. Your instructions must be clear and establish the level of authority for the task or project that is being handed over. But no matter how clear you think your instructions are, don't take it for granted that delegatees understand; let them tell you what *they* think the assignment is. Set expectations and priorities so that delegatees know what they should focus on first. Establish benchmarks and check in to ensure that the project does not go off track. And remember to evaluate performance and share the outcome of the task so that delegatees know the value of their contribution to the team.

## CHAPTER 4 ACTION STEPS

1. Make a list of the tasks you can delegate, using the questions on page 55 as a guide.

2. Make a checklist or set of instructions for a task that you often delegate.

3. Delegate your next assignment using the five steps you learned in this chapter.

# Chapter 5
## STRATEGIES FOR GETTING IT ALL DONE

So far, you've learned to prioritize; to eliminate unnecessary tasks, clients, and clutter; and to delegate important tasks that you do not need to do yourself. Now it's time to take care of the work you *do* need to accomplish.

The next two chapters will provide tips and tools to help you manage the many activities that make up a typical lawyer's day. We'll talk about how to determine what actions to take to pursue the goals you set and the priorities you established in Chapter 1 and how to combat procrastination and get down to the business of getting that work done.

## GET EVERYTHING OUT OF YOUR HEAD

Lawyers often have too many demands on their time and not enough resources to meet those demands, leading to increased stress and poor productivity. David Allen's book *Getting Things Done* describes a process for organizing all of your things and reducing anxiety about it at the same time.

Allen's basic premise is that you are not as productive when your mind is constantly busy trying to collect, process, and keep track of all of your commitments, or "open loops," pulling your attention from what you're doing right now. His concept focuses on managing commitments so you can free your mind to concentrate on the task at hand—and be more productive in the process.

The first step is to "get everything out of your head." When you don't have faith that the systems you have created will ensure that all of your important tasks will get accomplished, you rely on your brain to remember all of the things you have to do. But expending all that mental energy trying to remember makes it difficult to concentrate on anything else.

When Dan was a "pure solo," he relied on his memory—and a great case management system—to get things done. But as his firm grew, he "assumed" his new employees knew all the rules and procedures he kept in his head. They didn't. They came to him all the time with questions, and his office seemed to stop moving forward. As a result, Dan needed to do a brain dump (i.e., to take all of the information that was in his head and transfer it to his staff). He did the next best thing: he created checklists and started saving things into a "Law Firm Training & Procedure" file in his case management system. Efficiency improved, tempers calmed, and his office was a much better place to work.

Essentially, as Dan demonstrated in the illustration above, this step is an information dump: writing down *every single thing* you can think of that you need to do, whether short-term or long-term. You will notice as you do this exercise that some of the items on your list will be single tasks. Others will be projects that consist of multiple tasks. Don't worry about that too much now— just try to get everything down on paper.

Once you have "collected" all of this information, when you are confident that you aren't going to miss anything important, your mind will be clear and you will be better able to focus. Your mind (and your thinking) won't be cluttered up with trying to remember things and can be used to solve problems for your clients. As Allen says, you'll be using your mind to think *about* things instead of thinking *of* things.

## IDENTIFY NEXT ACTIONS

After your information dump, you'll have a list of projects and tasks to be accomplished. But how do you move forward? Looking at the big picture all of the time can get overwhelming. But breaking large projects down into individual, concrete steps makes them much more manageable. You've probably heard the old joke:

*What's the best way to eat an elephant?*

One bite at a time.

Or you've heard one of our favorite sayings:

*Yard by yard, life is hard, but inch by inch, life's a cinch.*

Simply put, taking things one step at a time instead of being overwhelmed by the entire project or the totality of work that needs to be done makes any task or project much more manageable. As David Allen says, instead of thinking about the impossibility of completing the entire project, just identify the *very next action* that needs to be done—the smallest possible task you can undertake to move the project forward.

For example, let's say you have to write a legal brief. Instead of thinking about the entire brief-writing project, break it into pieces and then concentrate on the first small step that you need to do. In this case, it might be gathering the documents for the record on appeal or doing some research to determine if the caselaw that addresses the legal issue in question needs updating. An even smaller first step might be simply putting the briefing deadlines on your calendar and scheduling a time to begin the work.

Let's consider another example: improving your online presence for marketing and business development purposes. It's easy to get overwhelmed by all of the potential places you could participate online and the time it could take to do so. Perhaps your first step might be calling a savvy colleague to see what is working for that person or scheduling a brainstorming meeting with your staff. Or it might simply entail reviewing your existing online presence to see if there are any glaring gaps or mistakes that need to be corrected.

Once you have identified the very next step that needs to be taken, schedule a time to complete that step using the techniques you'll learn in Chapter 6 or, if it is a small enough task, consider doing it right away (see the two-minute rule below).

A series of tiny steps will take you farther than you could have imagined.

## TIME YOURSELF

Whether you bill by the hour or not, you only have so many hours each day to accomplish productive work. Estimating the length of time it takes you to perform regular tasks can be invaluable in planning your days (which will help you when you get to Chapter 6), but it can also provide insight about how well you manage your activities now.

Try this exercise:

1. Make a list of the activities you perform on a daily, weekly, or monthly basis, by category.

2. Estimate the amount of time you spend on each category per day, week, or month.

3. Keep track of your activities and the amount of time you spend on each for a month.

4. Take note of activities that you failed to include in your original list.

5. Be aware of "time hogs" and interruptions and how they affect your day.

6. At the end of the month, compare your estimates with reality.

In today's hectic world, many of us try to accomplish too much or are unrealistic with our expectations. This exercise can be a real eye-opener and can help you see why you may be feeling overwhelmed and where you may need to make adjustments. It will also help you to plan better in the future and avoid—or, if that's not possible, make room for—the "time hogs."

## BEATING PROCRASTINATION

Even when we know exactly what we need to accomplish, sometimes we avoid doing it. As we saw in Chapter 2, procrastination can be a form of self-sabotage or self-interruption. Sometimes you need to force yourself to just do the work.

### Fifteen-Minute Timer

Using a timer can be an effective method for avoiding procrastination. Perhaps you've got a project or task that you are avoiding or that seems so overwhelming that you don't know where to start. You may be wasting more time worrying about what to do or how to begin than it would take to complete (or make significant progress on) the task!

Try setting a timer for fifteen minutes and committing only that amount of time to the task. Anyone can stand almost anything for fifteen minutes. You may be surprised at how much you can accomplish in that time. After the timer goes off, feel free to move on to the next task. But you may find that once you've gotten started, you're able to keep going and bring that matter to completion.

Another version of this strategy is known as the Pomodoro Technique®, pioneered by Francesco Cirillo, which uses a timer to break work into short intervals, punctuated by short breaks.[26] One of the main tenets of the technique is that each designated interval should represent uninterrupted working time—no answering the telephone, checking e-mail, or otherwise moving away from the task at hand.

This technique works even better if you have completed the exercise above and kept track of the length of time it generally takes you to accomplish specific tasks, because you'll have a better idea of what can be completed within your fifteen (or twenty-five) minute window.

## Two-Minute Actions

We mentioned the two-minute rule in Chapter 3 on eliminating clutter. But it's one of the more helpful tips in David Allen's book, so it bears repeating: when you're going through the stack of things that you need to do, if something can be done in two minutes or less, *do it* right away. Don't put it aside or make a note or anything else. By the time you put it down and pick it up again, or make the note, you could have completed the task.

## Make Procrastination Work for You

As we've seen, procrastination is often an obstacle to productivity; even if it isn't your main style, everyone has a bit of the procrastinator in them. Procrastination is usually a bad thing—it often means we're avoiding something, and it makes us feel guilty and unproductive. But sometimes procrastination can work *for* you, if you examine the reasons behind it.

Perhaps the task isn't one you enjoy or one that you are proficient at; in that case, procrastination may signal that the task in question is a good candidate for delegation.

Sometimes you procrastinate because you don't want to do something. If the task isn't a necessity or a priority, your procrastination may actually be a choice *not* to undertake that particular project. Perhaps you felt obligated to agree to do

---

26. The technique was named after a tomato-shaped kitchen timer; *pomodoro* is the Italian word for "tomato."

something that, in hindsight, doesn't serve your goals. If that's the case, release the guilt associated with your choice, fess up, and remove the item from your to-do list.

Procrastination can also result from an emotional response to a particular project or task. Can you get an objective viewpoint or otherwise remove the emotion from the situation?

Finally, you may be procrastinating for no reason. Perhaps you're just afraid of something new or you think the task will be worse than it actually is. Use reverse psychology on yourself and employ a version of the fifteen-minute timer. Put the task, or a representation of the task, in front of you. Then force yourself to do absolutely nothing. Stare at the task. Do not allow yourself to be distracted or to do anything else for at least fifteen minutes. Chances are that you'll be so sick of staring at it that you'll get started—and it's likely that the task won't be as bad as you think once you begin.

## GOOD ENOUGH IS GOOD ENOUGH

Here come the perfectionists again. One of the reasons why some important strategic tasks never get accomplished is that too many lawyers want to wait until they "'have time" to devote to "doing it right." They never complete the project because it isn't "perfect," or they fall into the trap of analysis paralysis, wanting to be 100 percent sure they are making the right decision before they proceed. This perfectionism can be another form of procrastination. Of course you shouldn't put out work product or business development materials that are sloppy or unprofessional. But most of the time, good enough is good enough, and you'll never be 100 percent sure if a decision is the correct one until you take action.

Analysis paralysis prevents action. For many lawyers, wasted time is wasted money. In addition, if they never take action, they never find out what works. Action is the key to breaking the pattern.

**Success is measured by the actions we take.**

Ultimately, the only way to make progress and to determine whether an idea will work is by taking action. That means being willing to take risks and accept that some actions may have to be changed or discarded over time. But action is what will determine whether your firm is thriving or just surviving.

This is the **success formula** that every lawyer needs to remember and look at daily:

### *Information + Implementation = Transformation*

Lawyers have the information part down. They're natural researchers and information gatherers, searching for precedent and what has worked in the past. But often they don't know when to stop researching. They fail on the implementation component of the equation. The irony is, of course, that the implementation is what yields the results.

Lawyers need to remember that every decision isn't going to be perfect and that an important part of this process is to discover what doesn't work and go from there. Just because you go down one road now doesn't mean that you can't change course later if it doesn't work out.

To avoid getting stuck in that endless loop of continuing to "tweak" or improve before rolling out a new procedure, plan, fee structure, or service, follow the 70 percent rule. Attaining perfection is unlikely, if not impossible. Focus instead on getting your project to 70 percent. Then introduce it, accepting its imperfection and recognizing that the best way to improve it is to expose it to and test it in the real world. *Then* you can tweak the parts that aren't working.

Think like software or technology companies: they roll out a product in "beta" form, allow some testing, feedback, and tweaking, and then release version 1.0. The beta versions always have bugs or are missing something, but the companies roll them out anyway, knowing that the products will perform some functions well and that other functions need improvement. Companies may even learn of some features that they were unaware were important to their customers. If these companies had simply kept the products in-house without real-world testing, two things might have happened: (1) a competitor might have introduced a similar product and beat them to the market, and (2) they would have missed the opportunity to engage with their customers and learn what features, benefits, or results their customers desired.

Instead of waiting until you think your website is 100 percent perfect or your plan for alternative fees is guaranteed to make more money than your current hourly system, get your project to 70 percent, take action, and start getting feedback. You can improve from there, with the help of your clients. Maybe you will even be able to put that project behind you and move on to something new.

## GET A BUDDY

As we've already seen with goal setting, when you really want to accomplish something, it can be helpful to let someone else in on what you're doing and ask for help. Even if you don't need help accomplishing the task, the "buddy system" can provide accountability. It's easy to break commitments to yourself—who would know the difference? But it's much more difficult to admit to someone else that you didn't do what you promised. Most people are embarrassed to admit that they haven't done something. That kind of friendly "peer pressure" can be a powerful motivator, particularly if you schedule regular appointments or progress reports.

Having an appointment with a buddy, coach, or consultant is often the only thing that makes you actually take action—even if it's at the last minute, right before your scheduled appointment or progress report. A buddy can also provide support and encouragement when you're having trouble and will be someone with whom you can celebrate your successes. And you'd be surprised how much you learn by supporting and teaching another person.

## GET OUT OF THE OFFICE/TAKE REGULAR BREAKS

Looking at the same four walls and sitting behind a desk for hours at a time, especially if you practice on your own, isn't exactly conducive to creative thinking. To be effective, your mind and your body have to breathe. This is another of the principles behind the Pomodoro Technique; regular breaks help you to be more productive during your working times.

A change of scenery is sometimes all you need to get going on a project or to get yourself out of a slump.

Getting out of your office or even just away from your desk is particularly helpful when you're working on planning and strategy. When you take a walk or work somewhere other than your office, you're less likely to be distracted by the telephone or the piles of paper that call out to you. Your attention is less likely to be divided between what you're working on now and the other things you could or "should" be doing.

## REWARD YOURSELF

One of the best motivators is a reward. If you've got a particular project that you've been avoiding, come up with a reward that you can give yourself when you've accomplished it or when you've finished each step or stage. Your reward can be some time relaxing, a meal at a favorite restaurant, or a piece of chocolate—anything that will help you complete the project.

## REPURPOSE

Why reinvent the wheel? Everything you do can be used more than once.

For example, when you give a speech or presentation, record it and use the audio on your website or make it into a CD to give or sell. Make notes from your speech outline and publish them as an article, both in print and on the web. Send the same article to a number of different places, both online and off-line, for publication. Create one seminar or presentation and give it in many different venues, for different audiences.

Create case studies or testimonials out of your experiences working with clients (be sure to get clients' consent when using testimonials). Write articles or blog posts or give seminars on a new twist on the law or new case law that affects your practice.

When you write an explanation of a legal concept or process for one client, turn it into a flowchart or handout to give other clients.

## WRAP-UP

It's often easy to identify all of the tasks we need to complete and then to become so overwhelmed with the sheer enormity that we become paralyzed and unable to move forward and take action. Or we're constantly distracted because we're not certain that our systems have captured all of the tasks we need to perform. These bad habits can be extremely demotivating.

By documenting everything that needs to be done, breaking it down into smaller pieces, and using some of the techniques described in this chapter, such as taking regular breaks or working with a buddy, you can reduce stress and retain your motivation.

## CHAPTER 5 ACTION STEPS

1. Make some time on a regular basis to do an "information dump" and get everything out of your head: all of the projects you'd like to accomplish and the tasks you need to complete.

2. Next, choose three of the items on your list and determine the next action for each. Share those projects and actions with a buddy and schedule time to follow up.

3. Set a timer for a short interval, such as fifteen minutes, to get started on your action steps.

4. Reward yourself when you have completed your action steps!

# Chapter 6
## ORGANIZE AND SCHEDULE TASKS WISELY

In the last chapter, we talked about some specific ways to ensure that your day-to-day work gets done, from identifying next actions on a project to working around the tendency to procrastinate. In this chapter, we'll talk about how to organize and schedule all of those projects and tasks and ensure that you have the time in your schedule to fit them all in.

## ORGANIZE TASKS

Sometimes it is easier to accomplish tasks in groups rather than as stand-alone actions. Tasks can be grouped in several different ways, including the following:

- by location (post office, law library, out of the office/errands)
- by tool (all tasks that require the computer, scanner, telephone)
- by type of work (all files to be closed, all complaints to draft, all bills to review)
- by category (administrative, planning, marketing, writing)

When organizing by category, don't create too many; a large number of categories can be difficult to keep track of and can result in wasted time trying to determine where a task belongs. Make the categories relatively broad, as in the example below:

- Administrative tasks
- Networking

- Planning
- Writing
- Family
- Social
- Clients
- Working
- Exercise
- Alone time

## Know Your Peaks and Valleys: Organizing by Energy

Not everyone operates effectively the same way or at the same time of day. Some people have more energy first thing in the morning, and others do their best thinking in the evening. Some people are energized by doing research and writing, and others are energized by interacting with others. Get to know your peak energy times during the day. Learn which activities energize you and which ones exhaust you. Plan accordingly.

## USE YOUR CALENDAR: BLOCK YOUR TIME

Your calendar is one of the greatest activity management tools in your arsenal. Use it wisely. One way to do so is time blocking. Time blocking is simple: it's all about planning. Instead of haphazardly choosing tasks with no rhyme or reason, you reserve a specific block of time on your calendar to complete a task or series of tasks. This is where estimating time well comes in handy, because if you know how long it will take to accomplish a task, you can determine how much time (or how many different blocks of time) you need to reserve on the calendar for that task.

Before you begin a particular activity, write down an estimate of the time you think it will take. When you finish the activity, compare your estimate with the actual amount of time it took. Adjust your estimates accordingly in the future. You may be wasting a lot of time or putting additional, unnecessary pressure on yourself by over- or underestimating the time it will take you to complete endeavors. When you are better at estimating how long tasks will take to complete, you'll make better use of your calendar.

There are several ways that you can block your time.

For example, the "success calendar" method on the Cotton Systems website (www.cottonsystems.com), run by Allison's friend Wayne Cotton, assigns each day a color:

**Blue Sky days:** Strategy and planning—one to two days per quarter if you're alone or have a small staff; four to five days if you're working with a team or larger staff

**Red Tape days:** Education and administration—one day per week (these are "nonbillable" workdays)

**Green Machine days:** Productive days—working on client projects

**Mellow Yellow days:** Personal/vacation time—one week at the end of each quarter

You may want to add some categories, such as marketing and business development or volunteer/pro bono time. Wayne suggests making every single day have only one color theme, recognizing that some of the other colors may "creep in" to those days, but most of the time will be devoted to one type of activity.

This system might not work for everyone, but it's worth trying. You might set aside half days, or just significant blocks of time, especially if you're an associate and don't have total control over your own schedule. But having one full day devoted to something like planning makes a big difference in your focus and productivity.

## SET DEADLINES

A goal isn't worth much unless there's a deadline. The same is true for a task. When you have a scheduled meeting with a client or a hearing date for a motion, somehow the work gets done on time. Those deadlines create urgency and provide a framework within which to structure your activities. But what about those tasks that Stephen Covey calls "important but not urgent" that we discussed in Chapter 1? Those are the items that often get carried on a never-ending to-do list.

Without a "drop dead" date for accomplishing those activities, chances are you'll never manage to get around to accomplishing your goal. When there's no deadline, it's far too easy to keep putting important but not urgent tasks on the back burner.

For tasks that fall into Covey's "important but not urgent" category, you must *create your own deadlines*. By assigning a deadline, you create urgency for otherwise non-urgent goals or tasks. For larger goals, choose a deadline that is a bit of a "stretch" or that will take a concerted effort on your part to reach. Don't make the deadline so short that it's impossible to meet, but don't make it so long that you put the activity or goal on the back burner again.

List the steps you'll need to accomplish to reach the goal or complete the project, then set a deadline for each step (or at least for the first step) and put it on your calendar. For example, if one of your goals is to get a website up and running, steps could include things like finding a web designer, deciding on a style, creating the content for the home page and other pages, and choosing a web host. Even those steps can be broken up into smaller actions.

But just because you've created a deadline doesn't mean you'll actually meet it. Indeed, some of you may be thinking that you've tried this before, and setting deadlines, or even putting them on your calendar, has never worked for you. But perhaps that is because you've missed the most important aspect of setting deadlines: they need to be *external*. Deadlines and to-do lists that remain private are easy to ignore because they are internal—you're the only one who knows about them, so they are easy to ignore. Setting external deadlines makes those deadlines have meaning outside of your own personal wish list or calendar. To improve your chances of meeting the deadline, make it external by *publicizing the deadline or sharing it with others* to make it real.

As we've already seen with goals and action steps, if you share them—and your deadline—with someone else and ask that person to hold you accountable, you'll increase your likelihood of reaching those goals.

The nature of your goal will determine whom to share it (and the deadline) with. Sometimes it's an attorney or staff member within your office. Other times, a consultant or colleague is a better choice. Whenever it is appropriate, share your goals and deadlines with clients; this is the most effective option since clients are the people you least want to disappoint.

## WHY EXTERNAL DEADLINES WORK

External deadlines use the power of peer pressure. They work because they act like commitments to other people, even if the only one who really benefits is you. None of us like to break our word or fail to fulfill a promise.

External deadlines also work because they can act as a support system for your efforts where you wouldn't normally have support. When you share your deadlines with others and ask them to keep you accountable, you've created a cheering section—and perhaps even an offer of help. At the very least, you'll have moral support.

Here are some examples:

- If your goal is to go through the publications on your office floor, your assistant may be the most appropriate person to share the deadline with. Most likely, your assistant will be just as happy as you are to see the clutter disappear. And your assistant can help you, either by actively going through them with you or by clearing your schedule and reducing or eliminating interruptions.

- Do you plan to ramp up your business development efforts this year? Devise a seminar topic and set an external deadline. Publicize the date on your website, do a press release, and/or send a mailing to your clients notifying them of the seminar.

- Do you want to finally get that website up and running? Choose a launch date and send postcards to clients and strategic alliances letting them know when you'll finally be online.

One of the advantages of external deadlines is that they force you to get over your perfectionism by letting good enough be good enough, as we saw in Chapter 5. The article or seminar presentation may not be perfect, but at least you've taken the first step. You can always refine it the next time.

## SCHEDULING TIME TO GET WORK DONE

Now that you've set a deadline, put the deadline on your calendar, and committed to someone else to complete the task or project by that date, it's time to actually do the work. Turn to your calendar and physically schedule that activity on a specific date and time.

You may find that using the time-blocking technique alone isn't enough to allow you to reach peak productivity. Often, the reason is that within the time you've blocked out, you're reverting to "reactive mode."

For example, perhaps you've blocked out a day to work on marketing. When that day arrives, instead of having specific tasks planned to execute during that time, you jump from task to task, checking on social media, then remembering you wanted to write an article, and finally deciding you want to create a follow-up letter for clients. Only at the end of the day do you remember that what you really should have done was work on your website. You blocked the time, but you didn't use it wisely. None of those tasks you began were completed, and your main marketing task—the website—received no attention at all. That's where planning, using your calendar and developing external deadlines can help.

If something is important enough to put on a to-do list, it's important enough to be an entry in your calendar, just like a court appearance, a closing, a client meeting, or a doctor's appointment. Your regular deadlines, like court dates or client meetings, are noted on your calendar. Your non-urgent deadlines need to be recorded on your calendar, too. But tracking the deadlines alone isn't enough. To avoid doing everything at the eleventh hour, schedule the time to get the tasks done. Make appointments with yourself and block the time on your calendar to write the motion papers, review your website copy, or develop a plan for the client's case.

When scheduling, leave room for the "chaos factor," otherwise known as Murphy's law, or "whatever can go wrong will go wrong." Emergencies, crises, and unforeseen circumstances are sure to arise. Priorities get shifted. You never know when an unplanned event is going to hit or how long you'll be sidetracked—the only thing that's definite is that it will come, probably when you least expect it, so you might as well be prepared.

Build a cushion into your deadlines, whether they are deadlines for clients, colleagues, family, or just for you. If you think you can get the document to the client within a week, give the client a date two weeks ahead. If you know the presentation is next month, put the deadline on your calendar two weeks in advance. That way, if the unexpected happens, you can still deliver on time. And if the chaos factor doesn't hit, you'll have impressed the client with your quick response—or you can actually take some time to enjoy yourself. Don't schedule every minute of every day. Leave some room in your schedule between tasks.

The advantage to setting specific times to accomplish important tasks and leaving some flexibility in the schedule is that as soon as the crisis or emergency has passed, you can return to your schedule without missing a beat and simply reschedule the tasks that were displaced by the emergency. But if those items were never on your calendar in the first place, they're even less likely to get done. A schedule gives you a blueprint or plan for every day. If a task needs to move, so be it; but at least you'll be choosing another specific time to get it done and it won't languish on a to-do list.

If it isn't on your calendar, it doesn't get done. Urgent gets done. Things that have deadlines get done. But setting the deadline isn't enough. Use your calendar to *schedule appointments to get the work done.*

## WRAP-UP: CREATE DAILY AND WEEKLY PLANS OF ACTION

Don't let yourself be overwhelmed or paralyzed by the amount of work you need to accomplish. Let's recap what we've discussed in the past few chapters and then create a plan of action:

- Determine every day which actions or tasks are the most important and make sure those take center stage. Don't let smaller "urgent but not important" activities get in the way. Put the big rocks in first! If you're a perfectionist, don't let your obsession with getting everything "right" overwhelm you or prevent you from accomplishing your goals. Delegate tasks that don't require your full participation.

- Create a Power of Three list every evening for the next day's work so that you start your day with action rather than with figuring out what you should do first.

- Eliminate distractions; say no to interruptions and bad clients. Multi-taskers: use the timing techniques and create "do not disturb" time. Give each task your full attention.

- Clear the clutter so you can focus on what's important. Pack rats: resist the urge to save everything, and make use of electronic filing!

- Determine the amount of time each prioritized activity will take to accomplish. Don't be stingy with your estimate; estimating too little time will add stress and confusion to your schedule.

- Decide when you will perform a specific activity and put the activity on your calendar. Make sure you leave some empty space or "downtime" on your calendar in addition to the personal and family time that you schedule. And leave room for the "chaos factor."

- Choose a time each week to review the work you need to accomplish and create a plan for the upcoming week. Many of Allison's clients have more success doing their weekly planning on Thursday rather than on Friday, when they are trying to get out the door for the weekend. Mondays work for some, but waiting until the week has already begun is not the best strategy for most. It's easier to enjoy the weekend when you know you can hit the ground running on Monday morning with a preset plan.

- Use your calendar to plan deadlines, but also use it to plan time to complete work. When unforeseen circumstances arise, revise the plan as necessary, moving your appointments to complete work the same way you would reschedule any other appointments.

- Be flexible: recognize that the schedule is not set in stone. It is likely that there will be last-minute emergencies, unforeseen circumstances, or client crises that must be addressed. As part of your weekly review, ensure that your plans cover all aspects of your practice, including marketing, management, administration, business development, and client work.

More often than not, you probably react to whatever is in front of you rather than determining in advance what you want to accomplish. If scheduling time on your calendar for important tasks allows you to complete them in even half the time, it's probably a lot more than you're doing right now. The advantage to setting specific times to accomplish important tasks is that as soon as the inevitable crisis or emergency has passed, you can return to your plan without missing a beat.

Don't leave your schedule to chance. Block time to create a purpose or plan for every day.

## CHAPTER 6 ACTION STEPS

1. Notice your work habits: when and where are you most productive?

2. Instead of simply creating a to-do list, put tasks or work to be done on your calendar for a specific date and time.

3. Block some time for important tasks over the next week. Make sure you're putting in the big rocks first.

4. Get into the habit of setting external deadlines by telling others when they should expect work to be completed.

5. When you encounter a new task that needs to be done, set a deadline, publicize it, and schedule time to complete the work.

# Chapter 7

EFFECTIVE MEETINGS

Lawyers attend (or host) a lot of meetings. Even solos are involved in bar association committee meetings, networking meetings, and client meetings, just to name a few. As technology has made scheduling meetings easier, with the ability to share calendars and send electronic appointments that automatically get added to the recipient's calendar, many of us are finding our days and weeks clogged with more and more meetings, whether they're in person or virtual (video- or teleconference). But meetings can be huge time wasters, as we discussed at the beginning of this book. Because scheduling meetings is so much easier now, it seems that less and less thought is put into determining who needs to attend them. And many meetings are unproductive due to the lack of a specific objective, an unclear agenda, or other problems. That lack of productivity is compounded when the wrong people attend or when meetings are unfocused; participants lose interest.[27] Some of those meetings are entirely unnecessary and can be eliminated completely. Others may require only a few participants.

Meetings can be invaluable tools to brainstorm, get input from a number of people at once, develop goals or strategies, discuss a problem, or choose an action or outcome. But just as e-mail isn't the best tool for all purposes, meetings aren't the best tool for all communications. If you're tempted to schedule a meeting simply to provide an "update" to a number of people, it may be more appropriate to provide that update using another method, such as a project management tool

---

27. Michael Mankins, Chris Brahm, and Gregory Caimi, "Your Scarcest Resource," *Harvard Business Review* (May 2014), http://hbr.org/2014/05/your-scarcest-resource/.

(like Basecamp), e-mail, or a note in the client or project file, unless the update is significant or is tied to an event or a celebration. Meetings should have a specific goal or intended action outcome.

If you can't eliminate the meeting, make it more effective and efficient by avoiding the most common meeting time wasters and following the steps below to develop a meeting system.

## BE MINDFUL OF POTENTIAL PITFALLS

Meetings can fail or be unproductive for a whole host of reasons, including the following:

**Lack of preparation.** Nothing gets accomplished during the meeting because participants did not know what the purpose or intended outcome was or because they failed to prepare by familiarizing themselves with topics of discussion or necessary documents.

**Lack of engagement.** It is difficult to keep meetings on track even when only a few participants are disengaged. Disengaged participants can be a distraction, particularly if they're doing other activities (such as surfing the web, texting, or checking e-mail) during the meeting. Frustration or bad attitudes of attendees who feel they are wasting their time or are not needed to achieve the meeting's intended outcome can bring down the energy of the rest of the group.

**Failure to follow through or implement.** Meetings can seem productive initially but can ultimately be a waste of time if there is no follow-up to ensure that results are documented and communicated, next steps are identified, and decisions are implemented.

**Lack of accountability.** Even when action steps have been set, we've seen a failure to implement (often resulting in additional meetings and wasted time) due to a lack of accountability. When clear responsibility for action steps has not been established, everyone can leave the meeting thinking that someone else will be performing the tasks that have been identified. And when no deadlines, check-in dates, or follow-ups have been confirmed, meeting action items often end up taking a backseat to other tasks.

As you read through our suggestions to make your meetings more effective, think about these potential pitfalls and how you can anticipate and circumvent them.

## DETERMINE YOUR PURPOSE

First, decide the purpose and goal for the meeting. What outcome do you want? Is this a brainstorming meeting to generate ideas, a meeting to identify and/or resolve issues, an action-based meeting to identify next steps and responsibilities, a task-based meeting to accomplish a particular assignment, or a meeting to make a decision?

Once you know what you are trying to accomplish, decide on the meeting structure that will work best: will it be a free-flowing discussion (good for brainstorming or generating ideas), or will participants have a set time to speak (perhaps better for check-in or status-based meetings)? Does the meeting involve a time-sensitive issue that must be addressed right away, or is it a future-oriented planning meeting?

## DECIDE WHO SHOULD PARTICIPATE

Attendance can make or break your meeting: inviting too many people can unnecessarily complicate it, but inviting too few (or the wrong people) can hinder progress.

Your knee-jerk reaction might be to invite everyone in the firm or everyone in a particular category to participate in every meeting, but we recommend that you give a little further thought to meeting invitations.

The meeting's purpose will also drive the attendance. Determine whose experience or expertise will be necessary to accomplish the meeting's purpose. For a decision-making meeting, it stands to reason that the decision makers must be present to accomplish the goal. But be sure to include other stakeholders and those who might be significantly impacted by the decision so that they may give their input or perspective on what factors should be considered.

You may also want to consider whether some participants should be present for only a portion of the meeting rather than for the entire meeting.

## SET THE AGENDA AND COMMUNICATE IN ADVANCE

Create an agenda with topics to be discussed and persons responsible. Show that you respect the time of all involved and set limits for discussion, with a concrete beginning and ending time for the meeting.

Advise invitees of the date and time of the meeting. Communicate the purpose and expected outcome of the meeting and its goals and agenda to all participants well in advance of the meeting so they can prepare. Include any supporting documents that may be needed for the meeting or that you expect attendees to have reviewed or to be familiar with. Advise participants of their expected roles at the meeting. Request that invitees confirm their attendance. Send out a meeting reminder the day before the meeting.

## HIGHLY EFFECTIVE MEETINGS

Start on time and stick to your agenda. Make sure introductions are made if you are not certain that all the participants know one another or if some are attending the meeting remotely. Have attendees indicate who they are and why they are there or what their role in the firm or group is.

Begin the substance of the meeting by repeating the goal or purpose. Advise participants of the format of the meeting. If there is a projected (or firm) end time, announce it in the beginning so that everyone is aware of it.

If issues arise that are unrelated but must be discussed during the meeting, request agreement of the participants to continue beyond the originally agreed-upon end time and establish that only those individuals involved in that particular project or issue be required to stay. If non-urgent issues arise, table them for a meeting to be held at another time specifically for that purpose.

Designate one person to be the meeting facilitator to keep the meeting on point and on time, or assign a timekeeper to keep an eye on the clock and remind the facilitator.

To obtain maximum participation, make the meeting a "safe place" for people to express their opinions without judgment or ridicule. Allow each attendee the opportunity to speak, but don't let one person take over. Obtain different perspectives by asking open-ended questions. Increase participant engagement by assigning different people to lead the discussion on each agenda item.

When controversy arises, look for points of agreement. ("Can we all agree that the goal is . . ." or "If I'm hearing correctly, everyone seems to think there is a problem with Y, but we haven't decided the best way to solve the problem yet. Let's see what we can come up with.")

Before concluding the meeting, develop an action plan based upon your initial agenda. If necessary, recap the decisions that were made, lessons learned, or options identified during the meeting. Confirm next steps, set deadlines for tasks, and assign responsibility for those tasks to specific groups or individuals. Determine whether additional or follow-up meetings will be required and, if possible, schedule them immediately.

## POSTMEETING ACTIONS

Even if you don't take minutes at the meeting, make sure that the main goals and decisions, deadlines, action steps, and responsibilities determined are communicated afterward, in writing, if necessary. Consider whether they also need to be disseminated to those who were not present at the meeting to make follow-up and future meetings more productive, even for those who were unable to attend. Follow up individually with those who have action steps to complete. If a follow-up meeting is needed, add the established tasks and responsibilities to the agenda or request that responsible parties submit a report of their progress to be attached to the agenda.

You may find it useful to send meeting participants a short questionnaire so they can rate the effectiveness of your meeting to help you improve efficiency in the future.[28] Ask participants to rate the meeting in each of the following categories:

- The meeting's **purpose** was clearly defined and was important to me.
- The **information** shared in the meeting was valuable to me.
- The **issue** being discussed was clearly defined and was important or significant to me.
- **Decisions** were made as a result of the meeting, there was clear **responsibility** defined for carrying out those decisions, and it was clear **who was responsible** for carrying them out.
- The meeting resulted in clearly defined **plans, next steps, and deadlines**. How valuable were the outcomes of the meeting compared with the time spent in the meeting?

---

28. Adapted in part from Russell Bishop's *Workarounds That Work: How to Conquer Anything That Stands in Your Way at Work*, McGraw Hill, 2011.

Use a scale of 1 to 5 as follows:

1. No value, a total waste of my time
2. Some value, but not really worth the time
3. Not valuable, but not a complete waste of time
4. Valuable, one of the better uses of my time
5. Absolutely valuable, one of the best things I could have done with my time

Multiply each participant's total score by 4 to get a score out of 100, and see whether your meetings rate an A, B, C, or worse.

## DIFFERENT MEETING FORMATS

Some kinds of meetings Allison's clients have found useful include the following:

### Stand-Up Meetings

A stand-up meeting is conducted with all participants standing to reinforce the brief nature of the meeting and ensure that they don't "settle in." These meetings are generally extremely short, often held simply to alert everyone in the firm or on the team of the status of projects or the activities undertaken by each member. An example might be a weekly briefing in which team members are given an opportunity to report on what they did in the past week, what they are working on this week (or intend to accomplish this week), what obstacles they anticipate, and where they might need help. These meetings can help supervisors and managers quickly determine whether resources (time, energy, staff) are being allocated appropriately or if projects are off track.

Given the time it takes to create and review reports or e-mail messages, stand-up meetings may be a more efficient and effective way to manage some teams.

### Departmental or Practice Group Meetings

Sometimes it's important to get all of the individuals working in a particular practice group or service area together to talk about changes, coordinate the handling of different matters for the same client, discuss changes in procedure that affect only that department, or even catch up on the status of matters. It isn't necessary for everyone in the firm to attend these meetings, but it can be helpful to hold them periodically to ensure consistency within a service or practice area.

## Partner Meetings

Many solo or small firms don't have regular partners' meetings, which can result in inconsistent decision making or lack of communication. It is often beneficial to conduct meetings with partners when firm-wide decisions will be made so that all partners can provide their input and perspective. In our experience, when this isn't done, there are often unintended consequences, since decision makers may not always realize the impact of their decisions on other partners or practice areas until it is too late.

## Staff Meetings

It can be extremely beneficial to conduct meetings solely with staff, or to include staff in larger meetings, particularly in small firms. In-person meetings foster communication and collaboration among staff members and between lawyers and staff. Regular meetings between lawyers and staff who work with them can help reduce interruptions, as we saw in Chapter 2, and may be useful for effective delegation, as we saw in Chapter 4. But don't overlook staff when meeting about policy or procedure changes, either; as frontline workers, they often have valuable contributions that can boost the overall efficiency of the firm.

## Interest Group or Committee Meetings

Small group meetings are often more effective than large group meetings. As we've already seen, in larger groups, it is almost impossible to keep everyone engaged the entire time, particularly if not every item on the agenda is important to every participant. Small meetings by interest or practice group or committee meetings to accomplish specific non-client-related work can be particularly effective.

## CREATE TEMPLATES

Do you routinely repeat meetings in your office? For example, does your firm have regular weekly or monthly partner or staff meetings that cover the same topics? If so, don't reinvent the wheel for every meeting. Create a template agenda that contains all of the items you routinely cover in the meeting, and adjust it only when special issues arise. This will help keep your meetings focused and on track and will let participants know what to expect and how to plan for them.

## MEETING TECHNOLOGY

Technology can help with some of the most onerous meeting planning and execution tasks. For example, one of the biggest meeting-related time wasters is the attempt to schedule meetings with a series of telephone calls and e-mails. Using scheduling programs such as Doodle (www.doodle.com), WhenIsGood (www.whenisgood.net), or MeetingWizard (www.meetingwizard.com) can allow meeting organizers to find the time that works for the most participants and to notify everyone quickly and easily of the scheduled date. Used in conjunction with Microsoft Outlook to send a final calendar appointment with meeting details, these tools can take a lot of the pain out of meeting planning.

Other programs or apps can also be helpful for creating meeting agendas and minutes or for following up on postmeeting tasks. For example, Beesy for iPad allows you to take notes on your iPad, create professional minutes, and automatically follow up on meeting tasks in the To-Do manager.[29] MeetingResult is a software program that helps you with meeting planning, execution, and follow-up.[30] You can develop an agenda based on defined objectives, invite participants, distribute the agenda, keep track of attendance, capture meeting notes, develop next steps, and prepare a meeting summary.

## WRAP-UP

Meetings don't have to be a black hole of wasted time if they are used properly. First, you must determine whether conducting a meeting is the correct way to accomplish your objectives. If it is, you'll want to develop an agenda based upon those objectives and invite only those people who are required to meet those objectives or make decisions necessary to move the project forward. Communicate the objectives in advance to allow participants to fully prepare. Then use facilitation techniques to keep the meeting on task and on time. And don't forget

---

29. https://itunes.apple.com/us/app/beesy-take-meeting-notes-automated/id499578384?mt=8.
30. http://www.meetingresult.com/.

to summarize what was accomplished and document next steps, deadlines, and responsibilities. Consider creating templates for agendas and minutes and using available software programs or apps to make scheduling, note taking, and follow-up easier.

## CHAPTER 7 ACTION STEPS

1. The next time you're planning a meeting, give some thought to the objectives to be accomplished, the type of meeting best suited to meet those objectives, and the people who will need to participate.

2. Consider using scheduling software to eliminate time-consuming e-mail chains.

3. Create an agenda for your next meeting and disseminate it, with the meeting objectives, well in advance. Communicate to all participants that you expect them to be prepared. Send calendar reminders to ensure that the meeting appears on participants' calendars.

4. For repeated meetings, develop templates for agendas and minutes to make preparation and follow-up easier and faster.

# Chapter 8
## CREATING SYSTEMS FOR YOUR PRACTICE

The practice of law uses a lot of mental energy, and anything that depletes mental energy unnecessarily or causes additional anxiety is a hindrance. As we've seen already, it's tough to do substantive legal work or to concentrate if you're distracted by piles of clutter in your office, if you waste precious time in unnecessary meetings, or if you're overcome with anxiety about how you're going to get it all done.

Developing systems and procedures helps you focus your mental energy on practicing law. You can better serve your clients when you know important tasks are being done consistently and effectively.

Although innovation, personal judgment, and creation of legal arguments and strategies on individual matters cannot be systematized, there are many things in a law practice that can and should be. In this chapter, we'll discuss how you can create systems and procedures for your practice to help reduce anxiety, increase consistency, and gain loyal clients.

## SYSTEMS LEAD TO LOYAL CLIENTS

Clients want to know what they can expect when dealing with their lawyer. They want to know their lawyer is watching out for their best interests and doing everything possible to bring their matter to resolution. Systems make it less likely that things will fall through the cracks. Your staff will be more comfortable because they will know what is expected of them. Outsourcing and delegating become much easier.

Clients like stability and reliability. When everyone in the office follows the same procedures every time, you create a consistent experience for your clients.

Systems allow you to more accurately set expectations with clients at the outset of the engagement, thereby reducing complaints and questions about bills.

Systems that provide for periodic follow-ups with current and former clients increase the trust clients place in you and increase your chances of receiving referrals or new business from those clients.

## SYSTEMS FOR SOLOS AND SMALL FIRMS

Firms of all sizes can benefit from systems and consistent procedures. Most large firms develop firm-wide or practice group systems and procedures out of necessity; the volume of work and the number of people is too large to allow everyone to develop their own way of working. But in our experience, solos and small-firm lawyers frequently operate with few or inconsistent systems, which results in wasted time, inefficiencies, loss of revenue, poor client experience, or even malpractice claims. For these reasons, we'll focus on systems for small firms and solo practitioners, but the principles apply regardless of the size of the firm.

In addition, we recognize that not everyone reading a book on personal productivity for lawyers will have the ability to implement—or even suggest—firm-wide systems. But individuals can create their own systems for consistency in dealing with their clients and matters that will stand them in good stead for the duration of their careers.

Small firms need structure just as much as large firms (if not more). As a solo practitioner or small-firm lawyer, it's likely that you're wearing many hats at once. You already have far too many things to think about during the course of the day. The better your systems are, the more you can focus your time on high-level, revenue-generating tasks.

For a solo or small-firm lawyer, spending too much time on tasks that don't generate revenue can be disastrous. That's why documenting your practices for others is so important. If the practice grows, if you need to hire an associate or legal assistant or even outsource work on a temporary basis, having documented procedures will make training much easier, quicker, and more effective.

Good documentation is also helpful if you want to take a vacation or need to hire a backup in the event of an emergency, illness, or scheduling conflict. Systems will also make for a smoother transition for clients if you decide to retire or sell the practice.

When everyone knows who is responsible for what, and when and how tasks should be performed, your office will run much more smoothly and your clients will have a much more consistent and enjoyable experience with your firm. And you can focus on bringing in more business and serving your clients well.

Look for Dan's recently published *Checklists for Lawyers* book from the ABA Law Practice Division, which contains procedures for creating checklists and checklists already started for you. These will give you a solid foundation for establishing your own procedures and checklists. Other good resources include the ABA Law Practice Division's *Law Office Policy & Procedures Manual* (as of this writing, now in its sixth edition) and the *Law Office Procedures Manual for Solos and Small Firms* (as of this writing, in its third edition).

Once you know why you need systems, you can determine what kinds of systems you need and how to create them, regardless of the size of your firm.

## WHAT TO SYSTEMATIZE

Anything that is done repetitively can be systematized, at least in part. Systems can include checklists, procedures, templates, and forms. Examples of tasks or processes that can be systematized within a law firm include the following:

- potential client interviews
- conflicts checking
- client intake
- opening files
- naming files
- reporting and notes on files
- depositions
- obtaining medical records and/or other evidence

- day-to-day file handling
- billing and accounts receivable
- closing files
- client contact
- client feedback
- marketing and business development

## HOW TO CREATE SYSTEMS

Once you determine what tasks or functions you'd like to systematize, you need to document the steps and the timing as you're performing them. Although this may take some time and effort up front that isn't billable *per se*, the time and mental energy saved in the long run is well worth the investment.

Here are some things to consider when creating a system or procedure:

- What is the purpose of this particular task or set of tasks? (strategy)
- How does this activity or set of tasks provide value for clients?
- How can this task be performed in the most effective manner?
- Who should be assigned to perform the task? Are we leveraging correctly here?
- Does this task require more than one person? If so, how will those people work together?
- If there is a series of tasks, is there a particular timeline that must be followed?
- What is the order the tasks should be performed in?
- Is there a way that we can perform this task differently than our competitors to make it a selling point or point of differentiation that will entice clients to hire us over our competition?
- Can we simplify this task or set of tasks?
- Is this activity really necessary?
- How can we use our existing office technology?
- Do we need additional training?

Think strategically about the best way to accomplish tasks within your practice and document the process. If necessary, carry a small tape recorder and explain what you're doing as you do it. You can have someone transcribe the tape later to begin creating your procedure manual. Or have someone take notes while you perform a task that you want to document.

## Example: Case Handling Systems

To create a system for day-to-day matter handling in your office, you might want to ask these questions:

- What steps does each matter of the same type need to progress through from intake to conclusion?
- How will these steps be accomplished?
- Who is responsible for accomplishing each step?
- When do these steps need to be completed?
- How often do we need to communicate with clients?
- How should communication with clients be handled?
- What systems can be put into place for consistent client communication and follow-up?

## Example: Client Intake System

You may need to create smaller systems within larger systems. For example, your system for client intake might be a subsystem of your file-handling system. A client intake system might be developed as follows:

- Determine what information you need to get from every client (or every client in a particular practice area). Although each matter is different, you should know at least the categories of information you must obtain from clients during an initial interview or consultation, the documents you'll need, and other important details.
- Create a checklist or questionnaire for use with every client so you don't forget anything.
- Create templates or form letters to follow up with potential clients.
- Create templates or forms for your retainer agreement and engagement letter.
- Create a timeline or list of items to follow up on after the initial intake, and enter any deadlines or follow-up dates into your calendar system. Part of your system will include *who* will do *what* (e.g., perhaps the lawyer does the initial consultation, but a staff member enters the information into the computer).

Even if you don't know all of the dates at the outset, you should be aware of the general steps or stages the matter will progress through. Document the steps and the deadlines for completing them. For example, if you're a personal injury lawyer, enter the statute of limitations date and the date you anticipate filing the complaint, as well as dates to follow up for the defendant's answer, to prepare default motions, and to perform other necessary activities.

One easy way to get started is by working on your systems and procedures as you're working on an individual case or matter; as the case progresses, keep track of the steps you (and others) take and the things you need to remember.

## Put It in Writing

Don't forget one of the most important rules we've discussed in this book: put it in writing—virtual plans are virtually useless. Documenting your systems makes it easier to share them with others, and it removes the burden of needing to remember every step in the process. Just follow the written procedure or checklist and it's more likely to be done right.

Don't let the idea of establishing systems and procedures for your practice overwhelm you. Instead of thinking about creating a checklist, procedure, or template as a separate activity, develop it as you perform the underlying task itself. For example, record the steps of your next client intake. Include the list of documents you ask the client to bring to the initial meeting. If it's easier for you to dictate as you're working, dictate the steps and have them transcribed into a written procedure.

Circulate your first draft to others in your office for their input and to ensure that you haven't missed any steps or other important items. Then add or revise as necessary as you perform that task or use the system over time. Test and revisit your systems to make sure they remain valuable to both you and your clients.

Over time, having systems and procedures documented will create a more effective practice and will allow you to focus your attention on the legal issues and the client's needs. You'll be more motivated to take action.

Don't give up because it's too distracting to keep up with everything that has to be done in your practice—making and following the rules will help you play the game to win and pave the way toward great lawyering and excellent client service.

# CASE AND FILE MANAGEMENT

It is crucial for every law firm to have systems for practice, case, and document management. Many large and midsize firms have implemented software to help them with these systems, but many solos and small firms have not. Some lawyers contend that these kinds of software programs are unnecessary, but we disagree. Those who believe document and practice management software is a waste of money miss some of the most important reasons for using these programs.

But before we discuss the software programs themselves, you must understand that no software will be valuable without systems or procedures in place to ensure consistent use of that software. It's the old "garbage in, garbage out" theory. If you spend the money and take the time to install practice, case, or document management software but do not develop and implement protocols for using it, this software will be of limited use. A directory/folder structure and good naming conventions are important whether you use practice or document management software or not; the difference is that with document management software, these protocols will be programmed in. Essentially, you'll be able to "set it and forget it."

We'll talk more about the kinds of software programs and platforms that are available a bit later in this chapter, but since it is unlikely that law firms will be able to entirely eliminate paper any time soon, and since many firms need to maintain paper files alongside or in addition to their electronic files, let's begin by talking about file systems and organization in general.

## File Organization

Before computers and electronic files became commonplace in law firms, all legal files were kept solely on paper. Generally, firms would create files for each client or matter, often with subfolders for different categories of documents and information. For the most part, this system of organization remains today, only it has become more complicated because now lawyers need to contend with electronic files, folders, documents, and information in addition to paper.

Although there is no one "best" way to organize files and folders, and each practice area or type of service you provide may require slightly different protocols, there are some general guidelines you should keep in mind when organizing both paper and electronic files.

We recommend that you create a separate file for each client or matter. If it is likely that you will represent the same client in more than one matter, creating files by matter rather than client is preferable to avoid confusion and misfiling. You can, however, cross-reference those matters or create file names that indicate there are other existing matters for the same client. This can be done in several different ways.

Some lawyers assign numbers as well as names to their files. Sometimes these numbers show how many new files have been opened in a given year. You could use colors or create file numbers to help easily identify different clients or practice areas. For example, if a firm has a client, ABC Corp., for whom they will be handling several matters, the firm might decide that ABC Corp.'s files will be green and that all of its file numbers will begin with a prefix, such as 01. If the firm also wants to keep track of files that are opened by year, the file number might also include the year. Let's assume the firm receives two different matters for ABC Corp. in 2014: *Smith v. ABC Corp.* and *Jones v. ABC Corp.* Both files will be green. But since they are two separate matters, they will not both be called "ABC Corp." Instead, the file names and numbers might be as follows:

*Smith v. ABC Corp.*, 2014-01-001

*Jones v. ABC Corp.*, 2014-01-002

In this example, the file name is the matter name (Smith v. ABC Corp.), 2014 represents the year the file was opened, 01 is the client code, and the final number represents the order in which the files were opened in 2014.

For multidisciplinary firms, numbers and/or color coding can be used to differentiate files in different practice areas as well. For example, instead of color coding by client, a firm might choose to color code by practice area, say red for personal injury and yellow for contracts. In the example above, if the *Smith* matter is a personal injury case and the *Jones* matter is a contract dispute, the file numbers might be the same, but the *Smith* file would be red and the *Jones* file would be yellow. You would still be able to tell from the number code (01) that both files involved the same client. Alternatively, you could assign additional number or letter codes to the file number to differentiate by file type, such as *RE* for real estate, *PI* for personal injury, and so on. Then the file name and number might look like this:

*Smith v. ABC Corp.*, PI 2014-01-001

Your electronic and paper file systems should mirror each other to avoid confusion, so the file name and number on the paper file must match those on the related electronic file. But do we need to keep paper files, and if so, how much information should be kept in "hard copy"?

## Electronic vs. Paper Files

Perhaps the worst thing we do is save every piece of paper. Why do we do it? Because we're accustomed to doing so. It's not efficient. In fact, it's terribly inefficient, as we've already seen in our discussion of clutter in Chapter 3. Why? Because every time you need to find something in a file somewhere else, you have to get up, go look for it, hope it's there, and then come back to your desk. This is simply a waste of time.

If you store files in a file room, it could take you one minute to get up from your desk and go to the room, another thirty seconds to find the file, and then another minute to go back to your desk. That's two and a half minutes, and if you do this ten times a day, that's two hours a week, or over 100 hours (two and a half weeks) a year, doing nothing but getting up to find files. And we haven't even factored in the time it takes to find what you're looking for *in* the file.

On the other hand, if every file-related item is scanned immediately when received and given a name you'll remember, you will be able to quickly and easily locate it on your computer, whether it is stored locally, on a file server, or in the cloud. If your system is set up correctly, you could do the same file search in a few seconds and save $20,000 per year in billable time (100 hours @ $200 per hour).

Having data available electronically will help you clear the clutter and provide better service to your clients. The more information you have at your fingertips as you're speaking to clients (rather than having to find the paper file itself), the fewer times you'll have to put them on hold or call them back; in other words, you'll be far more responsive.

Be aware that scanning and saving may eliminate or reduce paper clutter, but it's not the end of the clutter battle. Now that we're storing more and more information electronically, we're creating electronic clutter, which can have similar consequences to "real life" clutter: poor organization of electronic files wastes time and money.

## DEVELOPING A GOOD ELECTRONIC FILING SYSTEM

The keys to a good electronic filing system are first creating a directory structure that works—that is, having directories (folders on your computer) with names that are similar to the names you would have on file folders (a good case management system can make this part of the process even easier and more efficient)—and second, using a logical and consistent file- and document-naming convention/ protocol so that you always know where to find what you're looking for.

Begin with broad categories and name folders and documents accordingly. For example, to keep forms on your computer, you might create a folder called Forms, with subfolders for Pleadings, and a sub-subfolder for Complaints, and so on. Client files could be named for the matter (e.g., Jones v. Smith MVA Claim), with subfolders/directories for Memos, Correspondence, Pleadings, Discovery, Trial, and so on.

As we discussed in Chapter 3, paper clutter comes in many forms, including clutter not related to client files. Law firms have forms, templates, checklists, periodicals, reference materials, and other types of paper that represent information the firm may want to save, share, store, and reference; developing scanning and saving systems will help organize every type of file, including business files. For example, scanning and storing all of your financial records so that you can provide them in electronic format to your accountant will make it far easier to prepare your taxes (and reduce the time it takes, thereby reducing the accountant's fee). In each instance, you are taking far greater advantage of your computer system.

Documents and files must be named and saved consistently for easy sort and search. Use the tips below.

### Save Consistently

Most law firms have a server, whether in the office, off-site, or in the cloud, where all of their documents and information are stored. However, if you don't have a server or if you are using a laptop, save all documents only in the My Documents folder and nowhere else. Whether it's a spreadsheet, a letter, or a PowerPoint presentation, it should be saved in the My Documents folder. This will make it easier to find the files, and backing up this folder will automatically back up all of your documents.

## Create Subfolders in My Documents

Treat electronic files the same way you treat paper ones. Every client, matter, or topic should have its own folder. Use plain language to name your folders; you don't want to be looking at this list of folders in the future and wondering what "NTP" or whatever other interesting abbreviation you invented means, and if you share files with others, whether they are associates or staff, you don't want to create a situation in which the other person has to guess what your file names mean.

Your My Documents folder should mirror the way you would name and store physical documents and folders. Within each client or topic, create subfolders. For example, you might have a folder named Office Memos, which may contain subfolders called 2013, 2012, and 2011. Client folders might include the subfolders Pleadings and Correspondence. The goal is to have every file in a folder rather than having a list of orphan files.

## Use File-Naming Conventions

File names should be logical, specific, and consistent. There is no need for document or folder names to be all one word. Use spaces in file names. For example, a client file would be Jackson, Michael, not JacksonMichael. It's easier to read file names when they look more like normal words.

If you file documents in client subfolders, it is not necessary to include the name of the client in the file name. The document is already stored in that client's folder. The longer the file name, the more confusing it is and the less likely it is that you'll be able to see the entire name on your screen in some formats. Simple but descriptive should be the order of the day. Name documents in a way that allows you to tell at a glance what they contain so that you don't have to open multiple documents to find what you are looking for. While it is true that each operating system has its own search function, many of these search functions are not as robust as those in practice management software packages.

The goal when naming documents, files, and folders is to be able to tell what they contain without having to open them. If the document is a letter to a client about an upcoming hearing, name it something like "Ltr to client re hearing 2014-02-15" rather than just "letter." That way, you know who the letter is to and what the letter is about without opening the document. But don't go overboard—file names that are too lengthy or complicated will create additional confusion and inconsistency.

## Using Dates in File and Document Names

Lawyers often want to find documents and files based on when they were created or modified. Dan believes that one of the easiest ways to do this is to include in the name the date the file or document was created or modified. But you need to do it in a specific way if you want it to sort properly in Windows.

Don't use a date format such as 01012011 or 112011 for a January 1, 2011, document. Instead, use the year-month-day format and use consistent naming conventions. Dan's office requires that every file include the date it was created—or the date of the hearing or other event—in the name. For example, a letter to a client dated January 1, 2014 might be named "Ltr to Client 2011-01-01." While this format seems cumbersome, it makes reviewing file dates easy, it's clear, and, most importantly, it ensures that all files of a similar type will sort in order and in order by date. Dan's staff can easily search for the date in the file name and know that the date is accurate. They find the format to be essential to their case and document management systems.

On the other hand, Allison does not recommend including dates in document names unless absolutely necessary. She believes the simpler your system and the simpler your names, the easier it will be to maintain consistently. Operating systems allow you to *sort* documents by date created or modified regardless of how they are named, so naming them using the date is redundant and can lead to errors due to the complexity involved in keeping those naming conventions consistent. Including dates in file names makes them unnecessarily long and complicated and makes scanning through a list for a particular document type or name difficult.

Further, if you're scanning documents received from opposing counsel, your client, or others, the date of the document in your operating system won't be the same as the date the document was created; it will be the date it was saved to your system. But is the creation date important? There may be occasions when that is the case, but they will most likely be the exceptions to the rule. Often, the more important date (at least in searching for a document) is the date that your office received the document. On the rare occasion that there is some special reason that the date of the document itself is important, that date can be included in the document name, but as a general rule, Allison believes it is unnecessary.

Organizing documents by file type also isn't necessarily productive or helpful. Does it matter whether a document is a PDF or a Word file in most instances? When you are searching for a particular document, is its format most important?

Consider naming documents using criteria that you would use most often to search for them, or that give you some idea of the substance of the document itself, to make searching easier.

### Create a Junk Drawer on Your Computer

Every computer Dan owns has a folder in the C: drive known as Temp, and there is always a shortcut on the desktop to C:\Temp. That's the place he stores temporary files or things he wants to look at but doesn't need to keep; in other words, it's his electronic junk drawer. Periodically, Dan deletes the files in the folder without having to worry whether he's deleting something important.

## USING SOFTWARE TO MANAGE DOCUMENTS AND FILES

Software programs can help solve the consistency problem with file and document organization, naming, and storage by preventing individuals from creating their own naming and filing conventions rather than following those established by the firm. These systems can also make storage and search easier with features like full-text searching and more.

There are two main types of software that can help in this regard: case or practice management software and document management software. For the purposes of our discussion, we use case management and practice management software interchangeably. Although different programs have different features, most practice management software allows lawyers to effectively manage client, contact, calendar, and matter information. Essentially, your practice management system is a universal database of the files in your office. By contrast, a document management system is a system specifically for managing documents generated or received by the firm.

Keep in mind that each type of software program can be server based (accessed locally on your server or individual computer) or cloud based (accessed through the Internet).

Although many solos and small firms have what they call practice management or document management systems, a lot of these are homegrown and usually are document rather than database driven (i.e., the firm keeps a "master list" of all its files in a Word document instead of having a searchable database).

While home grown systems sound logical and can work for a while, as a practical matter, they have a number of pitfalls that we have, unfortunately, witnessed firsthand in the law firms where we've worked as lawyers, as well as in the law firms we work with as consultants. One of the main problems with these systems, as we've already discussed, is consistency.

## Practice or Case Management Software

Case management programs create a centralized database of client and matter information, resulting in easier searching, indexing, conflicts checking, and more. These programs also offer to-do lists, reminders, management of fee and billing information, and time tracking. Some packages come with integrated billing modules that generate client invoices and create billing reports; others will link to third-party billing and accounting programs. Some case management software also offers document assembly features, aiding in drafting documents and linking to word processing programs. Calendar features generally allow staff to view and schedule deadlines and appointments, set reminders, and calculate important dates.[31]

For solo or small-firm lawyers, less expensive options with fewer features may work reasonably well. One such program specifically for Outlook users is Credenza.[32]

## Document Management

Many lawyers manage their documents *without* using fully functional document management software, and this is the default position for many solos and small firms. Each individual creating a document determines where the document will be stored and what it will be called. This presents a number of problems, particularly when more than one person needs to access files. Time is often wasted trying to find documents (or determine if they exist at all) due to inconsistent naming and storage conventions. Effort can be duplicated if documents are generated more

---

31. For an interesting comparison of practice management software programs, see "The Best Law Firm Case Management Software—An In-Depth Comparison," on the JurisPage website at http://jurispage.com/2013/law-practice-management/the-best-law-firm-case-management-software-an-in-depth-comparison/. But be aware that these programs change frequently. Another resource you might want to explore is the ABA Legal Technology Resource Center's case management comparison chart. You can find it at http://www.americanbar.org/groups/departments_offices/legal_technology_resources/resources/charts_fyis/casemanagementcomparison.html.

32. For more details, visit the Credenza website at http://www.credenzasoft.com.

than once. Files can be inconsistent without established scanning procedures, and some (such as e-mails) may be lost entirely due to improper storage.

Of course, firms can develop naming and storage conventions and attempt to enforce them, but this depends on the cooperation of all attorneys and staff within the office. Similarly, some case management programs have a cross-reference system that will allow the user to note in the case management system where a document is stored—but again, this requires compliance with firm procedures.

Using a fully featured document management system will limit or eliminate many of these problems.

Fully featured document management systems do not allow users to circumvent or ignore the document management policy, which is integrated into the system itself. In other words, users cannot create or store documents without answering certain questions that will allow proper storage of the document. In addition, these systems have full-function search features, added security, and the ability to integrate with scanning and e-mail programs to properly store documents created outside of the system. Document management systems can even automatically archive older documents and keep track of different versions of a document so that users are certain they are viewing the correct one.

Some objectors opine that a special system for document management isn't necessary. They extol the virtues of storing documents in the regular computer operating system, which is the method for most solos and small law firms (and even some midsize firms). These systems use folders for each client and subfolders for individual document types, along with a naming system for those folders. On the other hand, a good case management system will eliminate the need for the Save As > Drive $X$ > Clients > Doc > File Name > Doc Type steps, and still allow users to find any document in seconds.

Another plus of practice management software is its ability to link clients with matters and documents with clients or matters. You can easily see what work has been done for a particular client across multiple files, and any document created on a particular file is also linked to that client and contact—along with to-dos or tasks for that client and upcoming dates or calendar entries. This is a big advantage when communicating with clients, because you have all of the information at your fingertips without having to search several different applications (word processing, e-mail, calendar, etc.) and individual client matters—you can get it all through the client interface.

Practice management software also is a huge time-saver when a client's information changes. Instead of having to go into each file separately to make changes such as address, contact name, or telephone number, the changes can be made once in the client's information screen and they will automatically be applied to each of that client's matters. Over and over, we have seen law firms struggle with address, telephone number, or contact changes when information is stored in individual file folders, because lawyers and staff either are not informed of the change or forget to make the change in each individual file.

Conflicts are another area of concern that can be addressed with practice management software. It may be easy to determine whether you've ever represented a particular party before, but without a robust database of information, it may not be as easy to determine whether you represented another party (such as a codefendant) with adverse interests. Many lawyers have gotten into a case only to realize some time later that a conflict or potential conflict existed. You could develop your own conflicts-checking system, but is it worth the time and effort when you can use one already created with lawyers in mind? If a grievance arises or your malpractice insurer inquires about what you're using to do conflicts checks, are you comfortable saying that you rely on memory or a local search on your system?

Practice management programs integrated with time-and-billing programs can help you create and assemble documents using information stored in the system (rather than constantly typing the same information over and over), and they can also help you track and bill your time for those activities as they're being performed (if you must bill hourly).

Some lawyers who are particularly tech-savvy might develop a series of systems using other applications that can work effectively for a solo practice. But once that solo practice expands—even with just the addition of a part-time paralegal or secretary—many of those systems will flounder or fail due to an inability to share information or inadequate training on how the systems work. In addition, although using several different applications, programs, or systems can be effective, it is less likely that information can be shared across those programs or linked effectively, creating the necessity to enter the same data in several different programs.

Purchasing (and being trained on how to use) practice management and document software is an investment in your practice. The gains in productivity, time, and organization should easily outweigh the up-front costs, especially if you're not a true solo and you need to share information with staff and other lawyers, or if you anticipate that you may need to do so in the future.

## WRAP-UP

Systematizing repetitive tasks or processes within your office can go a long way towards creating a more consistent client experience. In addition, creating these systems and procedures will allow you to stop thinking about logistics and what needs to be done next and focus instead on providing excellent client service and doing the best legal work you possibly can.

Lawyers waste a lot of time searching for documents and files because they don't have good file and case management systems in place. Creating protocols for naming and saving files can go a long way, but implementing software programs for case or document management automates these processes to create a much higher level of functionality.

Countless lawyers have told us, "Anyone who is starting a practice should invest in practice management software from the very beginning. It's the easiest and best way to stay organized. They may not think they need it right away, but it's an investment worth making, and it's much easier to have it ready from the start and enter clients as they come, rather than having to convert later when you've got a lot of clients and other work to focus on." Whether you're starting out or already experienced, consider practice management software.

## CHAPTER 8 ACTION STEPS

1. Make a list of the major components of each client matter your office handles, as well as the nonbillable components of your work, including marketing, business development, and client acquisition. Over time, ask the people responsible for each of those elements to write down the major steps involved. For example, if client intake is handled by both lawyers (interviewing clients in person or by phone) and by staff (taking basic client information, entering it into the computer), ask individuals to list the steps in their portion of the task. Circulate the lists around the office for input and clarification, and then use the finalized lists to create procedures and checklists, saving them in a centralized location where all employees can access them. Refine as necessary.

2. Develop your protocols for file organization, naming, and storage. Require that all firm employees use the same system.

3. Investigate case and document management software. Participate in webinars or demonstrations to find out which of these programs would work best for your practice and which have features that appeal to you. If you implement programs, get training at the time of the installation and then periodically to refresh your skills and learn about new features.

# Part II

## DOING 90 MINUTES OF WORK IN 60: TECHNOLOGY TIPS FOR INCREASED PRODUCTIVITY

## INTRODUCTION

In Part I of this book, we covered overarching strategies that you can use to manage your activities on a day-to-day basis. In Part II, we'll show you how to use the tools and technology you already have in your practice to their maximum advantage so that you can work more efficiently.

# Chapter 9
## MAXIMIZE YOUR USE OF EXISTING TOOLS

Lawyers are competitive. By the very nature of their profession, they want to win, and their clients hire them to win or, at a minimum, to get the best possible results. So imagine, if you will, a scenario in which lawyers lose—or fail miserably—again and again and again. Certainly you would think that if lawyers knew they were facing a difficult challenge, they would do everything possible to overcome it. Yet when that challenge involves technology, you would generally be wrong.

Think about this: When Dan's sons graduated from high school they and their classmates were required to be proficient in various subjects, including math and English. They were also expected to demonstrate proficiency in Microsoft Word, PowerPoint, and Excel. But there was one crucial difference. They took years of classes in the substantive subjects. They had *no* classes devoted to the software and only a few where the programs were mentioned or demonstrated in passing. Yet they were *expected to be* capable of using those products. Of course, in reality, they had to learn how to use the software on their own.

This lack of software training is no different from what happens in all types of organizations—including law offices—all the time. While knowledge of the law is a prerequisite for lawyers, and staff members must know their job duties, both lawyers and staff are *expected to know* how to use Outlook and Word. Were they trained in law school, college, paralegal school, or even high school to use these programs? Probably not. Computers, let alone the software, didn't even exist when many of these people graduated from college or law school. But businesses just assume that their employees are proficient in these products—as though staff emerged from the womb innately knowing how to use software. As a result, most computer users have never been taught how to use the technology they so heavily rely upon, or if they were, it was merely in passing. Many are self-taught and have likely picked up bad habits along the way.

In fact, as one tech commentator has written, "Adults have worn their computer illiteracy as a badge of pride for many years now so it shouldn't surprise anyone that their children share their digital inadequacies. Moreover, neither group is even willing to try to solve a problem when they encounter it."[33] Lawyers are an ideal example of this theory. These well-educated and intelligent professionals act as though the mere sight of a computer scares the stuffing out of them and learning about technology is beyond their otherwise impressive intellectual abilities. The problem is that people assume that just because they grew up without Word, Excel, and other software programs, they can't use these tools—or learn to use them better. And that's just not true.

In addition, for whatever reason, lawyers and law firms continue to place little effort on assuring that they and their staff get the most out of the technology they own, including basic programs such as Microsoft Outlook and Microsoft Word that are so critical to the efficient operation of their offices. And when it comes to more advanced technology, in our experience, lawyers seem to prefer to avoid it rather than learn how to use it to increase productivity and get better results for their clients. The reason is probably a simple one: most people don't like change.

Even the amendment to Model Rule of Professional Conduct 1.1, which requires lawyers to "keep abreast of changes in the law and its practice, *including the benefits and risks associated with relevant technology*" (emphasis added), has had little discernible impact on the profession. Most firms haven't suddenly investigated and implemented technology such as case management or litigation management software that would improve their efficiency and, potentially, help them get better results for their clients. And most firms haven't suddenly acknowledged that teaching their lawyers and staff how to use such basic programs as Outlook and Word would allow them to improve efficiency quickly and inexpensively.

---

33. Baldur Bjarnason, "Computers Are Too Difficult and People Are Computer Illiterate," *Studio Tendra* (blog), August 14, 2013, http://studiotendra.com/2013/08/14/computers-are-both-too-difficult-and-people-are-computer-illiterate/.

Whenever Dan has addressed this issue with lawyers and their staff or during presentations, he always gets a chuckle when he uses the following analogy: Lawyers would not want to receive medical care from a physician who won't use those "newfangled MRIs" because the technology wasn't invented when the doctor graduated from medical school. Yet they think nothing of avoiding almost every form of technology, not because it wasn't around when they were in law school—law schools still don't teach a lot about technology—but for other reasons that are just as nonsensical.

As a result, lawyers and their staff are less competent at using the technological tools they need to help them serve their clients better. And just as not prioritizing wastes time, so does using technology inefficiently. If a lawyer spends five minutes struggling to format a paragraph in Word or doesn't realize that using Outlook's Reading Pane can save lots of time, those precious minutes add up to weeks or months of wasted time over the course of a year.

This reality was brought into focus recently in a series of articles by D. Casey Flaherty ("Kia Motors Tests Outside Counsel Tech Skills," *Law Technology News*, January 24 and 25, 2013), in which he reported the result of his audits of the car manufacturer's outside counsel's competency with technology. The result was probably shocking to many lawyers: every associate at each of the nine firms tested failed a test that required them to complete mock assignments using Word, Excel, and Adobe Acrobat. Flaherty's conclusion was that "all of the associates approached the assignments in ways that would have required five to 15 times longer than necessary. At $200 to $400 per associate hour, such inefficiency suggests . . . that, indeed, waste is a righteous concern."

Although there are exceptions, many lawyers tend to ignore technology. Dan has spoken with managing partners who boldly boast that until their clients require them to become more tech-savvy, they are happy, and thriving, doing things the old way. But if Kia Motors is a client, they may not have the chance to change. And if Kia is any indication of client attitudes overall, it's time for lawyers to stand up and take notice.

Moreover, as Dan wrote years ago: "Attorneys often recommend that their clients make business decisions that may cost significant amounts of money, yet those same attorneys are often reluctant to make the decision to invest even small amounts in the technology necessary to improve their practices. On the other hand, attorneys tell numerous stories about how they informed clients that if they had come in for a consultation, they would have avoided a far more expensive lawsuit. By ignoring technology, or trying to do it for 'free,' lawyers do the same thing with technology."[34] In other words, rather than hire competent staff or hire consultants to help select and install technology and train their staff, lawyers often do without—or try to do it themselves, despite their lack of competence in the area.

What has changed in the six years since Dan's article? Not much. After all, Casey Flaherty couldn't find one law firm, or apparently even one lawyer, that had the rudimentary skills needed to use the software so essential to the practice of law. Consider the reality: Lawyers spend years learning how to be lawyers. They surrender months of their lives preparing to take the bar exam and devote at least twelve hours a year to taking continuing legal education courses. But those same lawyers won't spend one hour learning how to use Microsoft Outlook, the e-mail program used by more firms than any other.

Why does this matter? Today, fewer law firms employ one secretary per lawyer. Similarly, the days of merely dictating a letter or a brief are long past. Instead, lawyers often type their own letters, and many prepare their own briefs, contracts and other documents. Yet law school doesn't even introduce them to the basic programs needed to function, and neither do their law firms. As a result, the Casey Flahertys of the world, who expect their lawyers to have minimum levels of proficiency, become frustrated at how much time lawyers are wasting and how much that time-suck costs companies.

While there are still firms in which at least some of the lawyers do not prepare their own documents and reports, preferring to allow staff to undertake those tasks so that the lawyers may concentrate on doing legal work, staff rarely receive the training necessary to prepare those documents in an efficient manner. Where these tasks are billed to clients on an hourly basis (whether at a lawyer's rate or a paralegal rate), clients have every right to complain about the lack of technological competency. But firms that are not billing on an hourly basis should be equally concerned about their lack of technological competence because the more efficient they are, the bigger the impact on their own bottom line.

Flaherty's conclusions are instructive. He concedes that he employs partners whom he relies upon "for sage advice on esoteric topics [and] would continue to turn to these lawyers even if [he] discovered that they were disembodied heads

---

34. "Legal Technology: Investing in Technology Will Pay Off in Law Firms' Futures," *The Legal Intelligencer*, May 22, 2008.

locked in a closet, and incapable of turning on a computer." He contrasts that reality with the fact that "many commonly billed legal tasks are both essential and labor intensive. The proper use of technology cuts down on the labor required." Plus, because labor equals costs, he considers how well law firms "deploy labor-saving technology."

But Flaherty concludes that he doesn't choose between law firms based merely on his audits "unless performance on the audit is the only item that separates two firms vying for a project." There lies the rub. Many law firms are equally qualified to handle most legal tasks, and most would provide comparable results. In those cases, technological efficiency would, or should, be the difference.

This is not an earth-shattering revelation. Just think about projects at your home. If you are replacing your heater, when you obtain costs from various contractors, if all things are equal, won't you choose the least expensive proposal? That is what Kia is doing as well.

## A FIVE-STEP PLAN FOR IMPROVING TECHNOLOGICAL COMPETENCE

So how can a law firm bridge this technological chasm and become the first to pass the Kia audit?

Here is our five-step plan:

1. Don't cut corners.
2. Reduce your reliance on paper.
3. Train yourself and your entire staff on the programs your firm regularly uses, such as Outlook, Word, and Adobe Acrobat.
4. Use legal-specific programs, and train yourself and your entire staff on these products.
5. Engage your staff in every step of the process.

### Don't Cut Corners

Maximizing the use of technology helps make you more profitable. As we explained earlier, technology can save you money. If you bill at $150 per hour but can save six minutes a day using a computerized case management system, which is a highly conservative estimate, a $1,500 investment pays for itself in less than five months.

There are many ways you should use technology as though it were an additional employee—one who doesn't have to be paid a salary or benefits or get days off. First, consider hiring a technology support person rather than letting lawyers and staff "do it themselves." If a full-time support professional costs the firm $75,000 per year, that's only $36 an hour, a far lower cost than the time your lawyers will waste trying to do things on their own, and less than the cost of outsourcing. If your firm doesn't have that large a budget or that great a need, consider contracting with a support company to perform the role on a fixed hourly, monthly, annual or other basis, and let your lawyers do what they do best: practice law.

Second, hire a consultant to help you recognize where technology can improve your work flow. It may be that your network needs to be upgraded or that you simply need additional software. Perhaps your staff isn't well trained. There are network consultants who can spot the inefficiencies in your systems; similarly, there are law office work flow experts who can show you how to get more out of the programs you have or introduce you to products that can improve your efficiency, your results, and your bottom line.

Finally, create a budget, just as you do for marketing and other areas (we hope). This will help you plan for upgrades and avoid surprises.

## Reduce Your Reliance on Paper

You waste time whenever you handle paper. It takes time to get up from your desk, locate a file, go back to your desk, and then (hopefully) find the item you're looking for. And of course if an old client calls and the file is in storage, it can take days or weeks to find what you need, not to mention the costs charged by file storage services and how inefficient you look to the client. If you store files and documents electronically and cut the paper umbilical cord, you can find everything quickly, even when you're at home.

It is estimated that every lost piece of paper costs a law firm $120, that 15 percent of all paper handled in businesses is lost, and that 30 percent of all employees' time is spent trying to find lost documents. That's why the need to go "paper-less" (not paper-free; it is unlikely that we'll ever be completely paper-free) is so essential. As we have already seen, with proper scanning, file naming, and file storage systems, you reduce clutter, improve efficiency, and cut costs, including long-term file storage costs that often choke firms.

## Train Yourself and Your Entire Staff on the Programs Your Firm Regularly Uses, Such as Outlook, Word, and Adobe Acrobat

Ask yourself the following questions:

- Do I really know *how* to use the software programs, including Windows, Word, WordPerfect, Outlook, and Adobe, that are so essential to everything I do?

- Does my staff really know *how* to use those same software programs? Have I and my staff ever received training—real training, where a trainer demonstrates how to use the programs—on these items?

If you cannot honestly answer yes to each of these questions, it's time to get training for you and your staff.

There is simply no substitute for training. No one is born knowing how to use Outlook or graduates from college with a degree in Microsoft Word. Yes, it takes some time and commitment to train everyone in the firm, but the results will be tangible. A good trainer will generate lots of "I didn't know I could do that" moments, revelations that will lead to improved efficiency. Just as you would train new lawyers to be sure they know about the areas of law in which they are practicing, you should train them on the technology they will use.

## Use Legal-Specific Programs

Find out what software exists to help your firm be more efficient. It may be case or matter management software, document management or document assembly software, or a litigation tool that helps you annotate transcripts quickly and more effectively than doing it with Post-its and highlighters. These products improve work flow and provide better results for your clients while allowing you to take on more matters without hiring more staff. Remember, technology is, or should be, your "invisible" staff.

Jim Calloway, the Oklahoma Bar Association practice management advisor, offers some important criteria for selecting law firm software:[35]

---

35. "Picking the 'Best' Law Office Software," Oklahoma Bar Association Management Assistance Program (© 2003, 2006 Oklahoma Bar Association).

- **Know thyself.** Make a list of the features you want before looking at specific products. Rank features in their importance to you and then begin the search.
- **Test-drive the application.** The best way to pick software is to try it and see if it works for you. While it's important to test all software, it's particularly important to try case management, litigation support, and time-and-billing software because it's more difficult to move to a different product after you've committed to one.
- **Get some reviews.** Don't trust the lawyer next door. Many times, that same lawyer hasn't even used the software—the office staff has. Get references from the vendor, read independent reviews, and look for information online. TechnoLawyer can be a terrific resource, as can your bar association's practice management advisor, if there is one.

## Engage Your Staff in Every Step of the Process

The most ambitious plans will fail if the people implementing them refuse to cooperate. Staff members at all levels need to know what you are doing and why. Inform them, ask for input, and let them know you are investing in them.

We can't come to every office and teach everyone how to use technology, but in Chapters 10, 11, and 12, we provide lots of tips about how to use the most common law office software more efficiently. The genesis of these tips is a highly popular program Dan has given for years called "How to Do 90 Minutes of Legal Work in 60 Minutes," which was one of the inspirations for this book. The theory of the program is simple: if you learn one technology tip/shortcut that saves you fifteen seconds and use it four times a day, you will save about 250 minutes (more than four hours) per year from one tip alone. When you learn lots of other shortcuts and add the savings from those actions, you are suddenly saving hours and hours, if not days and weeks, of time—simply doing what you already do (but much more efficiently). Dan's program is very popular because it shows people how to use the software *they already have*—just better. It's like discovering a new route to work that saves you fifteen minutes each way. That's two and a half hours per week, or more than 125 hours (6 days) per year, that you aren't stuck in your car. That's the beauty and simplicity of learning how to do more in less time.

## CHAPTER 9 ACTION STEPS

1. Determine where your firm has knowledge and skills gaps with respect to technology, and ascertain whether those gaps can be filled competently, efficiently, and effectively in-house or whether outsourcing is needed.

2. Obtain the necessary training for all lawyers and staff on all essential programs.

3. Make technological competence a responsibility of all firm employees, and institute rewards for excellence and sanctions for failure, as you would with any other job requirement.

# Chapter 10

## TAKING CONTROL OF YOUR E-MAIL

Improving your efficiency happens in many ways. For example, in Chapter 1, we explained how to set goals and prioritize your work, planning ahead to get the most from each day. We then focused on why it's important to eliminate distractions and clutter. In Chapter 4, we helped you recognize that maybe, just maybe, you shouldn't be shouldering the entire load and that you'll benefit by delegating. Then we offered strategies for getting everything accomplished. In Chapters 8 and 9, we began to focus on systems, or the Rules of Procedure for your office. We then talked about global ways to use technology, including electronic filing systems, and how practice management and document management software programs can organize, store, cross-reference, search for, and retrieve electronic documents.

In this and the following chapters, we have arrived at the "techie" tips that you can use to make your computer work *for you*.

Because e-mail is one of the biggest time wasters lawyers deal with on a daily basis, we'll start by talking about e-mail management in general. Later, we'll give you some tips on using the most popular e-mail client for lawyers: Microsoft Outlook. Of course, we recognize that it takes time to wade through all of these tips. We've included screenshots of most of them to make the tips easier to understand and implement.

Let's get started.

## E-MAIL MANAGEMENT

E-mail may be the biggest form of electronic clutter we face each day, and keeping up with it can be a major hassle. As we discussed earlier, e-mail is one of the most often cited time wasters in modern offices. It can be overwhelming and one of the worst enemies of productivity. The following tips can help you get more control over your inbox and ensure that important messages don't get lost.

1. **Delete liberally—and quickly.** If an e-mail message is junk or a coupon or advertisement you won't immediately act on, delete it (advertisements, specials, and coupons will come around again). Don't let junk mail sit around and clutter up your inbox. If you haven't gotten into the habit of deleting e-mails right away, you may have a lot of backlog to take care of. To do that more easily, Ben Schorr, Microsoft expert and author of several books, including *The Lawyer's Guide to Microsoft Outlook*, advises:

    a. Temporarily sort your inbox by "From" rather than by date. You will likely be able to batch-delete a number of messages or move several at once to a client file or other archive or storage method.

    b. Next, sort by "Subject." This will group related messages together, and again, you may be able to delete several at once, such as e-mails scheduling appointments that have already taken place, duplicate messages, or e-mails that are part of a string.

    c. Finally, sort your inbox in reverse date order. The older the message, the less likely that it will be important and the easier it will be to delete.

    Remove yourself from one e-mail list per day. That's right. If you don't really participate in an e-mail list, get off it. No one will hate you for it, and if you find that you really need to be on the list, then resubscribe.

2. **Separate tasks from e-mails.** If an e-mail represents a task that you need to complete, move it to your tasks folder (in Outlook, just drag and drop the message onto Tasks; the body of the e-mail will remain intact as part of the task). Alternatively, you can create to-do lists and/or action folders for those e-mails or use third-party tools that help you manage e-mails as tasks, such as Toodledo (http://www.toodledo.com/) or Remember The Milk (https://www.rememberthemilk.com/). Just get e-mails out of your inbox.

3. **Move appointments to your calendar.** If you are keeping an e-mail simply as an appointment reminder, get the information into your

calendar right away and toss the e-mail. (If you use Outlook, just drag and drop the message to your calendar and all of the information in the e-mail will stay with the appointment.)

4. **Delegate.** If the e-mail requires action by someone else, forward it to that person right away with a note. Then get the original e-mail out of your inbox by deleting it, moving it to an alternate folder for follow-up, or converting it into a task for follow-up.

5. **Keep only business e-mail in your business e-mail account.** Don't clutter your regular e-mail inbox with newsletters, subscriptions, and the like. Create a separate account for them so they're not in the way of your main personal or business messages. Make a separate shopping account for e-mail such as sales promotions and shipping confirmations. There are many free services you can use for this purpose, including Google's Gmail.

6. **Respond immediately.** Don't make the mistake of "reviewing" your e-mails and planning to go back and respond to them later. It just creates extra work and may result in important client messages getting lost. If you're going to review your e-mails, respond when you first read the message if at all possible.

7. **Don't read e-mails first thing in the morning.** Doing so is the best way to ensure that your day will get out of control. For most lawyers, urgent messages don't arrive via e-mail overnight or first thing in the morning. If that's the case for you, schedule a specific time to blast through e-mail after you've already tackled your most important task of the day. If your clients *do* tend to send urgent e-mails before you arrive at the office, limit yourself to a quick skim of your inbox to ensure no urgent messages have arrived and then move on to another task.

8. **Don't let e-mail be a constant interruption.** Schedule specific times to review e-mail rather than checking it constantly throughout the day, unless you're waiting for something particularly urgent or your practice is *truly* emergency based. If you're waiting for a specific e-mail, don't get caught up in answering all of your e-mails or reading less urgent messages over and over during the day; simply scan periodically for the one message you are waiting for and leave the rest for your designated e-mail time.

9. **Keep your e-mails short and request a specific action or response.** If you're brief, those who respond to you are likely to be brief as well. When you give others good instructions and tell them what you expect, your e-mail becomes much more efficient.

10. **Know when e-mail is not the appropriate medium for your communication.** E-mail is fast and easy, but it isn't always appropriate. Sometimes picking up the phone to speak with a client or walking down the hall to see a colleague is a much more efficient way to accomplish a task or to get the answer you need than ending up in an endless back-and-forth exchange of e-mail messages.

11. **Flag important e-mails.** Some e-mails are more important than others. As a result, it can be helpful to flag messages that require immediate attention or that might otherwise get lost in your cluttered inbox. You can also create rules to automatically flag e-mails from certain people so that you can see them as soon as they arrive.

If you determine that e-mail is an appropriate method of communication for your purposes, remember these rules:

- E-mail is a form of communication. All e-mail messages should look professional and be properly written and spell-checked. Use complete sentences with appropriate punctuation.

- E-mail is part of a client's file and should be saved with the file. It's good practice, and it could be the documentation you need to avoid or combat a disciplinary claim.

- Move e-mails with important dates or deadlines directly to your calendar.

- Create folders and set up rules and filters for your e-mail so that messages are automatically routed to the correct folders. If you belong to several e-mail lists, forums, or similar groups, or if you need to respond to specific people's e-mails, this rule is absolutely critical to managing your inbox. You should create rules that automatically route e-mail that is from certain sources or is about certain subjects to specific inbox folders or to others in your office. That way, listserv e-mail is removed from all the client e-mail, and you can look at it another time. Similarly, e-mail from banks can be forwarded to your office manager or another person, as necessary. Finally, you can set up Outlook to flag e-mails from certain people so they stand out from the rest.

- Use your case management software. Most case management programs will allow you to save incoming e-mails directly to a client's file and will ask if you want to save outgoing e-mails to a client's file.

- Don't create paper versions of your e-mail.

- If you don't want to use folders and need to save e-mails, consider using Adobe Standard or Professional, which will create a PDF Portfolio containing specified e-mails or entire Outlook folders, and their attachments. Then you can remove these items from Outlook. Regardless, the best thing to do is to get the e-mails out of your inbox.

- Act on e-mail that can be addressed immediately.

- If the e-mail requires action by someone else, forward it to that person right away. If the e-mail is one you need to save for a file, move it into that file folder and get it out of the inbox. If it's a task you need to do, move it to your Tasks folder (the body of the e-mail will remain intact as part of the task). Create to-do lists and/or action folders or file trays.

- Get a planner, preferably electronic (you can always print it out if you need to), and enter appointments and any necessary notes right away and delete the e-mails. If you use Outlook for your e-mail and your calendar, you can drag and drop an e-mail directly into your calendar the same way that you can drag it to Tasks. Just drop it on the appropriate date, and the details from the e-mail will come with it.

## Outlook Tips and Tricks

Outlook is the most popular e-mail program for lawyers, yet many of them don't use most of the available features to help them manage the flow of e-mail.

### USE THE *SEND FROM* COMMAND

In the **File** menu of most Windows-based programs, such as the one shown in Figure 10.1, you will find ***Send From*** or a similar command (see Figure 10.2); in recent versions of some programs, it's called ***Share*** (see Figure 10.3). This feature enables you to send the item you are working on to another person through your default e-mail program (see Figure 10.4). Just select the command and it should open an e-mail window/dialogue and insert the file as an attachment, as shown in Figure 10.5. Then you can write your message, address your e-mail, and send it (Figure 10.6). *Before you use the command, remember to save the file you want to send so that you send the correct/latest version.*

**Figure 10.1** File Menu for Windows

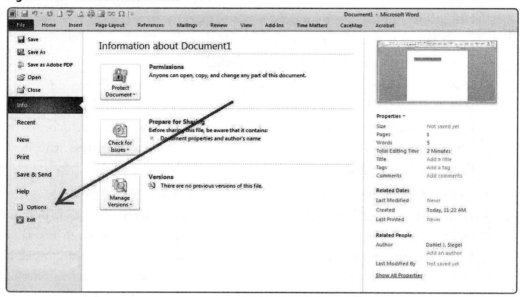

**Figure 10.2** Save & Send Option (Send From)

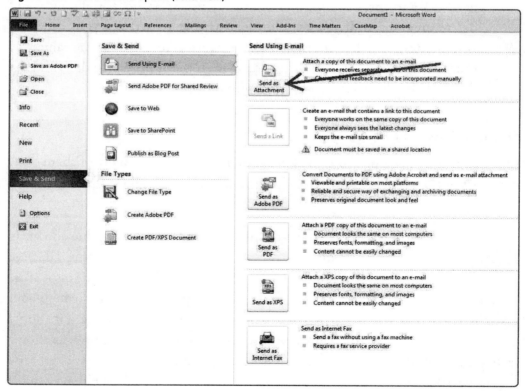

**Figure 10.3**   The Share Command

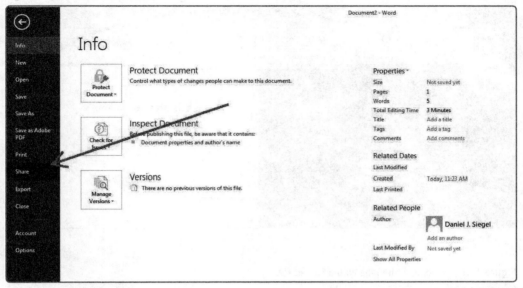

**Figure 10.4**   Share Using E-mail

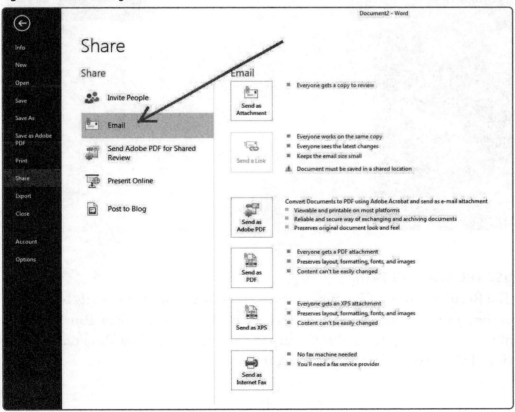

**Figure 10.5**   E-mail Attachment Using Share

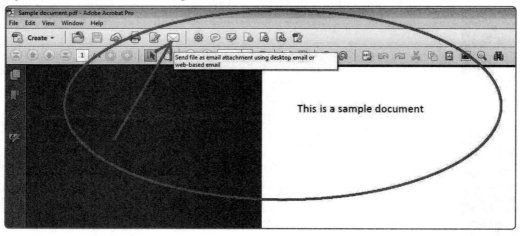

**Figure 10.6**   Sending a Message with a Shared File

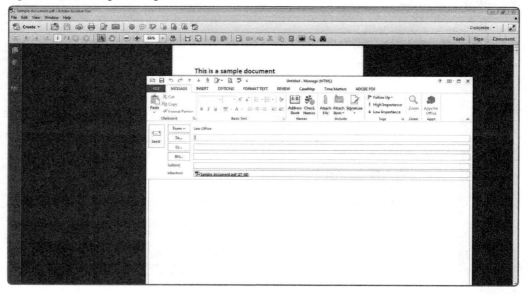

## USE THE READING PANE

The Reading Pane is a big time-saver with e-mails. Reading e-mails by clicking on one message after another is very slow. Using the Reading Pane makes it much easier and quicker. But the key is putting the Reading Pane on the right side of the screen. Here is how to set it up:

On the **View** tab, in the Layout group, click *Reading Pane*, and then click *Right* or *Bottom*, as shown in Figure 10.7.

**Figure 10.7**    Moving the Reading Pane

## MARK MESSAGES AS READ AFTER PREVIEWING IN THE READING PANE

Because you can view messages without opening each one, you can also set Outlook to mark messages as read either when you view them, after you view them, or after you view them for a specific amount of time. But you don't have to do it manually. Instead, follow these steps:

1. Click the *File* tab.
2. Click *Options* (Figure 10.8).
3. Click *Advanced* (Figure 10.9).
4. Under **Outlook panes**, click the *Reading Pane* button (Figure 10.9).
5. Select the check box at "Mark items as read when viewed in the Reading Pane" and then enter a number in the "Wait *n* seconds before marking item as read" box (Figure 10.10).

**Figure 10.8** Select Options

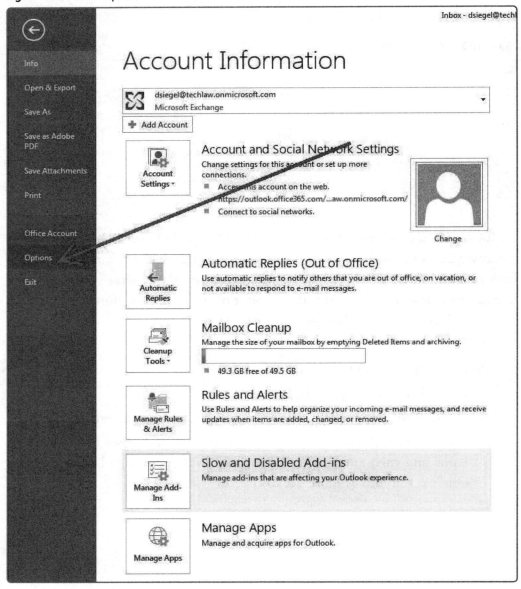

**Figure 10.9**    Select Reading Pane

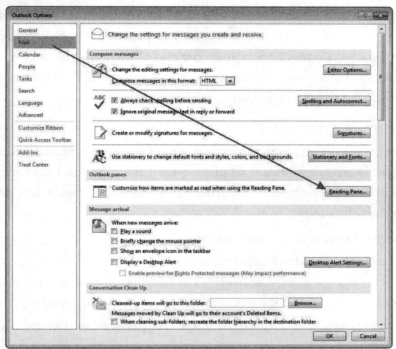

**Figure 10.10**    Set Reading Pane Options

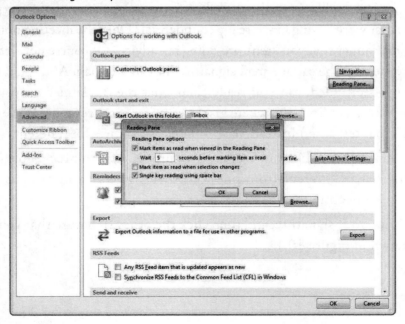

## TURN ON OR OFF SINGLE KEY READING

Single key reading lets you use your space bar to move quickly through your messages in the Reading Pane. Each time you press the space bar, the Reading Pane content scrolls down one page. At the end of the item, the next unread item in your message list appears. Follow steps 1 to 4 above and then select or deselect the check box for single key reading.

## NEVER PRINT AN E-MAIL

E-mail is electronic mail, which means it was meant to be created and stored on a computer. There is no reason to print e-mail messages and save hard copies. Instead, save them electronically. There are many strategies for doing this, including the following:

- Use your case management software.
- For e-mails that aren't client related and are just needed temporarily, create folders in your e-mail software. Create them logically—for example, by client or topic—and move e-mails there to avoid cluttering up your inbox.
- Alternatively, save e-mails into a PDF package or Portfolio in Adobe Acrobat.

## CHOOSE A SIGNATURE FOR DIFFERENT RECIPIENTS

Why do lawyers, and lots of other people, use the same signature on every e-mail? Is the fact that we're having lunch really confidential? Does the meeting notice really require a disclaimer that you aren't providing tax advice? Of course not, yet it seems that everyone uses the same e-mail signature for every e-mail. And, God forbid, if you end up being sued, can you really claim that the disclaimer on your e-mail should prevent a liability claim when it is the same for every recipient? (We wouldn't want to be that test case.) Instead, have different signatures for different e-mail.

If you want to use a different e-mail signature for different recipients (e.g., one for clients that is different from one for other lawyers), you can change your signature with two mouse clicks.

Right-click your signature, and then click the other signature that you want to use, as shown in Figure 10.11.

**Figure 10.11**    Changing an E-mail Signature

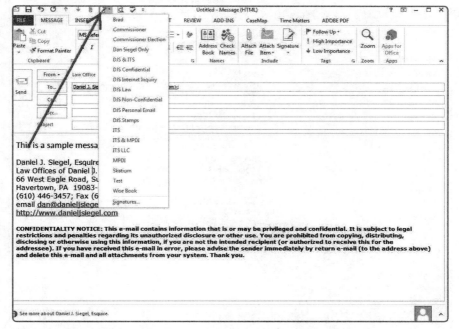

## WHEN YOU HAVE NOT DEFINED A DEFAULT SIGNATURE IN OUTLOOK

Add the signature drop-down to the **Quick Access** toolbar and every signature you have in Outlook will appear, as shown in Figure 10.12.

**Figure 10.12**    Signature List

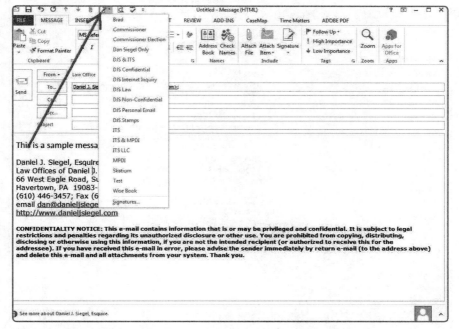

## FINDING E-MAIL MESSAGES QUICKLY

You can quickly search for a specific e-mail message. In the search box, type your subject—that is, the word or phrase you are looking for. For example, to find an e-mail message from Allison Shields, type "from: Allison Shields." This search quickly lists e-mail messages from Allison but not messages that contain her name. To find messages that mention Allison, type "Allison Shields" in the search box, as shown in Figure 10.13, to see all messages in which her name appears.

**Figure 10.13**   E-mail Search Results

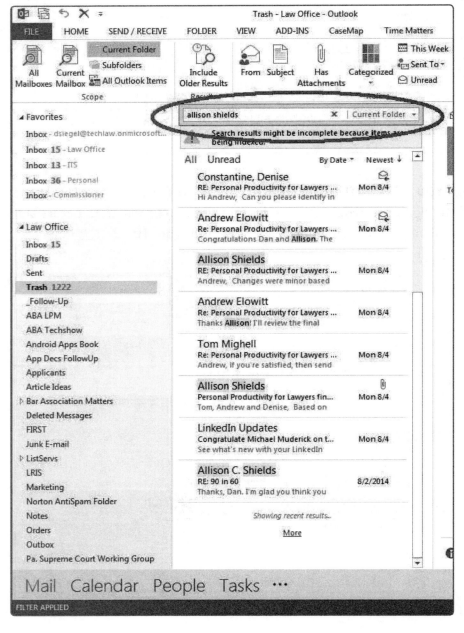

This tip also works for other criteria, such as folders. For example, a search for "folder: clients" quickly lists only those folders that contain the word "clients" as part of the subject.

You can also make important e-mail messages stand out by using color categories in Microsoft Outlook 2013. In **Mail**, click the **View** tab, then **View Settings**, and then click the **Conditional Formatting** button (shown in Figure 10.14). Here, you can change the color of unread e-mails in your inbox (the

**Figure 10.14**  Conditional Formatting for E-mail

default is blue) or change the font and color of all e-mails in your inbox. You can also click **Add** to create your own rules for different kinds of e-mails. See the dialog box in Figure 10.15.

For example, if you want e-mails from a specific client to appear in a different color in your inbox so you can find them easily, create the rule, choose the font and color for the messages, and then click **Conditions** to set the conditions for the rule (by choosing the client's name or e-mail address in the "from" field), similar to the way you would set up rules and alerts. See Figure 10.16 for a look at the Rules feature.

**Figure 10.15**   Conditional Formatting Dialog Box

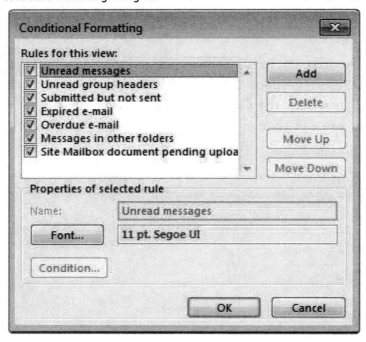

**Figure 10.16**   Creating and Managing Rules

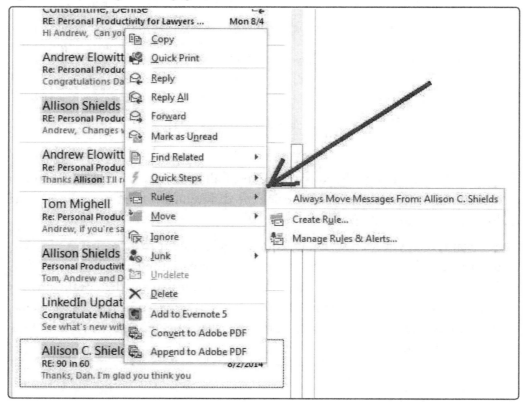

## FOLLOW UP ON E-MAIL

Sometimes you need to take action or follow up on an e-mail, but you can't do so right away. You can flag a message by using the **Insert** key. Select the message that you want to flag and then press *Insert*. This will flag the item and let you insert a start date and due date. If your To-Do Bar is active, the item will also appear in your task list.

## CREATING AND USING OUTLOOK QUICK STEPS

We often need to schedule an appointment as the result of receiving an e-mail. Outlook can make that task easy, and create so many other tasks, using Quick Steps. And when Outlook creates an appointment from the e-mail, it can include the e-mail text in the notes, making it easier for you to remember why you scheduled the meeting in the first place.

You must configure some Quick Steps the first time you use them. For example, if you want to use a Quick Step to move messages from one folder to another, Outlook requires you to specify the folder before you can use the Quick Step.

To create Quick Steps or modify existing ones, do the following:

- Under the Outlook **Home** tab, in the Quick Steps group, click the *More* arrow at the side of the Quick Steps box (Figure 10.17), then click *Manage Quick Steps*.

**Figure 10.17**    Accessing the Quick Steps Dialog Box

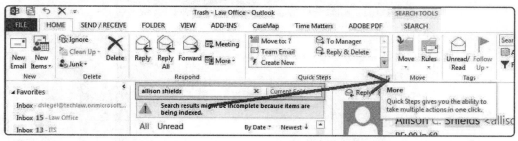

- In the dialog box, click the Quick Step you want to change, then click *Edit*, as shown in Figure 10.18.
- Under **Actions**, change or add the actions you want this Quick Step to perform. A list of actions is shown in Figure 10.19.

**Figure 10.18**   Editing a Quick Step

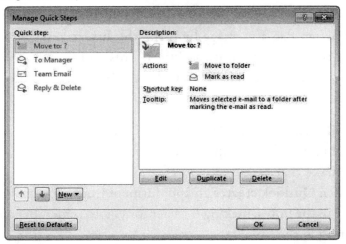

**Figure 10.19**   Quick Step Actions

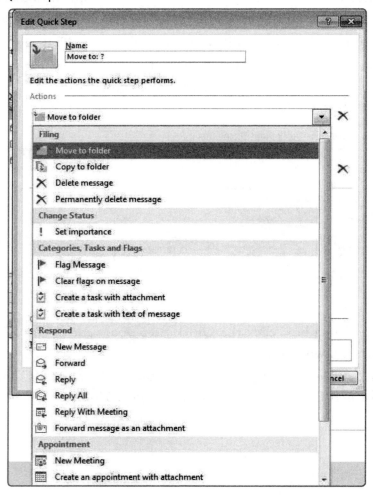

- You can also assign a keyboard shortcut to the Quick Step using the Shortcut key box, which is shown in Figure 10.20.

**Figure 10.20**   Shortcut Key Box

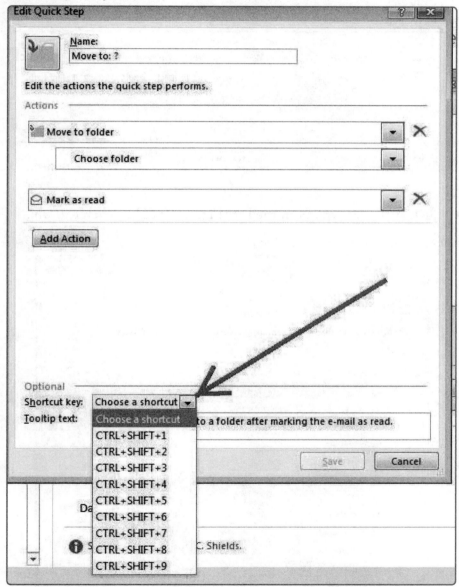

- To change the icon for a Quick Step, click an icon next to the Name box, click an icon to select it, and then click **OK**.

To create a new Quick Step, do the following:

- Under the Outlook **Home** tab, in the Quick Steps group (in the Quick Steps gallery), click *Create New* (see Figure 10.21).

**Figure 10.21**   Create a New Quick Step

- Click an action type from the list (Figure 10.22) or click *Custom*.

**Figure 10.22**   Choose an Action for the Quick Step

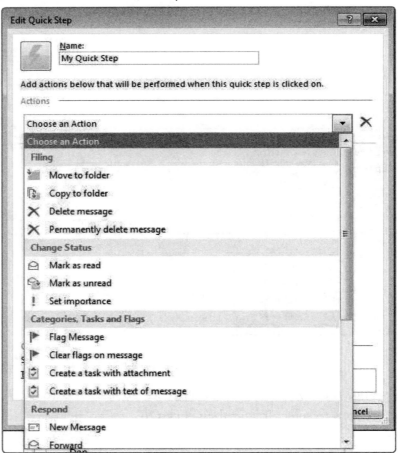

- In the Name box, type the name for your new Quick Step.
- Click the icon button next to the Name box, click an icon, and then click **OK** (see Figure 10.23).

**Figure 10.23**   Choose an Icon for the Quick Step

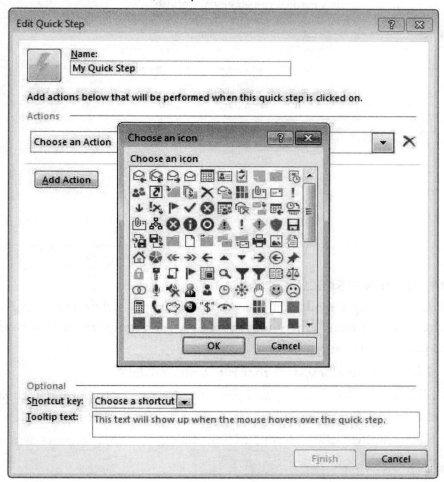

- Under Actions, select the action you want the Quick Step to do.
- Click **Add Action** for any additional actions.
- You can also assign a keyboard shortcut to the Quick Step using the Shortcut key box.

When you create new Quick Steps, they appear under the Outlook **Home** tab at the top of the gallery in the Quick Steps group. You can rearrange your Quick Steps using the Manage Quick Steps dialog box.

## CREATE REMINDERS TO FOLLOW UP ON E-MAIL YOU'VE SENT

In addition to flagging e-mails you receive for follow up, you can also set fol-low-up reminders on e-mails when you send them. When drafting an e-mail, click the Follow Up flag, as shown in Figure 10.24. Outlook places a flag in your To-Do Bar tasks for this e-mail message by default.

**Figure 10.24**    Flag a Message for Follow-Up (Before Sending)

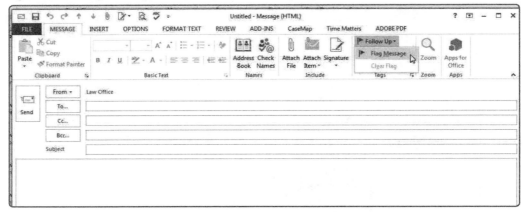

## DELETE E-MAIL MESSAGES PERMANENTLY

By default, deleting e-mails is a two-step process: you delete the e-mail and it goes into a trash folder, which needs to be purged later. Here is how to delete e-mails permanently in one step:

- Select the e-mail message that you want to delete.
- Hold down the *Shift* key and press the *Delete* key to permanently delete the selected e-mail message.
- Next, confirm the deletion in the dialog box that appears when you close Outlook.

## SWITCH TO YOUR INBOX OR OUTBOX

Switching between your inbox and outbox quickly can save time. Fortunately, there are shortcuts to help you do this:

- To go to your inbox, press Ctrl+Shift+I.
- To go to your outbox, press Ctrl+Shift+O.

## TURN OFF E-MAIL NOTIFICATIONS

If you receive a lot of e-mail (what lawyer doesn't?), then the e-mail notification icon is a pain in the you-know-what. So turn it off:

- Click *File, Options, Mail,* and then go to **Message arrival.** These steps are shown in Figures 10.25 and 10.26.
- Select or Deselect the *Display a Desktop Alert* check box.

**Figure 10.25**    Choose Options from File Menu

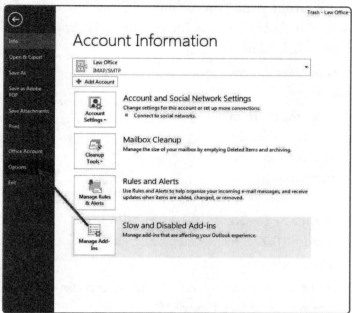

**Figure 10.26**    Select Message Arrival in Outlook Mail Options

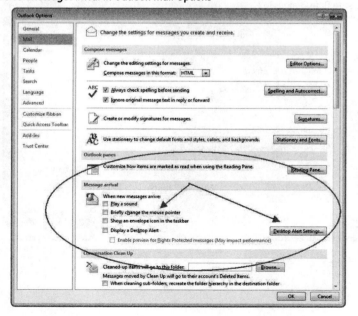

## CREATE A RULE

Outlook uses "rules" to automate common tasks. They're easy to create and can be used to streamline common e-mail-related tasks. Here's how to create a rule from a template or from scratch:

- In the Navigation pane (the column on the left side of the Outlook window that includes buttons for the Mail, Calendar, and Tasks views and folders), click *Mail*.
- On the **Tools** menu, click *Rules and Alerts.*
- If you have more than one e-mail account, in the "Apply changes to this folder" list, click the inbox you want.
- Click *New Rule* or *Create Rule* (see Figure 10.27).
- Do one of the following:
    - Use a template with prespecified actions and conditions and select the template you want (see Figure 10.28)
    - Create the rule by specifying your own conditions, actions, and exceptions

**Figure 10.27**   Rules Drop-Down Menu

**Figure 10.28**   Create Rule Dialog Box

To create a Rule  specifying your own conditions, actions and exception, use the Rules Wizard, which is accessed by clicking on the Advanced Options tab shown in Figure 10.28.

After selecting Advanced Options, Outlook will display the Rules Wizard (Figure 10.29), which walks you through all of the available options, including sender, recipient, subject, text in the email, and just about every other condition you can imagine. The Wizard allows you to move, copy or forward emails, delete certain ones automatically, etc., and is perhaps the best way to automatically move emails from listservs to specified folders you have created.

**Figure 10.29**   Rules Wizard

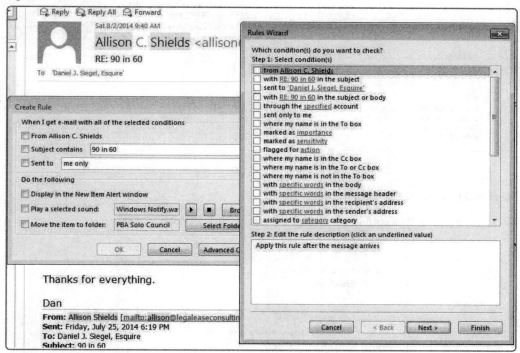

After creating the Rule, Outlook will ask whether you want to apply the Rule to all messages. Select Yes (see Figure 10.30). Next, Outlook will ask you to name the Rule, run it on existing messages and turn on the Rule (see Figure 10.31). If you have multiple email accounts, copy the Rule to use in your other accounts (see Figure 10.32).

**Figure 10.30** Applying a Rule

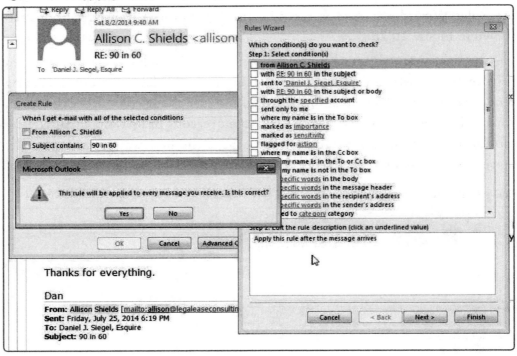

**Figure 10.31** Finishing Rule Setup in Wizard

**Figure 10.32**   Copying a Rule

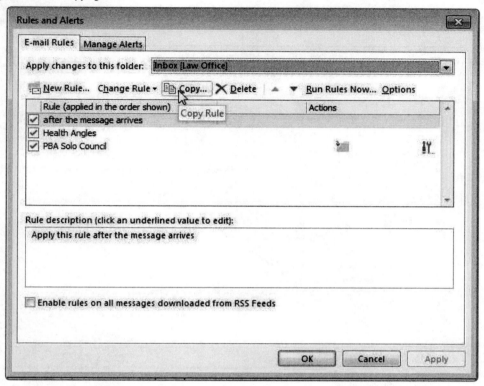

To have this rule apply to all your e-mail accounts and inboxes, select the "Create this rule on all accounts" check box on the last page of the Rules wizard.

## CREATE A RULE BASED ON A MESSAGE IN A FOLDER (GREAT FOR LISTSERVS)

- Open the folder that contains the message.
- Right-click the message you want to base the rule upon (see Figure 10.33).
- Click *Create Rule*.
- In the dialog box, select the conditions and actions you want to apply.
- To add more conditions, actions, or exceptions to the rule, click the *Advanced Options* button, and then follow the rest of the instructions in the Rules wizard.

**Figure 10.33** Creating a Rule Based on a Message

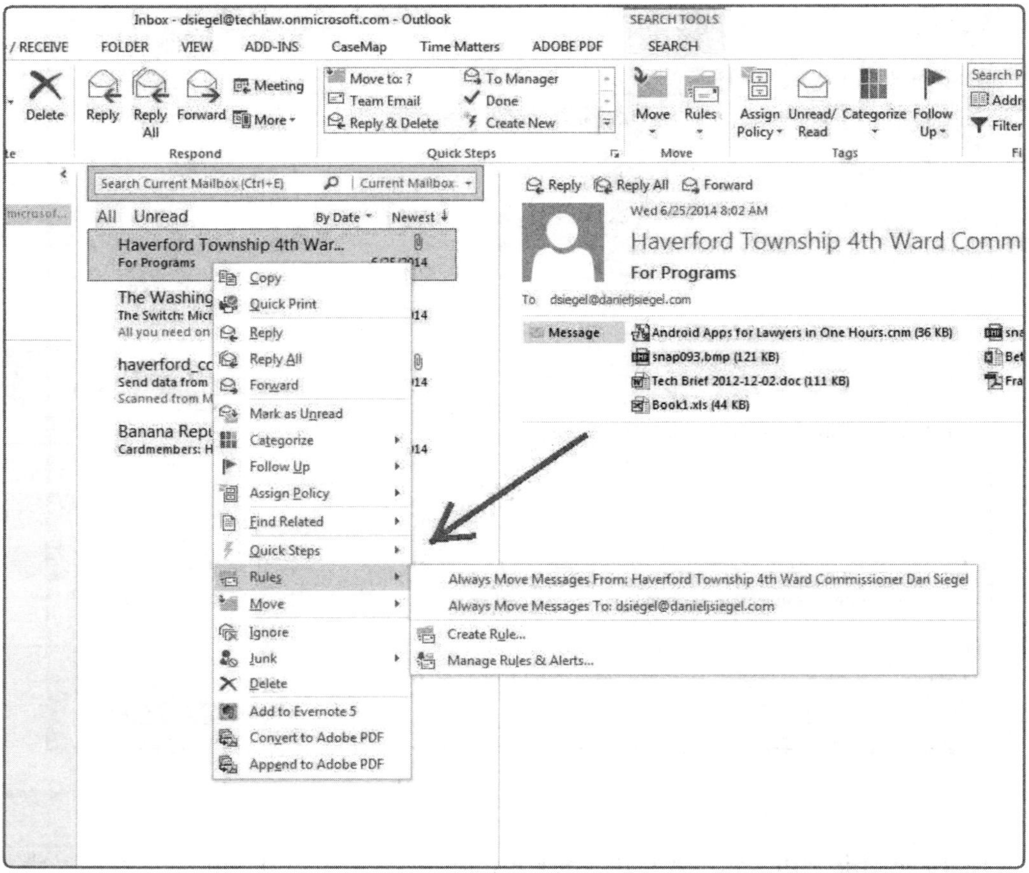

## CREATE A RULE BASED ON A NAME OR SUBJECT (INCLUDING FLAGGING THE SENDER)

- Open the message you want to base a rule on.
- On the toolbar or in the **Rules** menu, click *Create Rule*.
- In the dialog box, select the conditions and actions you want to apply.
- To add more conditions, actions, or exceptions to the rule, click the *Advanced Options* button, and then follow the rest of the instructions in the Rules wizard.

## DELETING A MEETING WITHOUT NOTIFYING INVITEES

At times, you may need to delete a meeting, but you don't want to send an e-mail saying that you have done so. Here's how to do that:

- Right-click the meeting and then click **Delete**.
- In the notification e-mail message, delete all the addresses from the To field, and type your own e-mail address.
- Click **Send**.

## USE ADOBE TO SAVE YOUR E-MAIL

While Adobe Acrobat is generally considered a program to create or work with PDFs, it is also a terrific way to save your e-mail, assuming you don't have case management software. Here's how to use it.

## SPECIFY WHETHER E-MAIL MESSAGES BECOME MERGED PDFS OR PDF PORTFOLIOS

A merged PDF simply combines PDFs into one large file, whereas a PDF Portfolio keeps them separate. It's like choosing whether to put everything in one folder or have separate folders for each item.

In Outlook, choose **Adobe PDF** and then **Change Conversion Settings**, as shown in Figure 10.34.

**Figure 10.34**   Changing Adobe PDF Conversion Settings

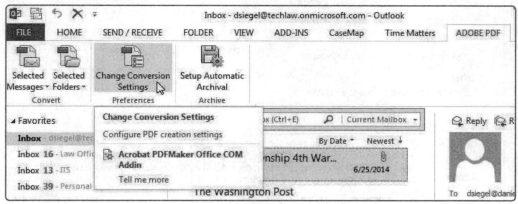

Do one of the following steps in the dialog box (see Figure 10.35):

- To convert and merge e-mail messages into a PDF as sequential pages of one document, *deselect* "Output Adobe PDF Portfolio when creating a new PDF file."

- To assemble converted e-mail messages as components of a Portfolio, *select* "Output Adobe PDF Portfolio when creating a new PDF file."

**Figure 10.35** Conversion Settings Dialog Box

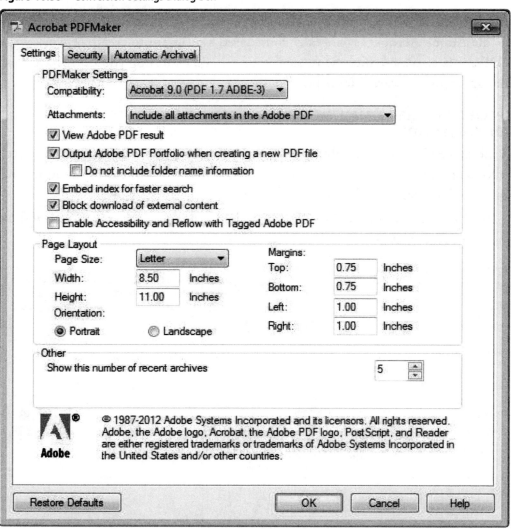

## CONVERT AN OPEN E-MAIL MESSAGE TO PDF (OUTLOOK)

Choose *Adobe PDF* and then *Convert this item to Adobe PDF* (Figure 10.36).

**Figure 10.36**   Converting an E-mail Message to PDF

You can also convert a different file to PDF from within an open Outlook e-mail message if the **Attach as Adobe PDF** toolbar is shown. Clicking this toolbar item opens a series of dialog boxes for selecting and saving the new PDF and also starts Acrobat, if it is not already running. The resulting PDF is attached to the open e-mail message.

## CONVERT E-MAIL MESSAGES TO A NEW PDF

In Outlook, select the individual e-mail messages.

Do one of the following:

- (Outlook) Choose *Adobe PDF > Convert Selected Messages > Create New PDF* (see Figure 10.37).
- In the "Save Adobe PDF As" dialog box, select a location, type a file name, and click *Save*.

**Figure 10.37** Creating a New PDF from E-mail Messages

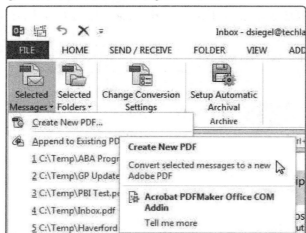

## ADD E-MAIL MESSAGES OR FOLDERS TO AN EXISTING PDF

In Outlook, select the individual e-mail messages or folders.

Do one of the following:

- (Outlook) Choose *Adobe PDF > Convert Selected Messages > Append to Existing PDF* (shown in Figure 10.38), or *Adobe PDF > Convert Selected Folders > Append to Existing PDF*.

  (Note: If you have already created one or more PDF Portfolios, you can choose from recently created portfolios in addition to the *Append to Existing PDF* option.)

**Figure 10.38** Appending E-mail to a PDF

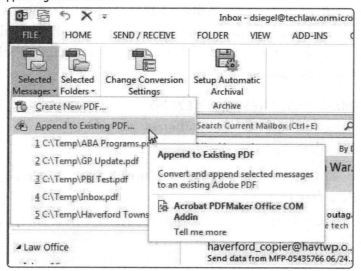

- Locate and select the PDF or PDF Portfolio to which you want to add the converted e-mails, and click **Open**. *Important*: Do not type a new name for the PDF. If you do, a warning message appears telling you that the PDF was not found. Click OK, and select a PDF without changing its name.

- (Outlook only) If a message appears alerting you that the existing PDF was created using an earlier version of PDFMaker (see below), do one of the following:

  ○ To create a PDF Portfolio from the original PDF archive, click **Yes**, and select a name and location for the new archive. (The default name adds _Portfolio to the original PDF file name.) When the conversion is complete and the Creating Adobe PDF dialog box closes, the new archive opens in Acrobat.

  ○ Click **No** to cancel the process.

Note: For PDF Portfolios of e-mail converted or migrated in Acrobat 8 or later, only new messages—that is, messages that are not already part of the PDF Portfolio—are appended.

## CONVERT E-MAIL FOLDERS TO A NEW PDF

Adobe Acrobat PDFMaker can convert multiple folders to PDF in one procedure. It is not necessary to select the folders at the beginning of the process because you can select them in a dialog box that appears automatically.

Do one of the following:

- (Outlook) Choose **Adobe PDF > Convert Selected Folders > Create New PDF** (see Figure 10.39).

**Figure 10.39**   Converting E-mail Folders to PDF

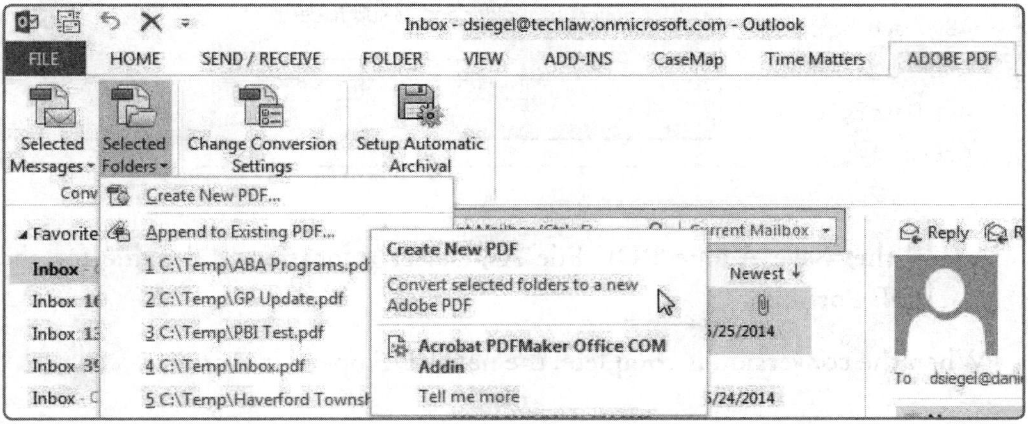

- o In the "Convert folder(s) to PDF" dialog box, select the folders. Then select or deselect the "Convert this folder and all sub folders" option (see Figure 10.40).

**Figure 10.40** Convert Folder(s) to PDF Dialog Box

- In the "Save Adobe PDF File As," select a location and name for the PDF Portfolio.

When the conversion is complete, the new PDF opens in Acrobat.

## CHAPTER 10 ACTION STEPS

1. Spend thirty minutes setting up your e-mail to work more efficiently in the future using folders, rules, and alerts.

2. Start developing the habit of deleting unnecessary e-mails immediately and moving e-mail messages out of your inbox to more appropriate places (such as your Calendar or Task list or to the client's computer file).

3. Set aside thirty minutes a week to clean out your e-mail using the e-mail management tips in this chapter.

# Chapter 11
## IMPROVING YOUR TECHNOLOGY IQ

In this chapter, we have chosen some of our favorite tips that you can use immediately to work better with electronic files, rename directories and files easily, and search for documents, whether or not you're using practice or document management software.

Mostly, we'll demonstrate many ways to use the products most law offices use—Microsoft Windows, Microsoft Word, and Adobe Acrobat—that are, or should be, the foundations of your office's technology.

We don't expect you to adopt every tip here. What we hope is that as you read, you'll recognize that these software programs have many features and shortcuts you never knew about and that you can do so much more with them by merely learning a few of these tips. Software is generally designed by computer geeks, not by the end users, and this can be frustrating. With these tips, we hope that you take back control of your computers and do things the way *you* want to, not the way some techie who works for Microsoft thinks you should do them.

Let's get started.

## MICROSOFT WINDOWS TIPS

### Open the Task Manager Faster

Admit it, Ctrl+Alt+Delete is your default keystroke when you want to go to Task Manager and shut down an ornery program that won't close. But the problem is that this command *used* to take you there. Now it takes you to a blue screen from which you go to the Task Manager. To go directly to the Task Manager, press **Ctrl+Shift+Escape** instead.

## Searching for Electronic Files

Saving files—on your computer or in a folder—doesn't do you any good unless you can find what you need when you need it. That's why naming files and storing them in a logical manner is so vital. Once you've established good naming conventions for files, folders, and documents, retrieving them should be much easier. Thankfully, there are many tools that you can use to help you to locate electronic documents and files.

## Where to Start Searching for Files

There are lots of ways to find files on your computer. Most of the time you'll start by using the search tools that appear for every folder. But there are a few other tools you should know about:

### SEARCH BOX

Usually, the quickest way to find a file is to use the search box at the top of the folder window, shown in Figure 11.1. Just type in the name and begin.

**Figure 11.1    Search Box**

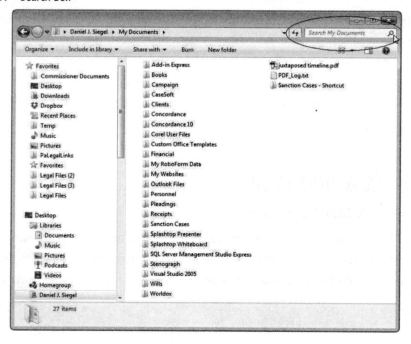

In addition, there is a virtually identical search box at the bottom of the Start menu that you can also use to find files. You can search by file name, kind of file (e.g., document), type of file (e.g., doc file), tag, or author.

## FILE LIST HEADINGS

When you want to find files that have similar criteria—for example, they're Word documents, or they were created the same day—you can use the headings above the file list (see Figure 11.2) to filter, stack, or group your files. But first, you'll need to use the drop-down box to select this method. Although it's generally not the most efficient way to view files, it can be a huge help sometimes.

**Figure 11.2**   File List Headings

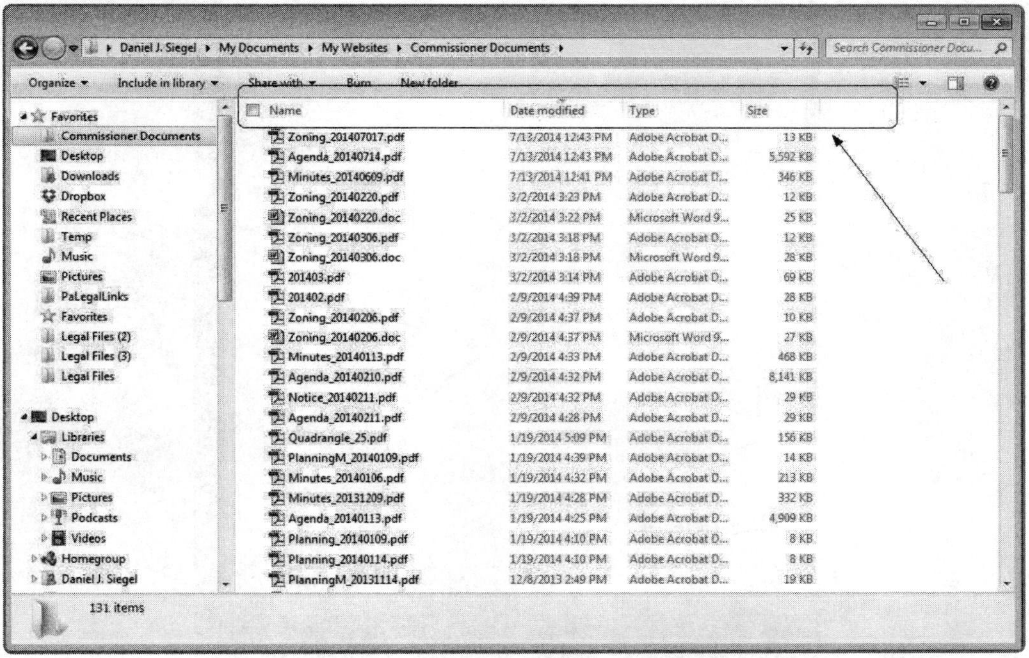

## SEARCH FOLDER

This is the best way to find files that are stored in multiple folders/directories. The nice part about using this method is that there is an Advanced Search option and you can save your searches and use them again. Thus, you can search by name and many other criteria. See the folder in Figure 11.3 below.

**Figure 11.3**   Search Folder

## RENAME DIRECTORIES AND FILES

The results for a file search appear in alphabetical order by default, so you may have to scroll quite a bit to find letters that are later in the alphabet. Renaming a file by adding an underscore or other symbol at the beginning of the file name will put it at the top of the alphabetical pile.

Windows users can also rename their files and directories by using one of the following four methods:

## Method 1

- Highlight the file or folder you want to rename.
- Right-click the file or folder and click **Rename** from the menu that appears. See Figure 11.4 for an example.

**Figure 11.4**   Method 1 for Renaming

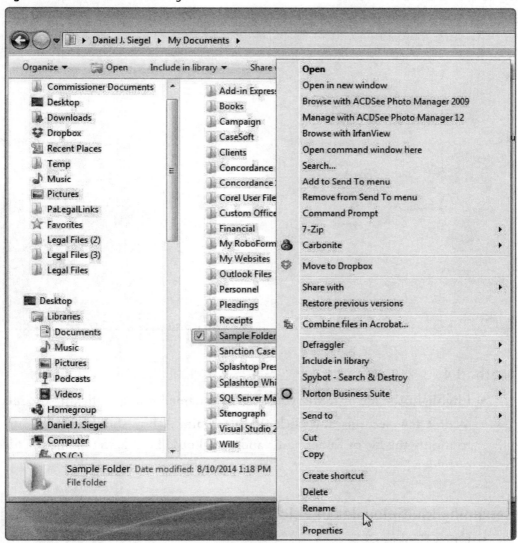

## Method 2

- Highlight the file or folder you want to rename.
- Press the **F2** key.

## Method 3

- Highlight the file or folder you want to rename.
- Click *File* at the top of the window and select *Rename* from the list of available options. See Figure 11.5 for an example.

**Figure 11.5**   Method 3 for Renaming

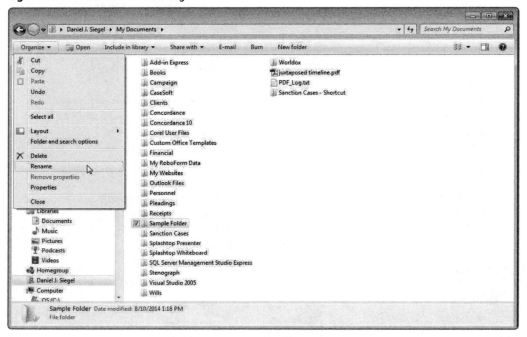

## Method 4

- Highlight the file or folder you want to rename by single-clicking the file.
- Wait a few seconds and click the file again. A box should appear surrounding the file or folder name and you should be able to rename the file or folder.

## Renaming Multiple Files or Folders at Once

- Open Explorer.
- Select all the files you want to rename.
- Press *F2* and type the new name for the files. For example, typing "test" will rename the files to test, test(1), test(2), test(3), and so on. If you have set your computer to display file extensions, also type the name of the file extension you're renaming.

## Windows Search

With each new version of Windows, the ability to search for files and folders improves dramatically. Windows Desktop Search can locate relevant documents, e-mails, programs, and other files almost as fast as you can type the information you want in the search box.

Windows Search lets you use various "operators" (keystrokes) to help you find the exact file or e-mail message you want. There are three ways to quickly access Windows Search: (1) go to the *Start* menu, (2) open *Windows Explorer*, or (3) press the *Windows key* + *F* to access the stand-alone search window. (When you use this option, Windows will offer hints and provide ways to perform complex searches more easily.)

Here are some examples of searches you can perform in Windows Search:

| Action | Keystrokes | Example |
|---|---|---|
| Find files that contain a particular word | ext:FILETYPE WORDSEARCH | To search for Word files with the word *lawyer* in them, type: ext:doc lawyer |
| Find file names that contain a particular word | ext:FILETYPE filename: WORDSEARCH | To search for file names that contain the word *lawyer*, type: ext:doc filename: lawyer |
| Find files that were created or modified during a certain time frame | ext:FILETYPE date: TIMEFRAME | To search for documents created or modified last week, type: ext:doc date: last week<br><br>You could also use times such as today, yesterday, last week, past month, or even "long ago" with the date search operator. This search also works with date ranges, such as: date:13-02-2013..24-09-2013 (finds files added/modified in this date range) |

| Action | Keystrokes | Example |
|---|---|---|
| Find files within a specified folder (By default, Windows Search finds files in every folder that have been added to the search index. You can limit your search to a specific folder or folders.) | folder:FOLDERNAME | To search only within the My Documents folders, type: folder:documents |
| Find files of a specific type saved in a certain folder on a specific date | folder:FOLDERNAME ext:FILETYPE date:DATERANGE | To find documents in the My Documents folders created or modified yesterday, type: folder:documents ext:doc date: yesterday |

## Find E-mails

You can use a similar method to search your Outlook e-mails. The search is similar to Gmail searches.

| Action | Keystrokes | Example |
|---|---|---|
| Find e-mails from a particular person that you received during a range of dates | from:NAME date: DATERANGE | To find e-mails from Dan Siegel last month, type: from:Dan Siegel date: last month |
| To find all e-mails containing specific words from a specific domain | subject:WORD from:DOMAIN.com | To find statements from PNC Bank, type: subject:statement from:pnc.com |

# MICROSOFT OFFICE TIPS

These tips apply to all of the Microsoft Office applications, but in particular to Word, PowerPoint, and Excel. While some of the commands work in Access and Publisher, we're confining our tips to the "big three."

## Keep Important Documents and Files Handy All the Time

The Recent Documents list is one way to keep important files or documents at your fingertips whenever you need them. To find the Recent Documents list, click the *File* or the *Office* button. Click the pushpin icon next to the file name to pin that specific file to the Recent Documents list (see Figure 11.6). When you click the pushpin icon, it changes in appearance to show that the pin has been activated for that document (see Figure 11.7). Doing this makes the document or file always accessible at a click.

**Figure 11.6** Using Pushpins

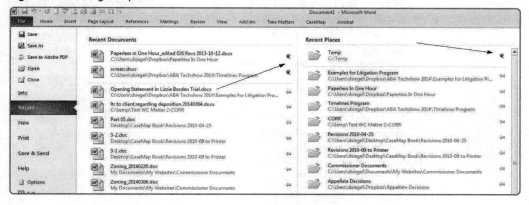

**Figure 11.7** Document "Pinned" to Recent Documents List

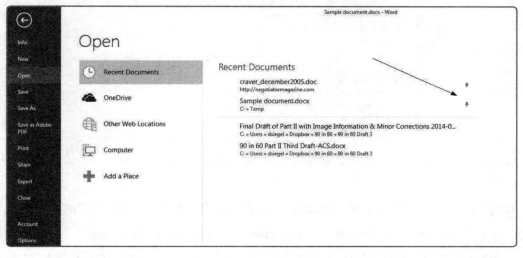

You can change the number of documents or files in the Recent Documents list. To do so:

- Click the **File** or the **Office** button and then click **[Program] Options** (for example, Word Options).
- Next, click **Advanced**.
- Scroll down to the Display section (Figure 11.8), and you will see an option for changing the number of recent documents displayed.

**Figure 11.8** Changing Number of Documents Displayed

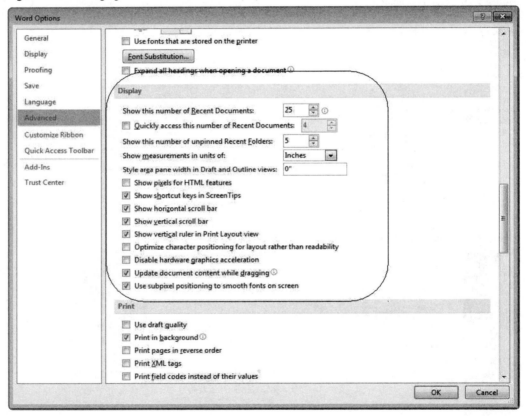

## Inspect and Remove Metadata Using the Document Inspector Tool

- To access the Document Inspector, first save your document.
- Click the **File** or the **Office** button and then click **Inspect Document** as shown in Figure 11.9.

**Figure 11.9**   Inspect Document

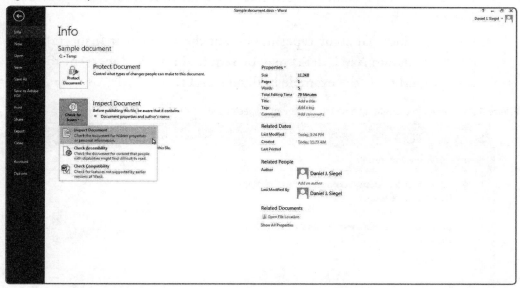

- Depending on the program you are using, this tool searches for different types of content, including comments, unresolved tracked changes, and headers and footers. A sample Document Inspector list is shown in Figure 11.10.

**Figure 11.10**   Document Inspector List

- Review the results and decide what you want to remove from your document.
- Keep in mind that some types of content the Document Inspector finds (such as custom XML data) may be required for the document to function properly. See the example in Figure 11.11.

**Figure 11.11**   Required Content Shown in Document Inspector List

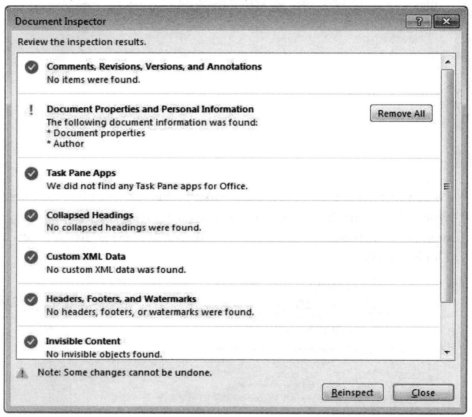

## Preview Formatting Before You Apply It

A Theme is a set of design elements, including backgrounds, colors, and fonts, that gives your document or presentation a professionally designed feel. Themes are located under the **Design** tab.

- You can preview many types of document formatting before you apply them.
- Point to a Theme style to see font, color, and graphic effect formatting changes all at once throughout the document. (More advanced users will find that this preview function also works for the SmartArt Styles gallery to preview a variety of formats for SmartArt diagrams.)

## Minimize the Ribbon

Sometimes the ribbon can take up too much screen space or is a distraction when you're working on a document. Here are three easy ways to minimize the ribbon if you don't want to see it all of the time:

- Double-click any tab name.
- Press **Ctrl+F1**.
- Right-click any tab name for the option to minimize the ribbon.

## Adding Line Breaks without the Bullets

When you are creating a bulleted or numbered list, you may want some items to appear in the list without a bullet or a number. To create a new line without a bullet or new number, press **Shift+Enter**. The next time you press Enter, however, the new line will continue the bulleted or numbered list.

## MICROSOFT WORD

### Customize the Default Word Document Template

When you start Word, it opens the Normal template (you may not have even known). This template is really Word's "memory." It's where Word saves all of your default settings, including styles, AutoText, macros, toolbars, and other customizations that determine the basic look of your documents. This template may not be set up the way you want your documents to look, but you can customize your own templates.

- First, make a copy of the default template in Word, which is saved in different places depending upon which version of Word you are using.
- Create the document that you want to use as a new template.
- Save the document on your desktop as a macro-enabled template by choosing **Word Macro-Enabled Template** as the file type.
- Close all instances of Word.
- Go to the location where you found the original default template and replace that template with the one you created. Your new template will now be the default.

## Change Default Document Formatting

To change the font and paragraph formatting defaults for an open document or all new documents based on the active template, do the following:

- Press ***Ctrl+Shift+Alt+S*** to open the Styles pane (or click the dialog box launch icon in the Styles section on the **Home** tab). The Styles pane is shown on the right in Figure 11.12.

**Figure 11.12**   Document with Styles Pane Open

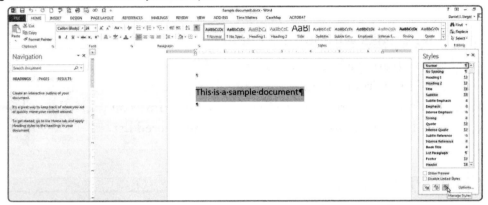

- Click the ***Manage Styles*** icon at the bottom of the pane to open the Manage Styles dialog box.
- On the **Set Defaults** tab of the dialog box, change font and paragraph formatting as needed. Then, at the bottom of the dialog box, click the option to apply settings either only to this document or to new documents based on the active template (Figure 11.13).

**Figure 11.13**   Applying Style Settings

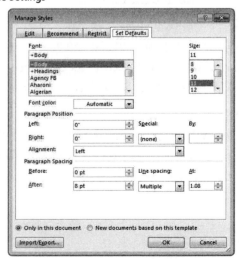

## Reuse Tables in Word

There may be times when you want to use a table again, either in the same document or in a future one. You can save a table so you don't have to start from scratch the next time you want to use it. First, you'll need to save the table you created:

- Select the table that you want to save.
- Under the **Insert** tab of the ribbon, click **Table**, choose **Quick Tables**, and then click **Save Selection to Quick Tables Gallery**. The steps are shown in Figure 11.14.

**Figure 11.14**   Using the Quick Tables Gallery

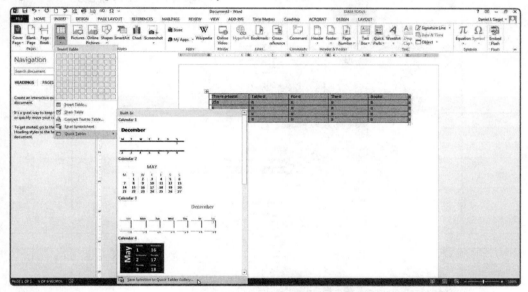

- In the Create New Building Block dialog box (Figure 11.15), give the table a name, classify it with some basic parameters, and then click **OK**.

Now you can reuse your saved table:

- Position your cursor where you want to insert a saved table.
- On the ribbon, click the **Insert** tab, click **Table**, and then choose **Quick Tables**.

**Figure 11.15**   Create New Building Block Dialog Box

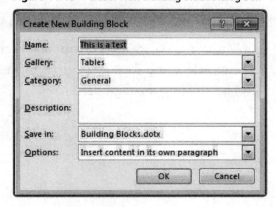

- From the list, click the table you saved previously. This table will now be inserted into the document. These steps are shown in Figure 11.16.

**Figure 11.16** Reusing a Saved Table

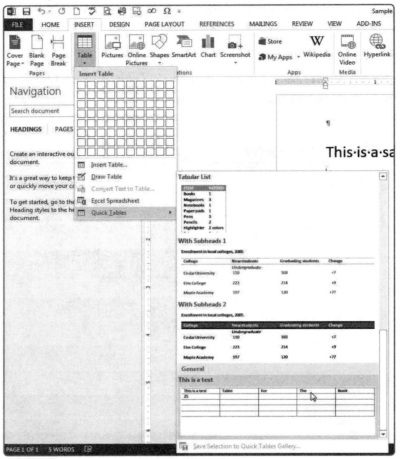

## Predefine the Format for Pasting in Word

In a Microsoft Word 2003 document, each time you paste some text or an image, you can select the format (source formatting, destination formatting, or text only) by clicking the clipboard icon.

In Microsoft Word 2007, Microsoft Outlook 2007, and later versions, you can do this manually by choosing the appropriate option from the **Paste** drop-down menu, or automatically by setting the default paste formatting mode.

Here's how to set the default paste formatting mode:

- Go to **Advanced Options** or click *Set Default Paste* when the clipboard icon appears (Figure 11.17).
- Choose your preferences from the options shown in Figure 11.18.

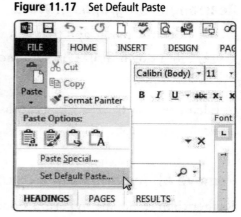

**Figure 11.17**   Set Default Paste

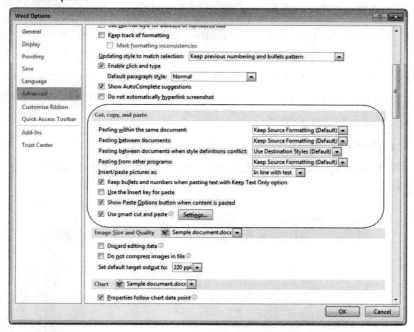

**Figure 11.18**   Paste Options

Pasted text and images will now be formatted automatically according to your settings.

## Rearrange Paragraphs in Word

- Click the paragraph that you want to move.
- Hold down *Shift+Alt* and move the paragraph up or down by using the arrow keys.

Each press of an arrow key causes your selected paragraph to jump over one adjacent paragraph.

## Remove All Hyperlinks in a Document at Once

Rather than removing hyperlinks one at a time, if you want a document with no hyperlinks at all, select the entire document using *Ctrl+A*. Then press *Ctrl+Shift+F9*, and all of the hyperlinks will be gone.

## Change the Smart Quote AutoCorrect Setting

Word sometimes uses "straight" quotation marks (also called "dumb") instead of true typographic quotation marks (called "smart" or "curly"). By default, Word usually replaces straight quotes with smart quotes. For consistency, it's best to use one style, generally smart quotes. Here is how you change this setting:

- Click the *File* or the *Office* button.
- Click *Word Options*.
- Click *Proofing*, and then click the *AutoCorrect Options* button (Figure 11.19).

**Figure 11.19**   AutoCorrect Options

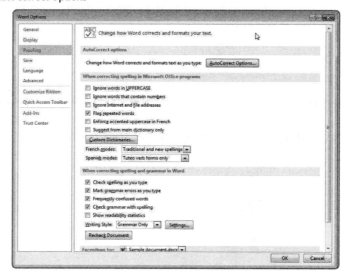

- Click the *AutoFormat* tab (Figure 11.20).

**Figure 11.20**   AutoFormat Tab Options

- Clear the "'Straight quotes' with 'smart quotes'" check box.
- Click the *AutoFormat As You Type* tab (Figure 11.21).

**Figure 11.21**   AutoFormat As You Type Tab

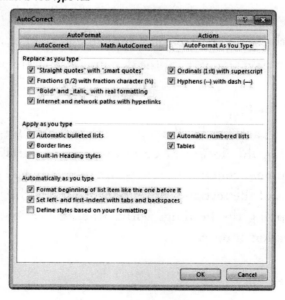

- Clear the "'Straight quotes' with 'smart quotes'" check box.
- Click **OK** twice.

## Find Tooltips for Keyboard Shortcuts

When working on a document, you can save time by not going back and forth between your keyboard and your mouse. If you press and hold the *Alt* key, tooltips appear above the commands in the ribbon, as shown in Figure 11.22. You can then press the appropriate letter for a simple keyboard shortcut.

**Figure 11.22** Tooltip

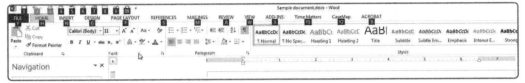

## Edit Long Documents Quickly

It can be tedious to scroll through a document to find the spot where you last worked. Fortunately, you can move to the location quickly. Use the shortcut *Shift+F5* to go back to wherever you were working last.

## Split Documents

If you ever want to see or work on two different parts of a document at once, you can. Just follow these instructions:

- On the **View** tab, click *Split*.
- Next, click the screen where you want the split to appear.
- You can then navigate parts of the document separately in each window.

## Finding Specific Terms

Use the Navigation pane (under the **View** tab) to search for—and jump to—specific terms within the document or to easily move parts of the document around. If the document contains headings and subheads, you can easily cut and paste large sections of the text and move them around within the document by dragging and dropping the headings within the Navigation pane, which will move the entire section at once.

## Using Quick Parts

The Quick Parts feature is a place where you can create, store, and find reusable pieces of content using AutoText; it's great for saving phrases, pleading parts, signatures, and just about any other information you type repeatedly. Quick Parts also contains document properties, such as title and author, and fields. Click on the *Insert* tab and go to the Text group to access Quick Parts.

## AUTOTEXT

You'll probably use AutoText frequently to store content that you can access again and again. You can save AutoText by selecting the text you want to save/reuse, opening Quick Parts and clicking on *AutoText* (see Figure 11.23), and then clicking *Save Selection to AutoText Gallery*. By filling in the new building block information, you save the content and store it to use again. To see stored items, simply click AutoText to access the AutoText gallery.

**Figure 11.23**  Accessing AutoText

After you save a selection to the AutoText gallery, you can reuse it by clicking on Quick Parts and selecting the item from the gallery. Or, when you start typing a saved phrase, Word will prompt you to press Enter if you want to insert the saved text.

## DOCUMENT PROPERTY

Click *Document Property* to choose from a list of properties (really metadata) that you can insert in your document, such as Author, Company, Subject, and more. This information stays with your document.

## FIELD

Use the field codes option to insert fields that can provide automatically updated information, such as the time, title, page numbers, and so on.

## BUILDING BLOCKS ORGANIZER

Have a large brief to complete? Or are you working on some other large project? Consider using Building Blocks Organizer to shorten the time it will take. This feature contains numerous Building Block galleries, such as Headers, Footers, and Cover Pages, to help organize your document.

In Quick Parts, click ***Building Blocks Organizer*** to preview all of the building blocks available to you in Word. You can also edit, delete, and insert building blocks.

## Find Out How Many Lines or Words You Have Typed

Right-click the status bar and then select a parameter to view line details or the number of words typed.

## Line Numbering

- Under the **Page Layout** tab, go to the *Line Numbers* drop-down menu, shown in Figure 11.24.

**Figure 11.24**   Line Numbers Drop-Down Menu

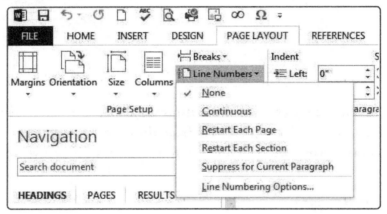

- The menu has options for continuous line numbers or numbering for each page or section, as well as the start number and increments.
- "From text" controls the distance between the numbering and the document text.
- Line numbering can be applied per paragraph or to the entire document.
- Line numbering can be stopped at any time or suspended for selected paragraphs: Click *Line Numbers > Suppress for Current Paragraph* or click *Home > Paragraph* (arrow in lower right corner) > *Line and Page Breaks (tab) > Formatting exceptions > Suppress line numbers*.
- You can change the look of just the line numbers using the Line Number style.

## MICROSOFT EXCEL

### Copy a Worksheet

Here's how to copy a worksheet to another place in your Excel workbook:

- Click the tab of the worksheet that you want to copy.
- Leave your mouse pointer on the tab.
- Press and hold down the **Ctrl** key.
- Press and hold down your left mouse button and drag the worksheet to the left or right (wherever you want to paste it). Watch for the little black arrowhead that follows your mouse pointer as you drag left or right.

When you release the mouse button, Excel inserts a copy of the worksheet where the arrowhead is pointing.

### Enter a Fraction in a Cell

To enter a fraction, simply prefix it with a zero and a space. To display the fraction one-third, type 0 1/3. This will display 1/3 but will have an underlying value of 0.33333333.

### Paste into Nonsequential Cells in Excel

Sometimes you want to copy a formula or piece of data into a series of nonsequential cells. You can do this quickly without having to paste into each cell individually.

- Copy the data from the source cell.
- Hold down the **Ctrl** key as you click to select each destination cell.
- After all the cells are highlighted, paste the data by pressing **Ctrl+V**.

You have to paste only once.

### Type Data into a Series of Cells Simultaneously

- While holding down the **Ctrl** key, click all the cells that you want to have the same text (or value).
- Type the entry and then press **Ctrl+Enter**.
- The text will be added to all the selected cells.

## Copy Data from a Table in a Web Page

To import a data table from a website, follow these steps:

- Copy the URL (address) of the page.
- In Excel, under the **Data** tab, in the **Get External Data** section, click *From Web*.
- In the **New Web Query** dialog box, paste the URL into the **Address** box.
- Select the table that contains the data that you want to work with, and then click *Import*.
- In the **Import Data** dialog box, indicate where you want the data to appear, and then click *OK*.

## Customize Records Storage

You can customize how you sort your records by activating a filter.

- Under the **Data** tab, click *Filter*, as shown in Figure 11.25.

**Figure 11.25** Activating a Data Filter

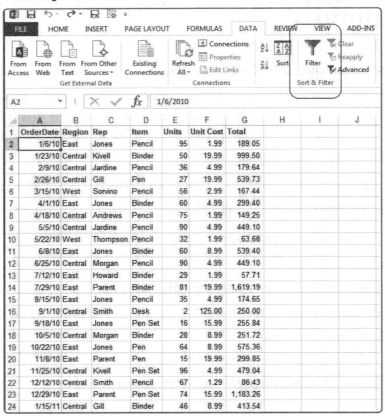

| | A | B | C | D | E | F | G | H | I | J |
|---|---|---|---|---|---|---|---|---|---|---|
| 1 | OrderDate | Region | Rep | Item | Units | Unit Cost | Total | | | |
| 2 | 1/6/10 | East | Jones | Pencil | 95 | 1.99 | 189.05 | | | |
| 3 | 1/23/10 | Central | Kivell | Binder | 50 | 19.99 | 999.50 | | | |
| 4 | 2/9/10 | Central | Jardine | Pencil | 36 | 4.99 | 179.64 | | | |
| 5 | 2/26/10 | Central | Gill | Pen | 27 | 19.99 | 539.73 | | | |
| 6 | 3/15/10 | West | Sorvino | Pencil | 56 | 2.99 | 167.44 | | | |
| 7 | 4/1/10 | East | Jones | Binder | 60 | 4.99 | 299.40 | | | |
| 8 | 4/18/10 | Central | Andrews | Pencil | 75 | 1.99 | 149.25 | | | |
| 9 | 5/5/10 | Central | Jardine | Pencil | 90 | 4.99 | 449.10 | | | |
| 10 | 5/22/10 | West | Thompson | Pencil | 32 | 1.99 | 63.68 | | | |
| 11 | 6/8/10 | East | Jones | Binder | 60 | 8.99 | 539.40 | | | |
| 12 | 6/25/10 | Central | Morgan | Pencil | 90 | 4.99 | 449.10 | | | |
| 13 | 7/12/10 | East | Howard | Binder | 29 | 1.99 | 57.71 | | | |
| 14 | 7/29/10 | East | Parent | Binder | 81 | 19.99 | 1,619.19 | | | |
| 15 | 8/15/10 | East | Jones | Pencil | 35 | 4.99 | 174.65 | | | |
| 16 | 9/1/10 | Central | Smith | Desk | 2 | 125.00 | 250.00 | | | |
| 17 | 9/18/10 | East | Jones | Pen Set | 16 | 15.99 | 255.84 | | | |
| 18 | 10/5/10 | Central | Morgan | Binder | 28 | 8.99 | 251.72 | | | |
| 19 | 10/22/10 | East | Jones | Pen | 64 | 8.99 | 575.36 | | | |
| 20 | 11/8/10 | East | Parent | Pen | 15 | 19.99 | 299.85 | | | |
| 21 | 11/25/10 | Central | Kivell | Pen Set | 96 | 4.99 | 479.04 | | | |
| 22 | 12/12/10 | Central | Smith | Pencil | 67 | 1.29 | 86.43 | | | |
| 23 | 12/29/10 | East | Parent | Pen Set | 74 | 15.99 | 1,183.26 | | | |
| 24 | 1/15/11 | Central | Gill | Binder | 46 | 8.99 | 413.54 | | | |

- Next, click the dropdown arrows to select the criteria for your filter (see Figure 11.26). Click **OK**. The table will now display the filtered data and any filtered columns will display a funnel where the dropdown arrow was.

**Figure 11.26**    Selecting Cells to Filter

- Click the filter arrow on the heading of the column that you want to sort, as shown in Figure 11.27.

**Figure 11.27**    Filter Arrows on Column Headings

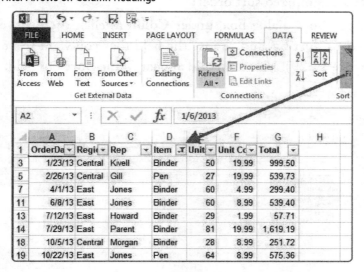

- Choose *Sort by Color*, and then click *Custom Sort*, as shown in Figure 11.28.

**Figure 11.28**   Sort by Color and Custom Sort

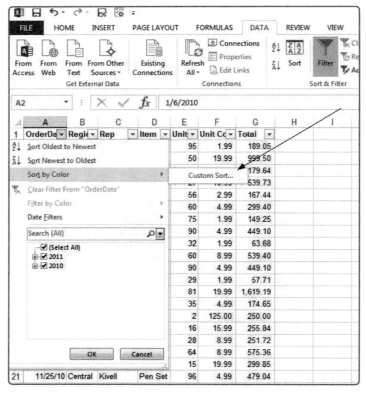

- Create a customized sort order:
  - In the **Sort** dialog box, under **Column**, click the drop-down arrow next to **Sort by**, and choose the field that you want to be sorted (see Figure 11.29). Values should appear in the **Sort On** field.

**Figure 11.29**   "Sort by" Box

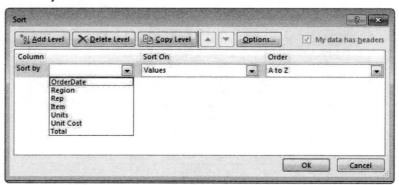

- o In the **Order** field, click *Custom List*. This will open a window that offers an entirely customizable sort list.
- o In the left pane, list the values (each separated by a comma) in the order that you want them to be sorted, and then click *Add*.
- o In the right pane, select the list you've created, and then click **OK**.
- o In the **Sort** dialog box, click **OK**.

Your records will now be sorted according to your customized list.

## Move the Cursor in Any Direction When Entering Data

By default, the cell pointer moves down when you press the **Enter** key after entering data in a cell. You can change the direction in which the cell pointer moves.

- Click the *File* or the *Office* button.
- Click *Excel Options*, and then click *Advanced*.
- Select the "After pressing Enter, move selection" check box if it isn't already selected (see Figure 11.30), and then in the **Direction** box, click the direction in which you want the pointer to move.

**Figure 11.30** Changing the Direction of the Cell Pointer

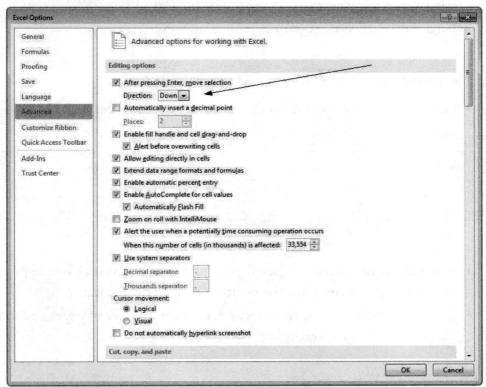

Also, when working in a document, you can make the pointer move in the opposite direction from the one you've chosen by holding down the *Shift* key while you press the *Enter* key.

## Zooming to Focus On Selection

- Select the range of cells that you want to focus on.
- Click the *View* tab, and then click *Zoom to Selection*.

## Change the Color of Every Other Row

Spreadsheets can be difficult to read. To make reading easier, change the color of every other row.

- Select the range of cells you wish to format.
- Go to the *Home* tab
- Switch to Styles group and click *Conditional Formatting*.
- In the drop-down menu, select *Use a Formula to determine which cells to format*.
- In the box, type: =MOD(ROW(),2)=0.
- Click the *Format* button and then click the *Fill* tab.
- Select a color for the shaded rows and click *OK* twice.

## Fit a Printout onto a Set Number of Worksheet Pages

- Click the *Page Layout* tab on the ribbon, shown in Figure 11.31.

**Figure 11.31**   Page Layout Tab

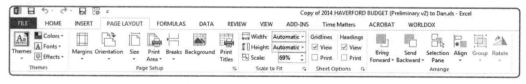

- In the **Scale to Fit** section (see Figure 11.32), in the **Width** box, type the number of pages you want the printout to span horizontally.
- In the **Height** box in the same section, type the number of pages you want the printout to span vertically.

**Figure 11.32**   Scale to Fit Options

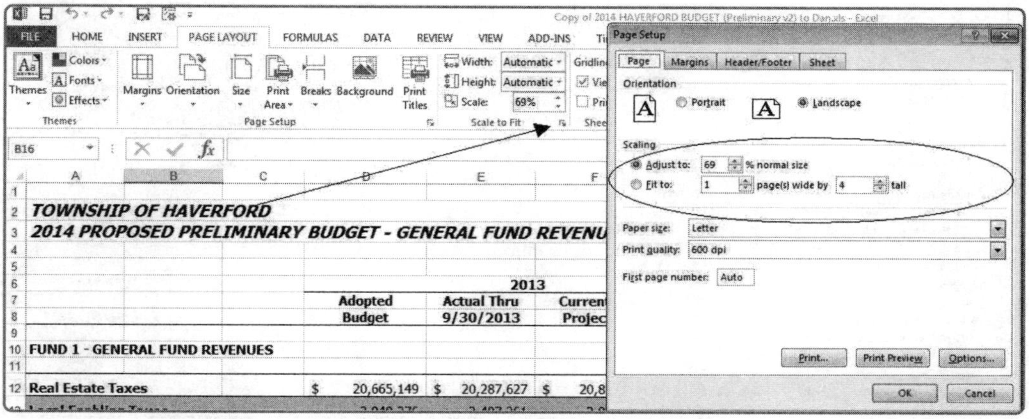

## Enter the Same Value into Multiple Cells Simultaneously

- Select the cells into which you want to enter the value.
- Type the value in the active cell.
- Press **Ctrl+Enter**.

## Enter a Series of Data

- Type the first value in the series into a cell.
- Type the second value into a cell below or to the right of the first cell.
- Select the cells.
- Drag the **Fill Handle** (a black square that appears at the bottom right corner of the last selected cell) over the cells into which you want to extend the series.

## Identify Duplicates

- Click the *Home* tab on the ribbon.
- In the Styles section, click *Conditional Formatting*.
- Select *Highlight Cells Rules*.
- Click *Duplicate Values*.
- Pairs of duplicates will then be highlighted, and you can choose which of each pair to delete. These steps are all shown in Figure 11.33 below.

**Figure 11.33**   Identifying Duplicate Values

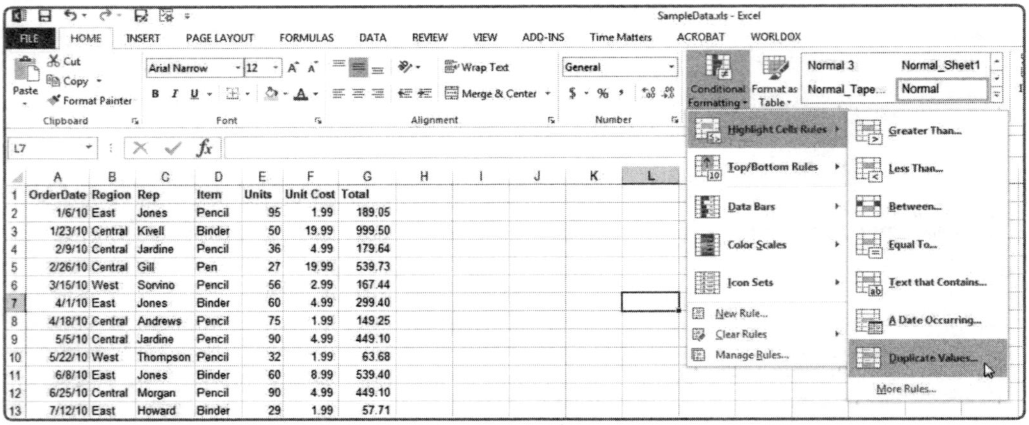

## Add and Delete Rows and Columns on Spreadsheets

- To add a row or column, select any row or column. Then press the **Ctrl** key at the same time as the + key (plus sign) on the numeric keypad.

- To delete a row or column, select the row or column. Then press the **Ctrl** key at the same time as the − key (minus sign) on the numeric keypad.

## View All the Text in Columns

- Select the columns where your text appears by clicking the column headings.

- To resize the columns to fit, double-click in the column heading, exactly on top of the border that divides any two of the columns you selected.

- All of your selected columns are resized based on the longest text string in each column.

- Sometimes this can make a column too wide. In that case, you may want to highlight the column (or cell), right-click, select **Format Cells**, and click **Wrap text** under the **Alignment** tab.

## Change the Color of a Sheet Tab

- Right-click the sheet tab.
- Click **Tab Color**.
- Choose the color you want from the palette that appears, as shown in Figure 11.34.

**Figure 11.34**   Color Options for Sheet Tabs

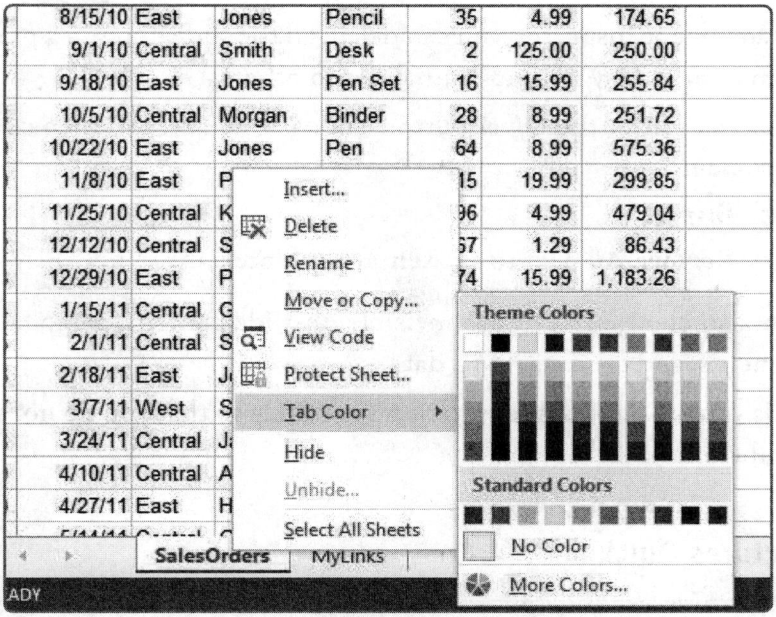

# MICROSOFT POWERPOINT

## Use Presenter View

Presenter view gives you more control over your presentation, including the ability to show slides out of sequence. It includes a blackout button that allows you to blacken the screen for the audience while you can still see the presentation and your notes on your own monitor. It also allows you to run your presentation from one monitor and let the audience view it on another monitor or a projector.

## Moving to Specific Slides during a Presentation

When a presenter quickly zooms through slides to make up time or to find information, it distracts from the presentation and annoys the audience. Before giving your presentation, print out the outline of your slides with page numbers on them or simply make a list of the slides with their corresponding numbers. Use this as a guide during your presentation. To jump to a specific slide, type the slide number and, voilá, you are there.

## Delete Slide Notes before Sending Copies of a Presentation

By using Document Inspector, you can delete all the slide notes in a presentation instantly, making it easy to send your slides to others.

- Click the *File* or the *Office* button, choose *Prepare*, and then click *Inspect Document*.
- Click *Inspect*.
- Click *Remove All* next to **Presentation Notes**.

You can also choose to remove invisible on-slide content, personal information, comments, and custom XML data.

Save this version of your presentation separately so that you do not write over the original version.

## Move Pictures Quickly

To move pictures around quickly in PowerPoint, just drag one picture over another. The top picture will become transparent, letting you position it accurately over the other.

## Select a Slide Layout

- Under either the **Home** tab or the **Insert** tab, click the *New Slide* icon.
- Select a layout option from the **Add Slide** gallery.
- On your new slide, click a placeholder to add text or content.

## Enter the PowerPoint Slide Show Mode at Any Point

To start your slide show with the current or selected slide, press *Shift+F5*.

## ADOBE ACROBAT STANDARD AND/OR PROFESSIONAL

While many lawyers are familiar with the *free* Adobe Reader, the Standard and Professional versions of Adobe Acrobat are the game changers. Using these programs can dramatically improve your efficiency and productivity. In fact, we believe that every lawyer and every support person needs Adobe Acrobat (either Standard or Professional). Plus, the software is essential to going paperless.

## Add Bookmarks to a PDF File

To create a bookmark, open the page where you want the bookmark to link and right-click to add a bookmark (see Figure 11.35).

**Figure 11.35**   Adding a Bookmark

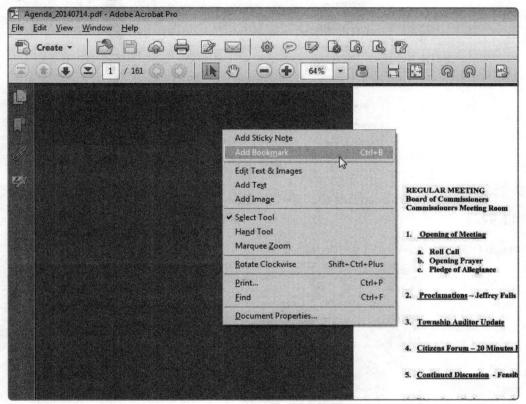

You can also use the **Select** tool to create the bookmark:

- To bookmark a single image, click in the image or drag a rectangle around the image.
- To bookmark a portion of an image, drag a rectangle around the portion.

To bookmark text, drag to select it, and right-click to get the *Add Bookmark* command (Figure 11.36).

**Figure 11.36**   Using Text to Create a Bookmark

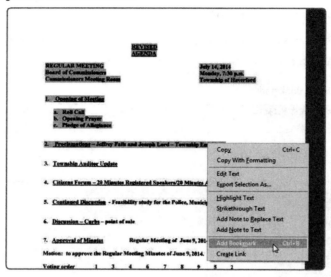

The selected text becomes the label of the new bookmark, as shown in Figure 11.37.

**Figure 11.37**   Bookmark Label from Selected Text

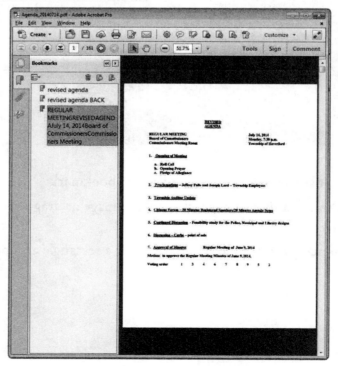

You can edit the bookmark label.

- Click the **Bookmarks** button. Select the bookmark under which you want to place the new bookmark. If you don't select a bookmark, the new bookmark is automatically added at the end of the list.
- Choose **New Bookmark** from the **Options** menu.
- Edit the name of the new bookmark.

## Add Menus to the Task Panel

It is important to know that, by default, not all menus are included on the task panel. You can add them easily by clicking on *View > Tools* and selecting the additional menus you want to see, as shown in Figure 11.38.

**Figure 11.38**   Additional Menus for Task Panel

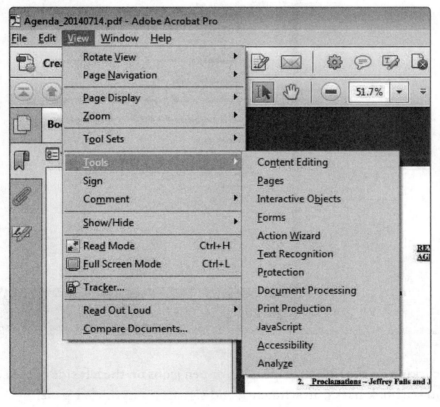

## View Thumbnails

As in previous versions, you can view thumbnails of pages, bookmarks, and signatures on the left side of the screen.

In Figure 11.39 below, page thumbnails are highlighted.

**Figure 11.39** Page Thumbnails in Adobe Acrobat

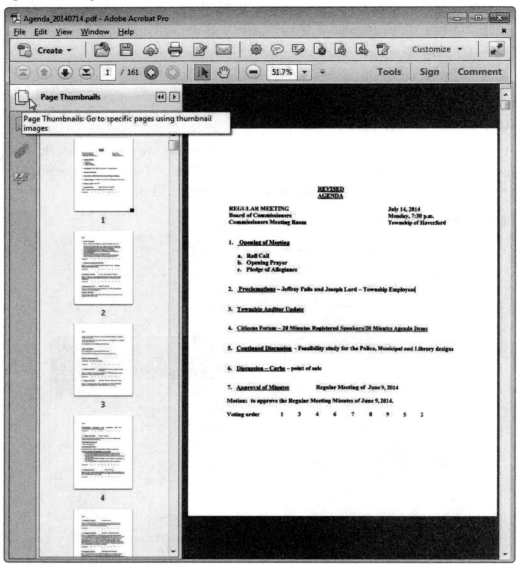

By clicking on the ribbon, paper clip, or pen icons on the left side of the screen, you can see bookmarks, attachments, and signatures in the left panel.

**Figure 11.40**   The Collapse Button to Close Thumbnail View

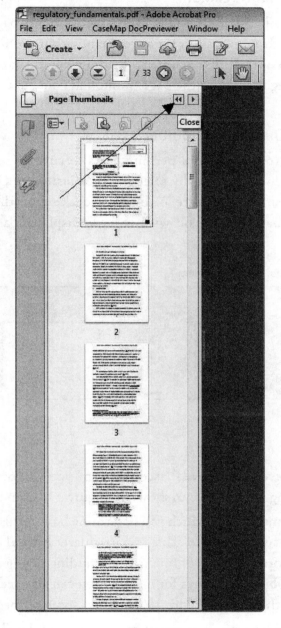

To close the panel, click the small *Collapse* button, highlighted in Figure 11.40 above. There is a corresponding **Collapse** button on the menus on the right.

## Arrange Pages in a Document

The page thumbnail view is especially useful for arranging pages in a document. You can drag and drop pages to rearrange them within the PDF and can easily copy between two open PDF documents by dragging the pages from one document and dropping them onto the page thumbnail panel in the second.

## Customize the Quick Tools Toolbar

Adobe Acrobat Professional still permits users to customize the **Quick Tools** toolbar, as in previous versions, by selecting the *Customize Quick Tools* button on the toolbar. Using this feature, or by right-clicking on the toolbar, you can select the additional features you wish to have displayed, as shown in Figure 11.41.

**Figure 11. 41** Options for Quick Tools Toolbar

## Saving PDFs

As with virtually every Windows-based program, you will open, close, and save files in Adobe using the **File** menu, shown in Figure 11.42 on the following page.

This is also the menu from which you determine how you save PDFs—that is, the specific format you will use. This is particularly helpful because the menu allows you to perform a variety of functions, including saving the file as PDF/A, the standard used by some courts for e-filing. You can also reduce the size of the PDF file through this menu. Figure 11.42 shows some of these functions.

The menu provides other important options as well. For lawyers, one of the most helpful is the **Reader Extended PDF** (see Figure 11.42) that permits you to create forms and other documents and send them to clients. The clients, who only need to have the free Adobe Reader, can then fill out a form, save it, and return it by e-mail.

**Figure 11.42**   File Menu and *Save As Other* Options

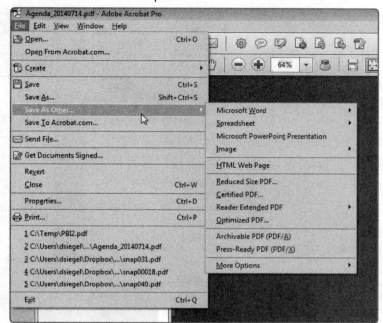

In addition, the **File** menu allows you to convert PDFs to Word files, images (Figure 11.43), and other formats (Figure 11.44), and to use many of the actions that automate the manner in which Adobe can process your documents.

**Figure 11.43**   Saving PDFs as Image Files

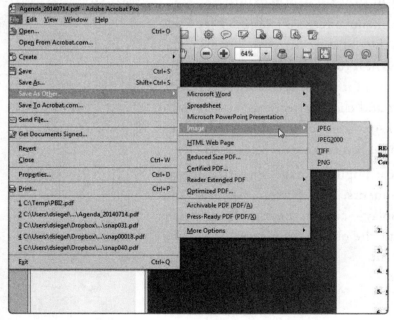

**Figure 11.44**    Saving PDFs in Other Formats

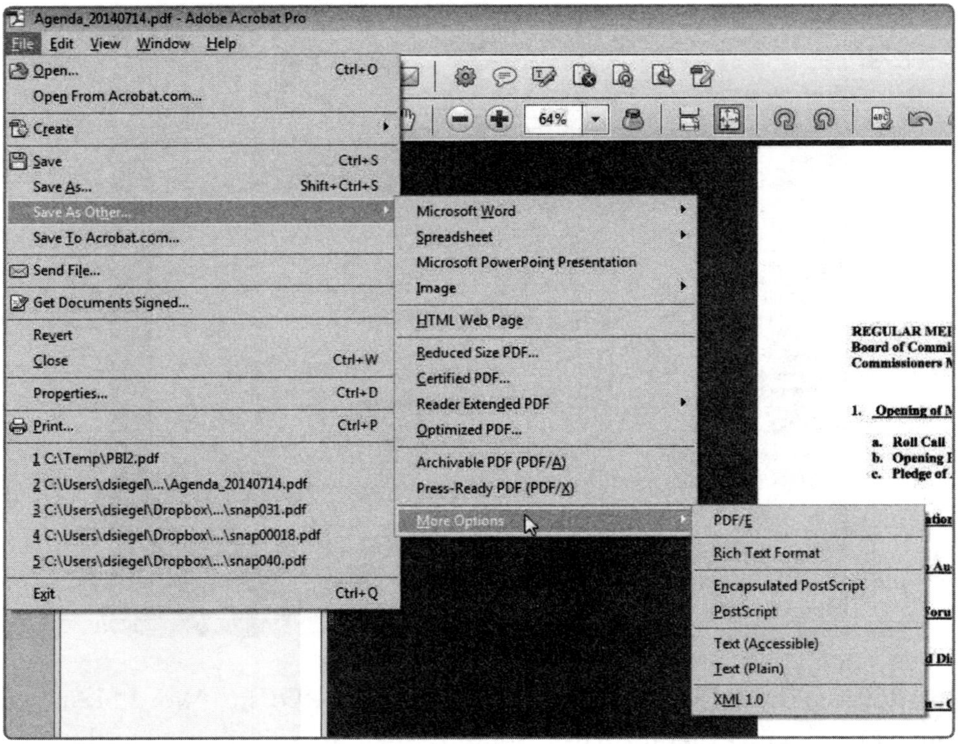

## Navigation and Customization

The **Edit** menu offers you options for customizing the software so that it works the way you want it to, not how the programmers think you want it to. To access these features, go to *Edit* and click *Preferences*, as shown in Figure 11.45. This opens the **Preferences** menu, where you make your selections.

The most popular categories—Commenting, Documents, Full Screen, General, and Page Display—are at the top (see Figure 11.46), but the other options can be equally as important.

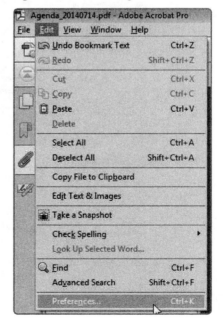

**Figure 11.45**    Accessing Preferences

**Figure 11.46**    Preferences: Categories

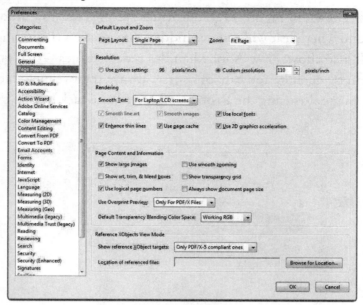

## COMMENTING

From this window, shown in Figure 11.47, you select the font used in Comments and specify how the comments will act and appear.

**Figure 11.47**    Comments Preferences

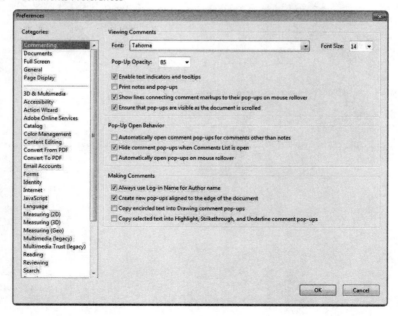

## DOCUMENTS

This window, shown in Figure 11.48, provides settings for how Adobe will save documents and whether it will remove hidden information (including metadata) by default. It also shows how Adobe handles redacted files—that is, whether it renames them by default. You can, of course, always remove metadata and other hidden data manually using the **Protection** tab on the task bar.

**Figure 11.48**    Documents Preferences

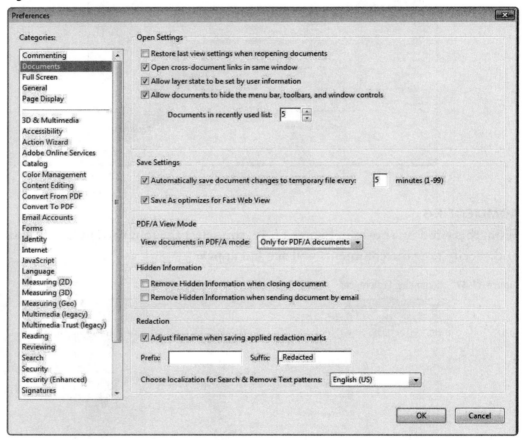

## FULL SCREEN

This window, shown in Figure 11.49, gives you the opportunity to customize how documents are opened, how they appear, and how they are navigated. In most cases, you can modify these for any particular document without having to modify your general preferences.

**Figure 11.49** Full Screen Preferences

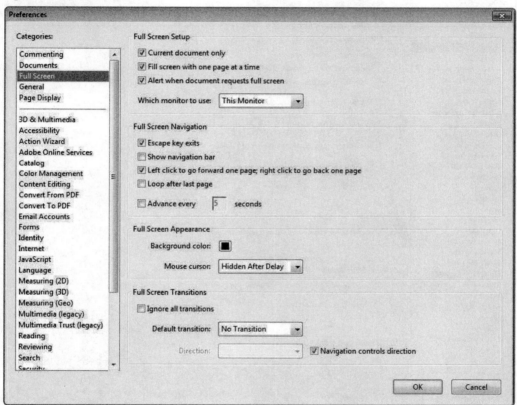

## GENERAL

From this window, shown in Figure 11.50, you can change some of the program's most common settings.

**Figure 11.50**   General Preferences

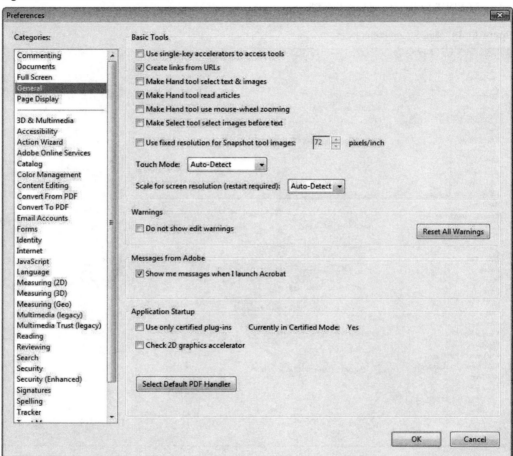

## PAGE DISPLAY

Every user tends to prefer a different method of page display—for example, one page or two pages at a time, the full page or the page fit to the width of the screen, or some other setting. You can modify your defaults here, as shown in Figure 11.51.

**Figure 11.51**   Page Display Preferences

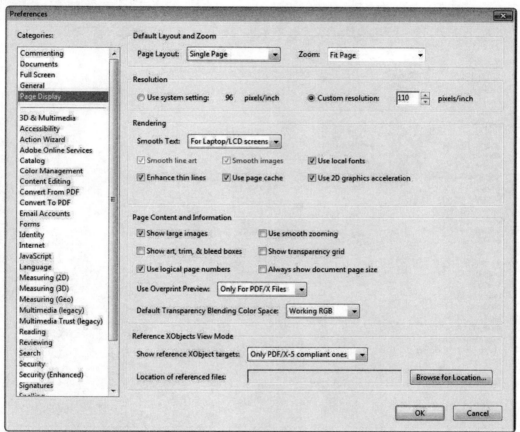

You should also review and modify the other categories of preferences to be sure that Acrobat works for you. Among the most important of these categories are Identity and Internet.

## IDENTITY

From this screen, shown in Figure 11.52, you specify the default data that will appear in the metadata of the file: the name, title, and organization of the PDF's "author." Many users prefer to leave this blank so that no identifying information appears in the document's metadata. Others include the information to avoid any questions about who created the document.

**Figure 11.52** Identity Preferences

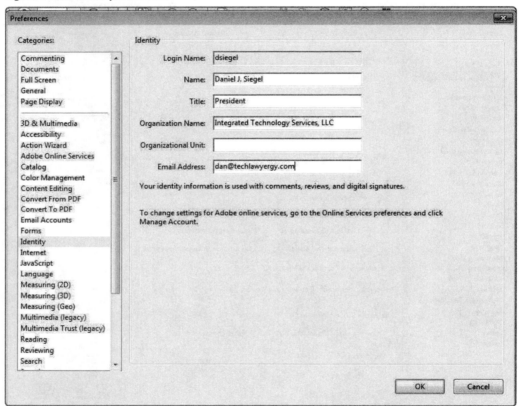

## Help Using Adobe

Adobe also offers numerous keyboard shortcuts, enabling you to perform many tasks quickly. You can locate the tools from the Help menu or by going to http://helpx.adobe.com/acrobat/using/keyboard-shortcuts.html

## Creating PDF Documents

You can create PDFs in several ways with Adobe Acrobat.

You can select **Create** on Acrobat's **File** menu (Figure 11.53) or use the **Create** menu on the toolbar to select the way you will open a new file (see Figure 11.54).

**Figure 11.53** Creating a PDF Document from the Opening Screen

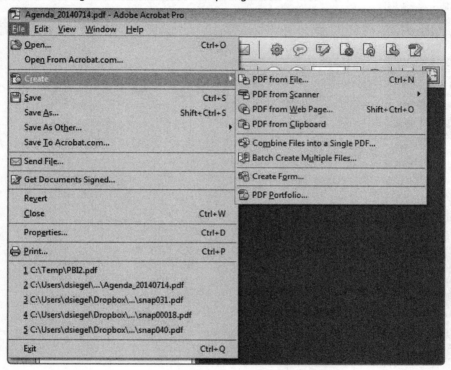

**Figure 11.54** Creating a PDF Document Using the File Menu

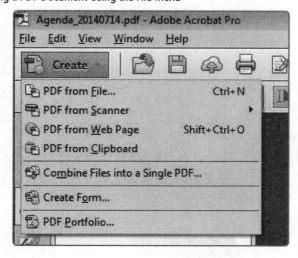

You can create a PDF from other programs, such as Word or Excel, in the same way you would print to any printer. The process is shown in Figure 11.55. Simply select Adobe Acrobat from the list of printers in one of those programs, and the document will print to a file that you can then save.

**Figure 11.55** Creating a PDF with the Print Function

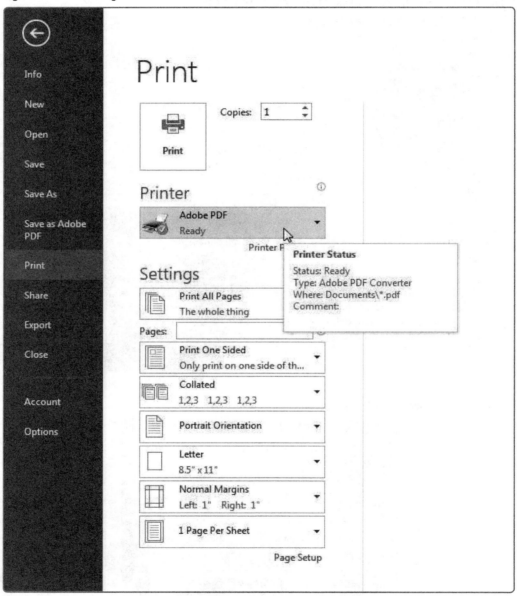

You can also create a PDF from an existing document directly from Windows Explorer without opening the document: right-click on the file and select ***Convert to Adobe PDF***, as shown in Figure 11.56.

**Figure 11.56**  Creating a PDF from Windows Explorer

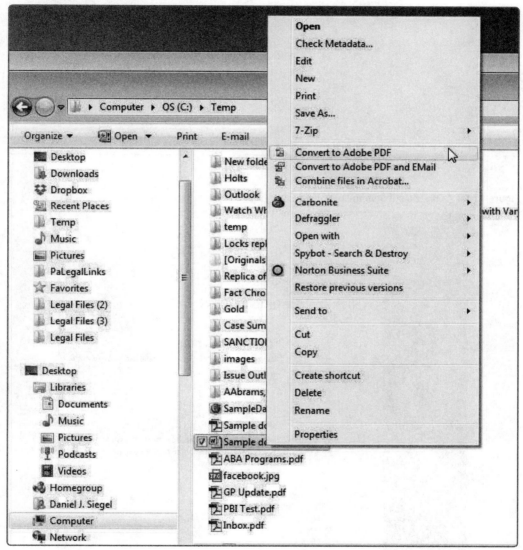

Microsoft Office programs link directly with Adobe Acrobat Professional, allowing you to convert a document created in Word, Excel, Outlook, or Power-Point to a PDF without leaving Office. For example, in Word 2010, an **Acrobat** tab appears on the ribbon at the top of the Word document (Figure 11.57), or you can create a pdf from the **File** menu (Figure 11.58).

**Figure 11.57**   Acrobat Tab in Word Document

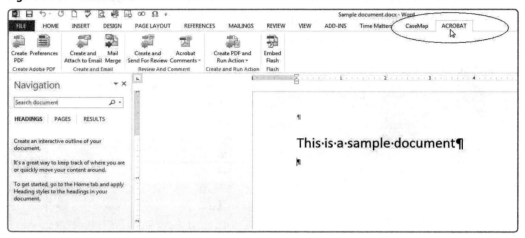

**Figure 11.58**   Create a pdf from the File Menu

An **Acrobat** tab also appears on earlier versions of Word.

## E-MAILING PDF DOCUMENTS

E-mailing a PDF is simple. With one mouse click, you can send a PDF as an e-mail message or an attachment. You can send an image just by clicking on the envelope on the toolbar (see Figure 11.59).

**Figure 11.59**  Attaching a PDF to E-mail from the toolbar

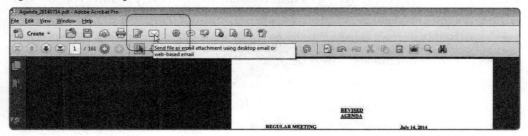

Alternatively, you can click on the *File* menu, and then *Send File*. Either option attaches the PDF to an e-mail in your default e-mail program (see Figure 11.60).

**Figure 11.60**  Attaching a PDF to E-mail from the Share option

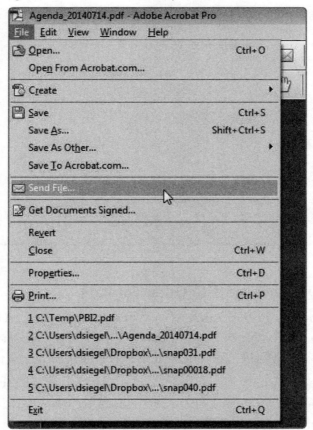

E-mailing a PDF preserves the formatting of the document and eliminates the issue of whether the recipient has the right program to read the file. PDFs are also more difficult to edit and change than Word documents.

### CREATING PDFS FROM WEB PAGES

You can also save web pages as Adobe documents. This permits you to save online receipts and confirmation pages without wasting paper. In Windows Internet Explorer, there is an Adobe Acrobat icon at the top of the toolbar that, when clicked, will convert a web page to a PDF file. You can also use the print feature to print a web page to Adobe.

Adobe also allows you to select the web content you desire, not merely the entire page. In addition, the program has extremely advanced website capture capabilities that are accessed by clicking **Create** and then **PDF from Web Page**, allowing you to capture one page, part of a website, or the entire website (see Figure 11.61).

**Figure 11.61** Creating a PDF from a Web Page

## Converting PDF Documents to Other Formats

You can also convert a PDF document to Word. It may not be an exact reproduction, but the quality continues to improve with each version. Just select **File > Save As > Microsoft Word** and you are done. Then open the document in Word.

There are other options. For example, you can export a PDF to rich text (a generic word processing format that can be used by most word processors), or XML (the format used in newer word processors), or as a spreadsheet. You can also save your document as an HTML or web-based format, or as a picture (usually a JPG or JPEG). Finally, you can save a PDF document as a generic text file. With text files, you have two options: plain or accessible. In plain text, each paragraph retains its formatting (hard returns at the end of the paragraph); in accessible text, each line from the PDF becomes a line with a hard return. Thus, you probably prefer plain text.

## Creating PDFs from Multiple Files

The days of having to merge multiple files into one large PDF are over. Using PDF Portfolios, you can assemble PDF files (including PDF forms) as well as non-PDF files into a single Portfolio. Merging PDFs into a Portfolio is the equivalent of making a stack of documents in separate folders, rather than creating a PDF document that is the equivalent of having a pile of documents that are merely placed into a stack.

In a PDF Portfolio, files are not modified when packaged, permitting signatures and security options to stay intact. Documents within a Portfolio are viewed in the same window, so you can scan quickly, without needing to scroll through all the pages of the document to get to the next one or creating bookmarks. It is also easy to delete or extract documents from a Portfolio. Finally, you can search and print the current or selected document, or all documents, from within the Portfolio.

Creating a PDF Portfolio takes only a few steps, and the choices you make in the Combine Files wizard determine whether the files are merged into a single PDF or combined into a PDF Portfolio.

- Click *Create > Combine Files into a Single PDF* (see Figures 11.62, 11.63)

**Figure 11.62**   Combining PDF Files from the Opening Screen

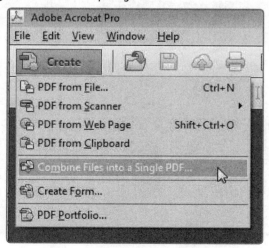

**Figure 11.63** Combining PDF Files Using the File Menu

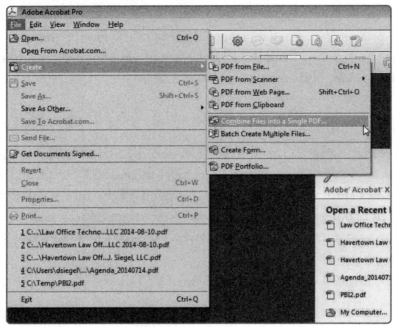

- Next, in the Combine Files wizard (Figure 11.64), do any or all of the following:
  - To add individual files, click **Add Files**, navigate as needed, select the files, and click **Add Files**.
  - Repeat these steps, if necessary, to add files in other locations.
  - To select all of the files in a specific location, click **Add Folders**, navigate to the needed folder, select it, and click **OK**.

**Figure 11.64** Combine Files Wizard

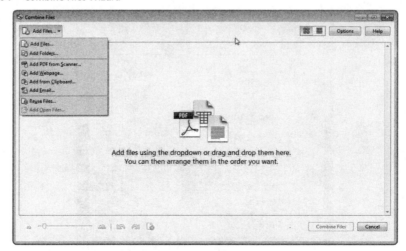

You can also change the order of the files in the Portfolio using the **Move Up**, **Move Down**, and **Remove** buttons to adjust the file sequence. In the top right-hand corner of the Combine Files screen, you can select whether to create a single PDF or a PDF Portfolio. At the bottom right of the screen, you can choose the file size to create. (There are many options and methods to create a Portfolio. For more detailed instructions, use Adobe's excellent Help feature in the program.) Once your files are in the correct order and you have the appropriate format and file size, click *Create*. A status dialog box will appear, showing the progress of the file conversions. Some source applications may start and close automatically.

When the conversion is complete, the document opens and permits you to change the layout of the Portfolio. You can add additional files (*Layout > Add Content > Add Files*); you can review the thumbnails and rearrange the documents if necessary. When you are satisfied with the final product, click *Save*, and select a name and location for the PDF Portfolio.

## Reading and Working with PDF Files

Now that you have documents saved as PDFs, you can begin to use the features that make Adobe Acrobat such a powerful product. Some of the most significant tools for lawyers are the abilities to make scanned PDFs searchable, to index multiple PDFs, and to annotate documents.

### SEARCHING

One of the biggest benefits of receiving legal documents, such as medical records, as PDFs rather than as hard copies is the ability to quickly search for a particular word or phrase instead of shuffling through a stack of papers. If you have scanned in medical records or opposing counsel's brief, you won't be able to search immediately, however, because scanning a document to PDF is like taking a picture of it. You wouldn't be able to edit the text of a picture, so you can't edit the text of the scanned document. You need to make the text editable, and you do so by using the OCR function.

OCR stands for "optical character recognition" and denotes a type of computer software that translates images of text into editable and searchable text. In Adobe, you can use OCR on a freshly scanned or previously scanned document. (In some cases, such as when Word documents are converted to PDF files, the OCR process is completed simultaneously.) Using OCR will make typewritten text (not handwriting) searchable within the PDF.

The OCR process in Adobe is done through the **Tools** menu and is found under **Text Recognition** (Figure 11.65). You can apply OCR to text in the file you have open or to multiple files.

**Figure 11.65** Text Recognition

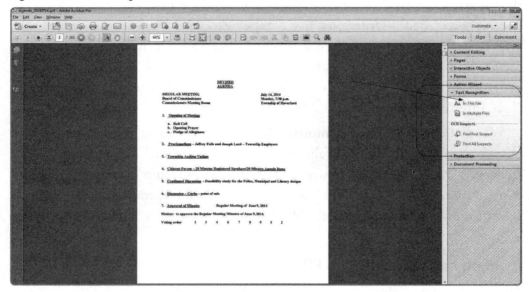

When you select *In This File*, a Recognize Text dialog box appears (Figure 11.66), prompting you to select an option under **Pages** to determine whether you want to apply OCR to the whole document or just a particular section. You may also, if you desire, click *Edit* and open the Recognize Text Settings dialog box to select the options you want to use.

These settings are extremely important and should be edited. The default for PDF Output Style is Searchable Image, which means that Adobe may actually change the appearance of certain characters so that they match the internal fonts stored in Adobe.

**Figure 11.66** Recognize Text Dialog Box

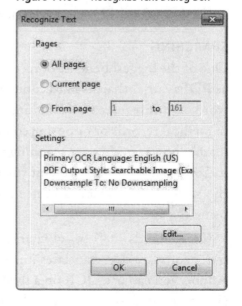

We do not recommend using the Searchable Image or the ClearScan setting. ClearScan will revise fonts to appear the same as the closest font within Adobe. In contrast, the Searchable Image (Exact) setting preserves the original fonts so that the output is identical in appearance to the original, which is critical for most lawyers. Fortunately, once you change this setting, Adobe remembers it every time.

Once a document has text that can be searched, there are multiple ways to search for words and phrases.

A valuable corollary to using OCR on documents is the ability to index and search them. From within a PDF, you have two choices: **Find** or **Search**, both of which are found either on the toolbar or in the **Edit** menu on the top left of the Adobe Acrobat window.

- **Find** (Figure 11.67) will search for a word or phrase one instance at a time.
- **Search** (Figure 11.68) brings up a separate window that searches for every instance of a word or phrase in the current PDF and creates a list, allowing the user to go directly to each instance. **Search** offers other options as well, including searching for whole words only and the ability to search Comments.

**Figure 11.67**   *Find* Function

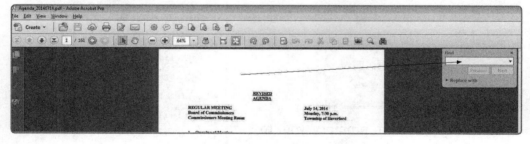

**Figure 11.68** *Search* Function

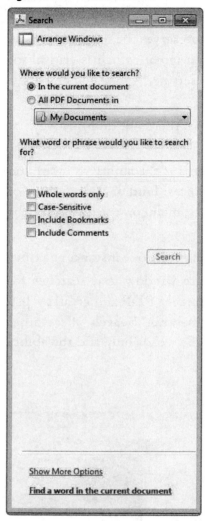

The real strength of Adobe is its ability to index groups of documents, including multiple files or directories, and permit a global search, with the immediate display of each instance of a word or phrase in every document indexed.

Create an index by clicking *Tools > Document Processing > Full Text Index with Catalog*. These steps are shown in Figure 11.69 below.

**Figure 11.69**　Creating an Index

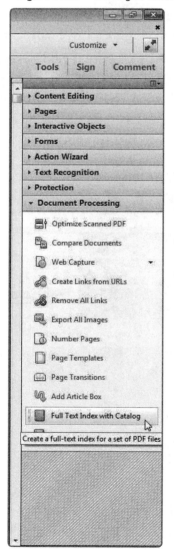

The program then prompts you to select the files to be indexed (Figure 11.70) and the location of the index file, as well as other indexing parameters (Figure 11.71). To search an index (indexes are PDX files, not PDF files), just open it (double-click on the file name or use the **File** menu, remembering to change the file parameters from *.PDF to All Files so that the PDX file will be displayed). Then type in the word or words you are searching for and wait for the results.

**Figure 11.70**   Selecting Files to Be Indexed

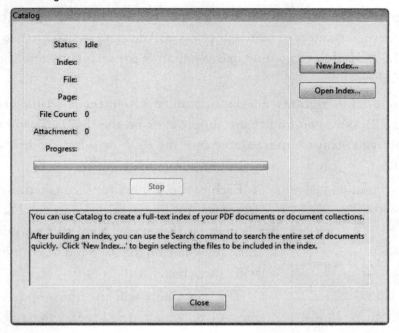

**Figure 11.71**   New Index Definition

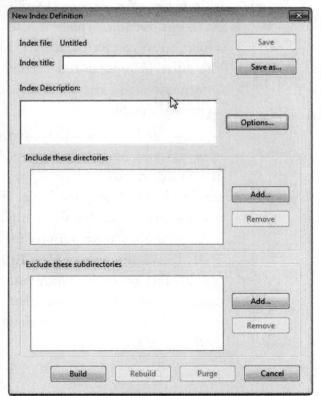

## ANNOTATING PDF DOCUMENTS

Once you have indexed and searched a document or documents, you may want to annotate the instances of words or phrases. Adobe allows you to use the same tools in the PDF that you would use to annotate paper documents: sticky notes and highlighters.

The annotation options are found under **Comment > Annotations** (see Figure 11.72); once you find them, simply click on the tool you want and then click where you want to insert a note into the PDF or select the text you want to annotate.

**Figure 11.72**   Annotation Options

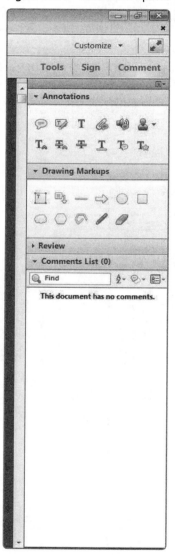

Each of the Annotations icons represents a different way to annotate the document. For example, clicking on the Sticky Note tool permits you to click anywhere on the page and insert a sticky note with a text box.

The sticky note will also show up in the Comments List, which makes it easy to navigate to the annotations in a document or you can build an index to search annotations.

Below the Annotations section is the Drawing Markups section, which is useful for drawing attention to certain parts of a document. Using the different tools in this section, you can circle information, add arrows, or create a call-out box as part of the document.

Back in the Annotations section, the Stamp tool in Adobe Acrobat Professional includes many preloaded stamps, such as "Approved," "Confidential," and even "Sign Here." (See Figure 11.73 for an example.) This tool also permits you to create custom stamps from various formats, including PDF, JPEG, and bitmap files. To add an image to a PDF, just paste the image into the document. Pasted images used as stamps have the same characteristics as other stamps: each includes a pop-up note and editable properties.

**Figure 11.73**   Stamp Tool

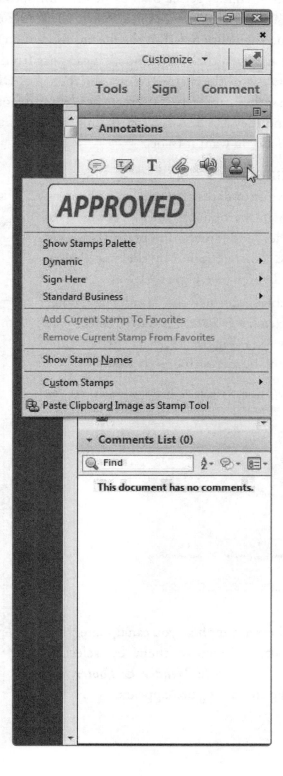

To create a custom stamp, select **Stamps** in the Annotations section of the **Comment** menu. Then click **Show Stamps Pallet**. Click **Import**, choose the file you want to use, and then click **Select**. If the file has more than one page, scroll to the page you want and then click **OK**. Choose a category from the menu or type a new category name, name the custom stamp, and then click **OK**. The real advantage of stamps is that they can be used to create headers and footers, backgrounds, and watermarks, and they can be saved for use in other documents. A stamp can be as large or small as you want it to be.

## OTHER CUSTOMIZING TOOLS

You can also remove or update existing headers, footers, watermarks, and backgrounds; shrink content to accommodate headers and footers; and preview changes in real time. These tools are found by clicking **Tools > Pages > Edit Page Design** (see Figure 11.74).

To add page numbers, you use the Header & Footer tool. First, select **Header & Footer** and then select **Add Header & Footer** (see Figure 11.75). This method works for adding any header or footer as well.

**Figure 11.74**   Adding, Removing or Editing Headers and Footers

**Figure 11.75**   Adding Page Numbers Using the Header & Footer Dialog Box

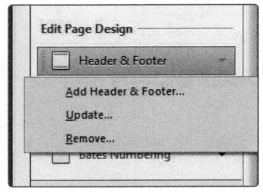

Once page numbers are applied, you can update them by selecting **Update** or remove them by selecting **Remove**. Once you select **Add Header & Footer**, the Add Header and Footer dialog box appears.

**Figure 11.76** Add Header and Footer Dialog Box

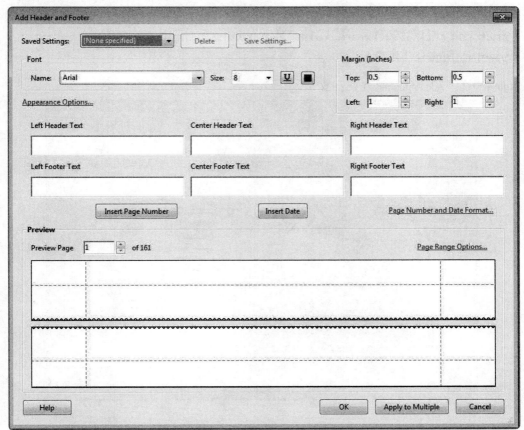

This dialog box (Figure 11.76) permits you to select the font and size of any text in the header or footer. You can also control the page margins. If you select *Appearance Options* below **Font**, you can instruct Adobe to shrink each document so that the page number does not overlap the document information.

To add the page number, select the location where you want the page number to appear—for example, Left Header Text or Center Footer Text—and click *Insert Page Number*. To the right, you can control the format of the page number and date.

Just as with Word and Excel, any text you put in the header and footer shows up on each page. Thus, if you are preparing an appellate reproduced record, you can type "R." and then click *Page Number* to get the correct numbering format of R. 1, R. 2, and so on. You can also save these settings for later use.

If you want to send clients a draft document that clearly shows it is a draft, use the Watermark tool. You access this tool just below the Header & Footer tool. When you click *Watermark > Add Watermark,* a similar dialog box appears, as shown in Figure 11.77.

**Figure 11.77**    Add Watermark Dialog Box

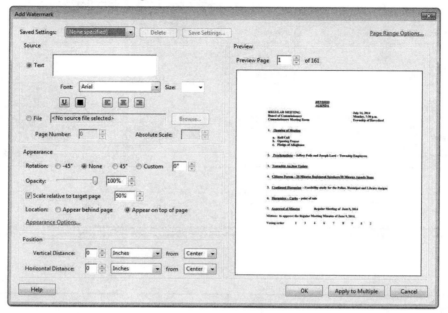

You can have the watermark load from text you type or from a file you select. The text or image will then appear on every page of your document. You can apply watermarks to multiple documents and can save settings you frequently use.

Adobe offers different tools for different types of documents. For example, perhaps you are working with a form downloaded from a website. Adobe Acrobat Professional permits you to type on the form with the Typewriter tool. If it is a form you will use again and again, you can create form fields in the document so that you can type into it without using the Typewriter tool. Also, if a form uses fonts you have on your system, you may be able to type directly into it.

The following tools are found in the Content Editing section of the **Tools** menu:

**Add Text** (Figure 11.78) permits you to simply start typing anywhere in a document that has searchable text. (In previous versions, this was the TouchUp Text tool.) If a form is still a "picture," use *Add or Edit Text Box.* Once you click on the appropriate command, a text box titled Typewriter will pop up and you can click anywhere on the PDF and begin typing. The menu contains options to change the font, size, and spacing of the text you type, as shown in Figure 11.79.

**Figure 11.78**   Adding Text to a PDF Document

Once you have your document the way you want it, you can *Save* and *Print*. Both of these functions are in the **File** menu and can also be added to the **Quick Tools** toolbar.

When printing, you have several options. You can elect to print the document as it shows on your screen, print it without markups or annotations, or print only the markups and annotations. Although these second two options may sound odd, they are fantastic for legal professionals.

Using the *Print Form Fields only* option, you can scan a form to PDF, type on the form using the Typewriter tool, and then print the "typewritten" text back onto the original paper form.

**Figure 11.79**   Formatting Options for Adding Text

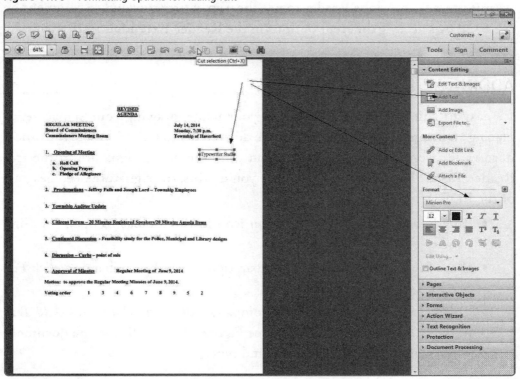

## Working with Forms in Acrobat

As discussed above, you can use the Typewriter tool to fill out forms, but Adobe Acrobat Professional X also gives you the ability to automatically or manually create forms, distribute forms, and manage the data received from forms. Acrobat X also comes with LiveCycle Designer form creation software as a standard feature and has improved the form field recognition features. The Forms tools are found under the **Tools** menu in the Forms section. The **More Form Options** field, which is where you can import and export data received from forms, is highlighted below.

To obtain data from clients or other individuals to import or merge, you can use forms you create or can highlight existing fields, which allows Adobe to select the areas the software recognizes as form fields. Once you have created a form, you can send it to anyone, even if the person only has Adobe Reader. One of the great frustrations users had with prior versions was they could not save any documents filled in with Adobe Reader; they had to print the documents to retain the changes. There are now several options for allowing users with Adobe Reader to modify PDFs.

If you have a form you want users with Adobe Reader to be able to save, you save the form as a Reader Extended PDF in the **File** menu. By enabling additional features, you permit users with Adobe Reader to save files. You can also permit users with Adobe Reader to use the Typewriter tool and to comment on the PDF by selecting different options in the **Reader Extended PDF** menu.

## ADDING SIGNATURES TO A PDF

It's easy to add a signature (by typing your name, drawing your signature, or placing an image of your signature in the document) to a PDF. While the procedure varies from version to version, you can even add a signature in the free Reader. Regardless of the method, once you do this, the signature becomes part of the PDF.

- To add a signature, click the *Sign* icon in the toolbar to open the **Sign** pane or click the *Sign* pane.
- If the **Sign** icon is not in the toolbar, right-click the toolbar and click *File > Add Text or Signature.*
- To add text, such as your name, company, title, or the date, click *Add Text* in the "I Need to Sign" section (see Figure 11.80). Click in the document where you want to add the text, and type.

- If the document requires you to indicate a selection, click **Add Checkmark.** Click on the document to place the checkmark.
- In the **Sign** pane, click *Place Signature.*
- The first time you sign, **Place Signature** opens a dialog box to allow you to create or import your signature.
- (First time signing) In the dialog box, choose how you want to place your signature:
  - Type my signature
    - Type your name in the "Enter Your Name" field. Reader creates a signature for you. You can choose from a small selection of signature styles. Click *Change Signature Style* to view a different style. When you are satisfied with your signature, click *Accept.*
  - Draw my signature
    - Draw your signature in the "Draw Your Signature" field. When you are satisfied with your signature, click *Accept.*
  - Use an image
    - Click *Browse* and locate your signature file. When your signature appears in the dialog box, click *Accept.*
    - If you don't have an image of your signature, use black ink to sign your name on a clean blank sheet of paper. Photograph or scan your signature and transfer the image file (JPG, PNG, GIF, BMP, TIFF, or PDF) to your computer. Don't crop the image; Adobe only imports the signature.
    - Adobe will then use that signature on future PDFs you sign.
- Click in the PDF where you want to place your signature.

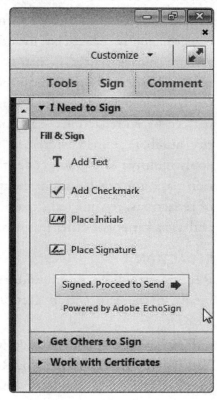

**Figure 11.80** Adding a Signature to a PDF

## Acrobat Features for Lawyers

Adobe Acrobat Professional permits users to permanently redact text, including being able to repeat redaction across pages to remove headers, footers, and other consistently placed text or images; perform pattern-based redactions (e.g., Social Security numbers, e-mail addresses, etc.); and apply multiple exemption codes to a redaction mark. You can determine the appearance of redactions, rename redacted documents, and use a variety of other features.

### REDACTION

Redaction tools are found under the **Tools** menu in the **Protection** section (Figure 11.81):

First, mark the text or pages to redact. You can do this using **Mark for Redaction, Mark Pages to Redact**, or **Search and Remove Text**. Then determine how the redactions will appear by using the **Redaction Properties** menu. Finally, click *Apply Redactions*, and you will be prompted to save the document to a different file.

### BATES NUMBERING

If you are producing documents for discovery, it is also useful to apply Bates numbers to the documents. Bates numbering allows you to place a unique identifying number on every page of every document so that there is no confusion later. With Adobe, you can Bates number one or many documents and save and reuse the Bates numbering formats.

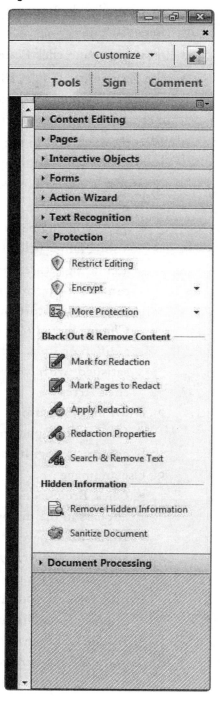

**Figure 11.81**   Redaction Tools

Adobe makes it easy to apply these identifying labels to a batch of related documents. Bates numbers appear as a header or footer on each page of each PDF in the batch and are created in virtually the same manner as page numbers. Adding Bates numbers, which you create in a wide range of styles, is done in the **Pages** section of the **Tools** menu (Figure 11.82).

As with page numbering, once you click Bates numbering, you are prompted to determine whether you want to add or remove Bates numbering (Figure 11.83).

**Figure 11.82**   Bates Numbering Function

**Figure 11.83**   Adding or Removing Bates Numbers

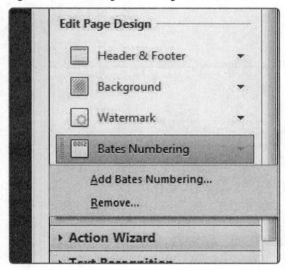

If you select *Add Bates Numbering*, you are then prompted to identify the files to add Bates numbers to and in the order in which they should appear (Figures 11.84, 11.85, 11.86).

**Figure 11.84** Select Files for Bates Numbering

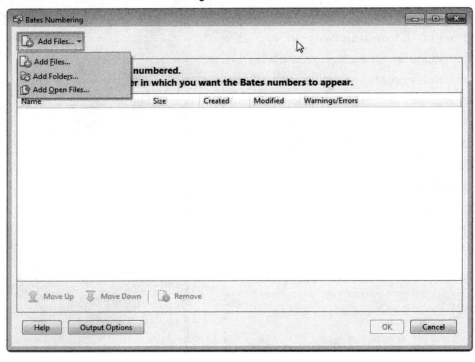

**Figure 11.85** Add Files for Bates Numbering

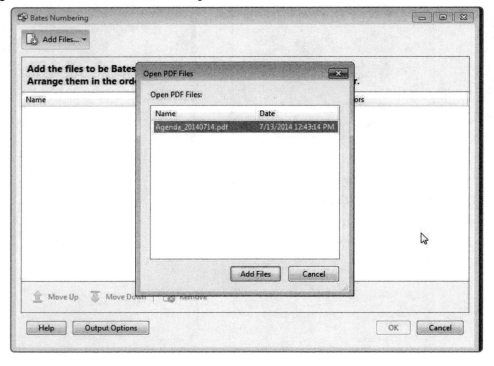

**Figure 11.86**   Order Files for Bates Numbering

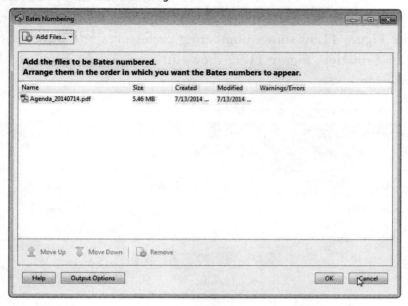

Once you have selected the files, you are prompted to add the Bates numbering in the style you would like and indicate the location on the page where you
would like it to appear (Figure 11.87).

**Figure 11.87**   Style and Placement of Bates Numbers

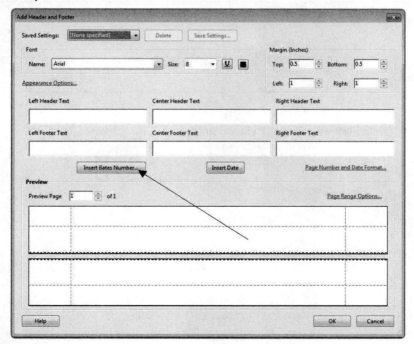

The following images show the steps in the rest of the Bates numbering process. Figure 11.88 shows numbering options; Figure 11.89 shows a sample prefix and suffix; Figure 11.90 shows numbering preferences and placement; Figure 11.91 is confirmation; Figure 11.92 shows an example of a Bates number on a document page.

**Figure 11.88**   Bates Numbering Options: Digits

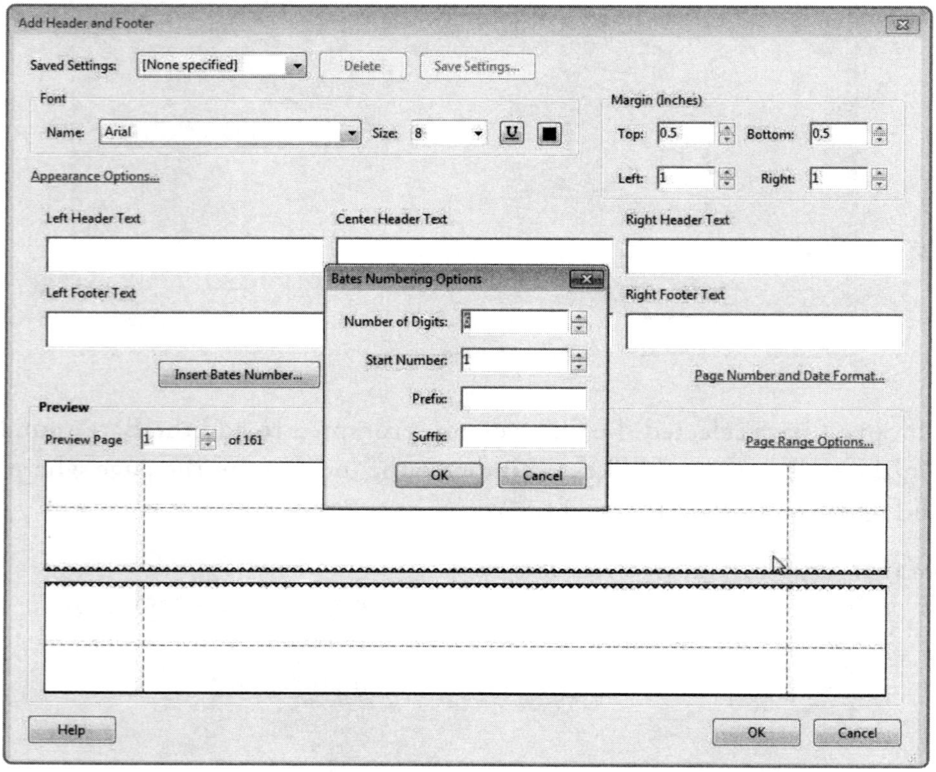

**Figure 11.89**   Bates Numbering Options: Prefix and Suffix

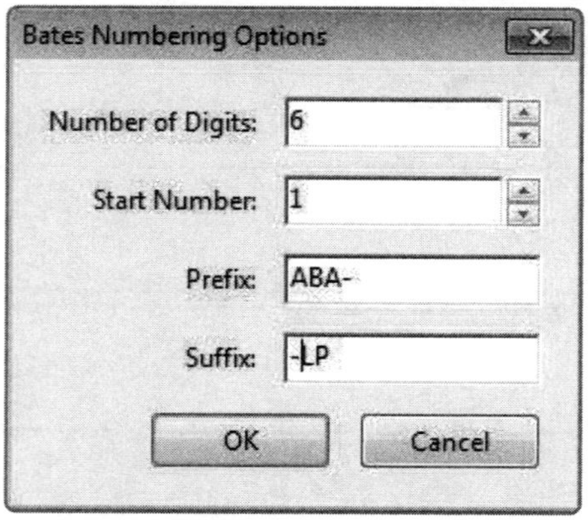

**Figure 11.90**   Bates Numbering: Preferences and Placement

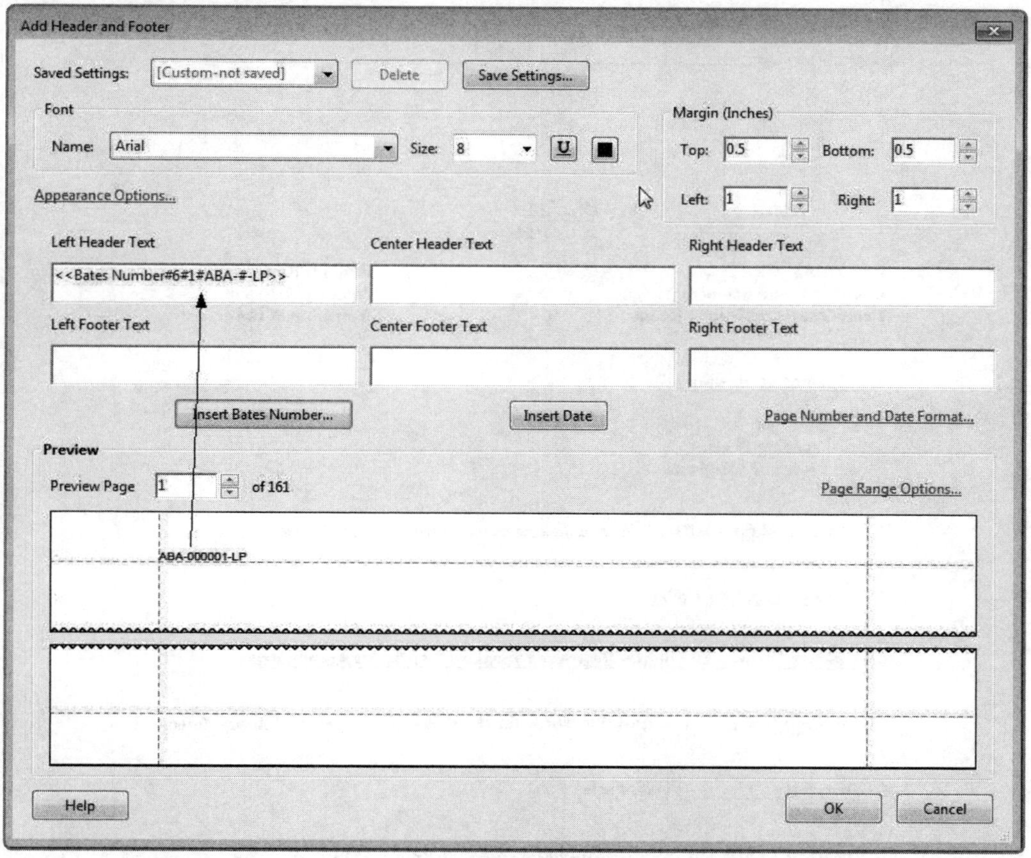

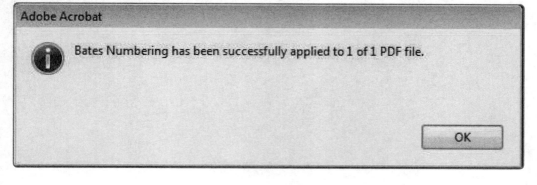

**Figure 11.91**   Confirmation of Bates Numbering

Adobe Acrobat

Bates Numbering has been successfully applied to 1 of 1 PDF file.

OK

**Figure 11.92** Document with Bates Numbering Applied

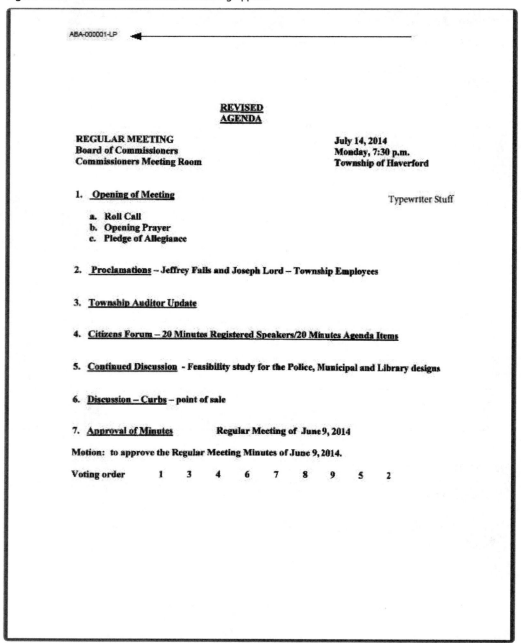

You can also save the settings for future projects.

## METADATA REMOVAL

Another function in the **Protection** section involves metadata removal. Most common software programs, including Word, Excel, and PowerPoint, contain metadata, or "information about data." This can include names of individuals who worked on a document, editing time of the document, and more. Adobe also contains metadata, although not the same data in the original document or other object that was converted to a PDF file. There may still be reasons, however, that you would want to remove the metadata from a PDF.

With Adobe Acrobat, you can easily view an object's metadata by using **Remove Hidden Information** in the Protection section (see Figure 11.93). The metadata is displayed in predefined groups of related information. In Windows, you can display or hide the information by clicking the plus and minus signs next to the group. (Adobe calls each group a schema name.) If a schema does not have a recognized name, it will be listed as Unknown. The XML name space is in parentheses after the schema name.

Adobe Acrobat has taken metadata removal a step further with the **Sanitize Document** function (see Figure 11.94). With one click, you can remove metadata, embedded content and attached files, scripts, hidden layers, indexes, stored form data, review and comment data, hidden data from previous saves, and other information.

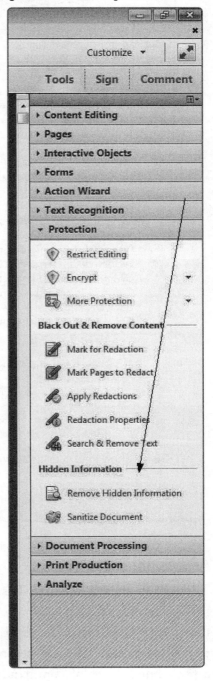

**Figure 11.93**   Removing Hidden Information

Selecting *Remove Hidden Information* gives you a chance to review the information you are removing, whereas *Sanitize Document* removes all the hidden data with one click.

**Figure 11.94**   Sanitize Document Function

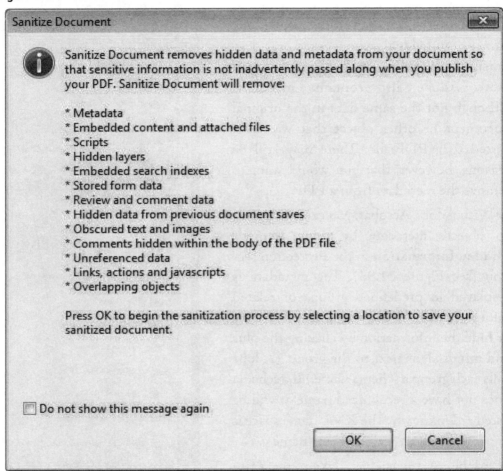

## Additional Features

The Action wizard in Adobe has improved upon the Batch Processing feature of previous versions. This wizard permits you to automate a series of frequently performed tasks (see Figure 11.95). By applying one or more routine sets of commands to files, users save time and keystrokes by using an automated sequence—that is, a predefined series of commands with specific settings performed in a specific order that can be applied in a single step. You can apply a sequence to a single document, to several documents, or to an entire collection of documents.

**Figure 11.95**   Action Wizard

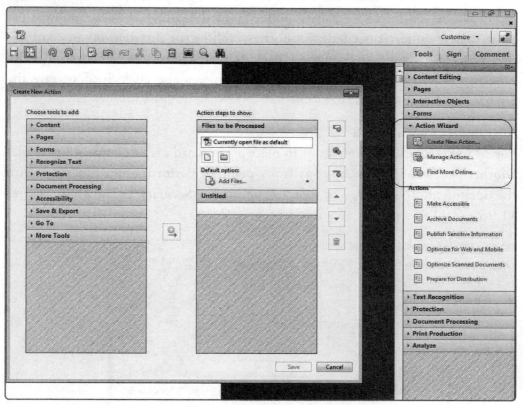

Selecting *Create New Action* will allow you to choose actions from the tools available in the **Tools** menu. You can also select from Adobe's preloaded actions. For example, **Prepare for Distribution** will prompt you to apply a header and footer, a watermark, and bookmarks to an open file and will then remove hidden information (metadata) from the file.

Here are some other actions you might want to consider using:

## PASSWORD PROTECTED ENVELOPES

With this feature, you can add security to any document by storing it in an encrypted envelope, which is called a security envelope, and sending it as an e-mail attachment. This method is especially useful for sending secure file attachments without modifying the attached files. When the recipient opens the security envelope, he or she can extract the attachments and save them to disk. The saved files are no longer encrypted when saved. To use this feature, click *Tools > Protection > More Protection > Create Security Envelope*.

Just add the files you want to attach, select an envelope template, select a delivery method, and select a security policy from the list of available policies (or create a new policy, if needed). From there, follow the instructions to complete the security envelope. If prompted, provide your identity information. Finally, type an e-mail address in the message that appears and click *Send*, or save the security envelope to send later.

## DOCUMENT PASSWORDS

For added security, you may want to place a password on a document or restrict another user's ability to edit, copy from, print, or perform other functions with the document. To do so, go to *File > Properties > Security*, as shown in Figures 11.96 and 11.97.

Figure 11.96    Accessing Document Security Menu

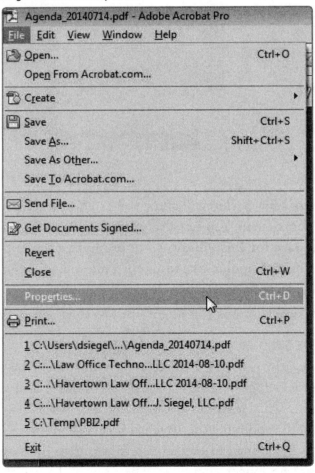

**Figure 11.97**   Document Security Options

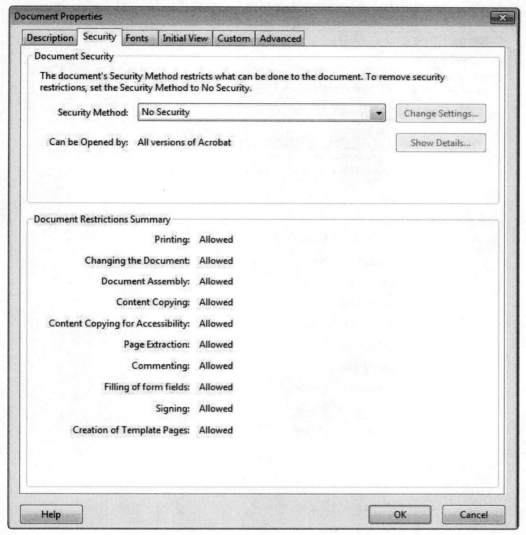

To change the type of security, click on the down arrow next to the **Security Method** box and select the type of security you desire, generally **Password Security** (see Figure 11.98). This will bring up the **Password Security** settings dialog box (Figure 11.99), which allows you to specify the encryption (security level), password (Adobe even tells you how strong the password is), and other permissions. Just follow the prompts.

**Figure 11.98** Accessing Password Security

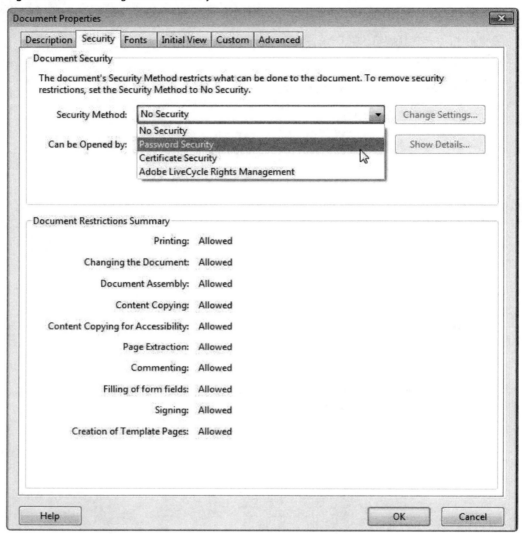

**Figure 11.99**   Password Security Settings

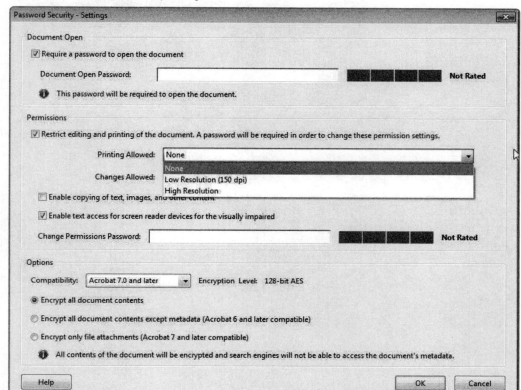

Of note, at this location, and when you use *Save As > Reduced Size PDF*, you can specify with which prior versions of Adobe your PDF will be compatible.

This is an important setting because, unlike you, many other computer users only have the Adobe Reader or are using an earlier version of Adobe Acrobat. Thus, it is recommended that you make documents compatible with Adobe 6.0 and later, or perhaps even Adobe 5.0 and later. Otherwise, you may discover that other users cannot open your PDFs. Please also remember that when you change version compatibility, certain features may be disabled, so be careful when doing so.

# Chapter 12
## TIME-SAVING TIPS TO MAKE YOUR COMPUTER DO WHAT *YOU* WANT

In this chapter, we continue with more tips and shortcuts designed to save time, including tips for using the Internet effectively, using technology in litigation, configuring your computer to work better for you, and other shortcuts. If you adopt only a handful, you will save days (and perhaps even weeks) of time simply by doing your work more efficiently. And the best part is, no computer skills are required.

## SEARCH WISELY: USING THE INTERNET MORE EFFICIENTLY

### Google

Everyone uses Google. Well, almost everyone. When looking for something on the web, most searchers rarely do more than type a brief query (a word or short phrase) into the search box on the main Google page. But you can obtain better, more tailored results by tweaking your queries just a little. Here are some of our favorite search shortcuts and features (sample queries appear in boldface).

### SPECIFIC PHRASES

When you place quotation marks around a group of words, like "book shelf," Google will display only results that include that phrase. Of course, by default, the results you get will be based on the order of the words you entered. So if you search for "shelf book" instead, your results will differ. Similarly, when you place the plus sign in front of one word (without a space), Google will display results

241

that include only the word you typed. For example, a search for **+siegel** will display only those web pages that include Dan's last name.

## SPECIFIC PAGES IN A SITE

The query [word/phrase] site: before a URL (a web address) allows you to search for something within a specific website. Google will display any page at that site that contains the searched word or phrase. For example, the query **siegel site:www.justice.org** will return every page or link on the American Association for Justice (AAJ) website that references Dan's last name.

## SPECIFIC FILE TYPES

Google can display results for a specific word or phrase in a document that exists in particular format, including Microsoft Excel (xls), Microsoft PowerPoint (ppt), Microsoft Word (doc), Microsoft Works (wks, wps, wdb), Portable Document Format (pdf), PostScript (ps), rich text format (rtf), Shockwave Flash (swf), and text (ans, txt). For example, **siegel "PDF"** displays only PDF documents that contain Dan's last name.

## EXCLUDED TERMS

If you include a minus sign (without a space) before a word, Google knows that your results should exclude web pages that contain that particular word. For example, **former presidents—carter** will display websites discussing former presidents *not* named Carter. Google also knows the difference between the minus sign and a hyphen.

## WILD-CARD SEARCHES

The asterisk, or wild card, instructs Google to treat the symbol as a placeholder for unknown words and to display only the most relevant results. Unlike in other programs, in Google the asterisk works only on whole words, not on parts of words. For example, **lawyer * jones** will search for web pages that contain the words "lawyer" and "jones" with a word or name between them, like "lawyer Cyrus Jones."

## OR

If you want results to include any one of a few words, use the word "OR" (in all capital letters). Google will display results with one or more of the desired words. You can also use the "|" symbol instead of "OR." For example, **sotomayor OR scalia** or **sotomayor | scalia** will display pages containing one or both of those names.

## DEFINITIONS

If you type define: at the beginning of a query, Google will return sites that include a definition of the word or words you entered. Note that the definition will be for the entire phrase you entered, not just the first word. For example, **define:summary judgment** will return a list of several websites that offer a definition of that phrase.

## WORDS IN URLS

The term allinurl: at the beginning of a query yields a display of sites that have web addresses that include the specific words entered. Try querying **allinurl:justice department** to see what we mean.

## SYNONYMS

If you place the tilde symbol immediately before a word in a query, Google will display websites that include synonyms for that word. For example, when you search for "**~vehicle parts**," you will also see results that include "auto parts."

## SAVED VERSIONS OF WEBSITES

Typing cache: along with a URL (with no space between the two) will display the page as it appeared the last time you visited it—in other words, the cached version. To see your cached version of Google's home page, type **cache:www.google.com**.

## WEBSITE LINKS

Placing link: before a URL will display pages that have hyperlinks (clickable links) to the specified page. Try this: **link:www.justice.org**.

## SIMILAR SITES

When you type related: before a URL, Google will display web pages that have content similar to what is found at that address. See what a search for **related:www.justice.org** turns up.

## WEBSITE INFORMATION

Using info: in a search will yield links to information about a particular site and some additional search suggestions. For example, **info:www.justice.org** brings up a description of AAJ and a link to its home page, and Google also offers several AAJ-related search options.

## GOOGLE CALCULATOR

Google includes a sophisticated built-in calculator that works by entering the desired calculation into the Google search box or the Google toolbar (an add-on to most Web browsers). The calculator can perform basic arithmetic (addition, subtraction, multiplication, and division), advanced math (trigonometry, logarithms), and computation of units of measure and conversions (currency, weights, distances). You can find excellent examples on Google Guide (www.googleguide. com/calculator.html).

## WEATHER

When you type weather and the name or ZIP code of a specific place, Google will display the location's weather. For example, Dan types weather 19083 or weather Havertown, PA to learn what weather conditions to expect in his area.

## Internet Explorer

### TYPE SHORTER URLS

Never type www. and .com. Instead type the website name (e.g., amazon) and then Ctrl+Enter. Internet Explorer (and most other browsers) will add www. and .com and take you to the site. However, if the site you are searching for has an extension other than .com (such as .org, .biz, etc.), you will want to include those in the URL when you search

### USE INTERNET EXPLORER'S LINKS TOOLBAR

Never type website addresses more than once. When you use the Internet Explorer Favorites bar, shown in Figure 12.1, you can save and organize your bookmarks by category or topic—for example, all federal court websites or all social media websites. Here's how to do it:

It is even more helpful to synchronize your bookmarks so that they are the same everywhere (i.e., on your home computer,

**Figure 12.1**   Internet Explorer Favorites Bar

on your office computer, and even on your phone). You can do this using a bookmark manager such as one of these:

- Linkman (http://www.outertech.com/en/bookmark-manager)
- Xmarks (http://www.xmarks.com/)
- Mozilla Weave (https://mozillalabs.com/en-US/weave/)
- Google Bookmarks (https://www.google.com/bookmarks/)

## ORGANIZING FAVORITES

Use "favorites" to keep track of the websites you visit frequently or want to remember in Internet Explorer. If you're on a site that you want to make a favorite, click the *Favorites* button, *Add to favorites*, and then *Add*. You then select where to add the website, such as in a folder, etc. To show the Favorites bar, right-click the **Favorites** button and click **Favorites bar**. It will appear below the address bar.

To go to a favorite site, click the *Favorites* button and then click any site in the list or click the site on the Favorites bar. If you want to keep the Favorites list open all the time, pin it to your browser window.

Keep track of your favorites more easily by organizing them into folders. For example, group news sites into a "Daily news" folder, or shopping sites into "My shops."

- Open Internet Explorer by clicking the Internet Explorer icon on the task bar.
- Click the *Favorites* button.
- Click the down arrow next to *Add to favorites*, and choose *Organize favorites* from the drop-down menu.
- Click *New Folder* and enter a name.
- Drag favorites into the new folder.

To delete folders or favorites, right-click the folder or favorite you want to delete, and then click *Delete*.

To rename folders or favorites, right-click the folder or favorite you want to rename, and then click *Rename*.

To sort your favorites alphabetically, right-click any favorite or folder, and then click *Sort by name*.

## IMPORT AND EXPORT FAVORITES

Internet Explorer lets you import your favorites from other browsers, so switching between sites doesn't mean switching browsers. You can also import favorites from older versions of Internet Explorer and back up your favorites by exporting them to a file.

Here's how to import favorites from other browsers:

- Click the *Favorites* button.
- Click the down arrow next to **Add to Favorites**, and then select *Import and export*.
- Click *Import from another browser*, and then click Next.
- Select the browser or browsers you want to import favorites from, click *Import*, and then click *Finish*.

## BACK UP YOUR FAVORITES

Even if you use a bookmark-syncing service, it's still a good idea to back up your favorites every few months, or if you're going to download a newer version of Internet Explorer. You can also export favorites to another browser using your backup copy.

To back up your favorites, follow these steps:

- Open Internet Explorer by clicking the **Internet Explorer** icon on the task bar.
- Click the *Favorites* button.
- Click the down arrow next to **Add to favorites**, and then select *Import and export*.
- Select *Export to a file*, and then click *Next*.
- Select favorites (and any other settings) that you'd like to export, and then click *Next*.
- Click *Browse*, select a folder or drive to export your favorites to, and enter a name for your bookmarks file. Click *Save* when you're done. (For example, after you click *Browse*, select *Documents*, and then enter the file name "bookmarks." Your bookmarks will be saved in your Documents folder.)
- Click *Export*, and then click *Finish*.

To import favorites into Internet Explorer, follow these steps:

- Open Internet Explorer by clicking the **Internet Explorer** icon on the task bar.
- Click the **Favorites** button.
- Click the down arrow next to **Add to favorites**, and then select **Import and export**.
- Select **Import from a file**, and then click **Next**.
- Select **Favorites**, and then click **Next**.
- Click **Browse**, find and select the backup file you created earlier, click **Open**, and then click **Next**.
- Click **Import**, and then click **Finish**.

## Get It and Send It Electronically

Since Dan opened his own firm in 2005, he has never provided discovery or other materials in paper form. Instead, he either sends the items as e-mail attachments or on a CD. This enables him to Bates number every item using Adobe Acrobat Professional (assuring no one claims something was missing) and to reduce or nearly eliminate the costs of printing, copying, postage, envelopes, and the time involved.

Another advantage to Dan's process is that when you receive a document related to a client's case, you can scan it, save it, and then send the document to the client, further reducing the number of copies made and the amount of paper used. It's more economical all around.

## CONFIGURE YOUR COMPUTER FOR INCREASED PRODUCTIVITY

Computers were designed by tech geeks, not by the people who use them. After all, no one would ever intentionally format a document with the line spacing that comes with Microsoft Word, yet many users never change these settings.

We recommend that you make some changes right out of the box.

First, right-click on the Windows **Start** button/icon. (Its location and appearance will vary depending on your operating system). Next, click **Properties** (see Figure 12.2). From here, you can control how things look on your computer.

**Figure 12.2** Accessing Properties

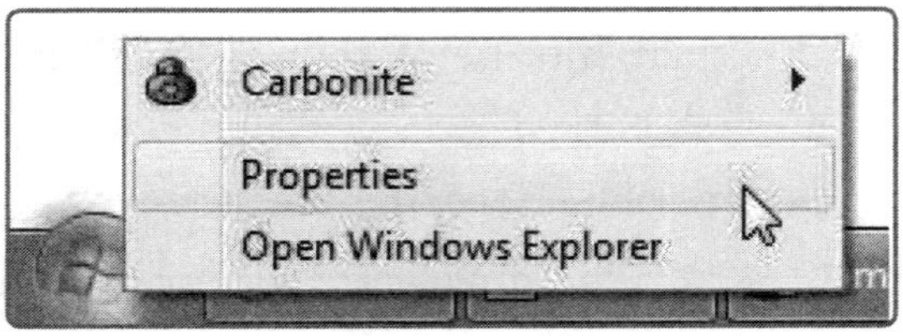

## Configuring the Task Bar

You can find the task bar settings under the **Taskbar** tab in the **Properties** dialog box, as shown in Figure 12.3.

**Figure 12.3** Task Bar Settings

- **Lock the taskbar** prevents any changes.
- **Auto-hide the taskbar** allows you to hide it unless you mouse over it (giving you more desktop space)—highly recommended.
- **Use small icons** reduces icon size so the task bar takes up less space.
- **Notification area** lets you see which notifications appear on the task bar.

## CHANGING THE TASK BAR LOCATION

The task bar is the long horizontal bar that is almost always at the bottom of your screen. Most users keep the task bar visible. It has three main sections: (1) the **Start** button, which opens the **Start** menu; (2) the middle section, which shows the programs and files that are open and lets you switch between them; and (3) the notification area, which provides the time and date and the status of certain programs and computer settings.

By default, the task bar is located at the bottom of the screen, as shown in Figure 12.4. We recommend that you move the task bar to the left (or to the right if you're left-handed). Doing so will allow you to see more. When you want to see what programs are open, they are not all bunched together; you can see them all and read their titles very easily.

**Figure 12.4**   Default Task Bar Location

Because monitors are wide-screen, you have more screen real estate horizontally than vertically, especially when you consider that users scroll up and down web pages, not left and right. Thus, placing the task bar on the left or right is a more efficient use of space.

When your task bar is along the bottom, it usually takes up just one line. But because of the ample space on the side, you can bump it up to two or three columns. This means that you can see more icons in your system tray and your Quick Launch bar, and your running task buttons are all of a uniform height and width, instead of scaling based on how many are open. Figure 12.5 below shows an example of a task bar set to the side of the screen.

If you have the task bar on the bottom of the screen, combining buttons makes it easier to see information. There are three options for combining task bar buttons: always, never, or when the task bar is full. (These options are accessible through the task bar settings, shown in Figure 12.3 above.)

## Start Menu (Windows 7 and Earlier Versions)

Customizing the **Start** menu is the key to your computer (see Figures 12.6 and 12.7). This lets you control how everything works on the menu and gives you instant access to areas of your computer that aren't automatically available without multiple mouse clicks. To begin, go to the *Start* button and right-click, then select *Properties*.

**Figure 12.5**    Task Bar on the Side of the Screen

**Figure 12.6**    Accessing the Customization Feature for the Start Menu

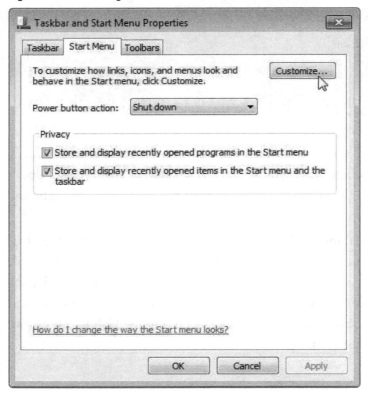

**Figure 12.7**   Customization Options

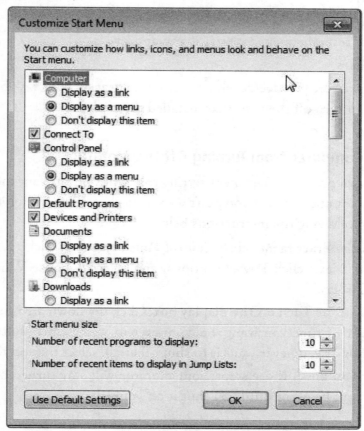

- **Display**

  **Display as link; Display as menu; Don't display.** These options let you show various categories (Computer, Control Panel, Documents, Downloads, Games, Music, Personal folder, Pictures, Recorded TV, Videos) from the **Start** menu, a huge time-saver.

- **Icons**

  Change the size of icons, which can be a big improvement, depending upon your vision or other issues.

- **Power Button**

  Most people want the power button to turn off their computer, yet the button isn't programmed to do that. Here is where you change it.

- **Privacy**

  If you work on a shared computer, or just want privacy, you can control which "recently opened items," if any, appear.

- **Toolbars**

  This is where you decide which toolbars appear on your task bar or where you can turn off the ones that installed themselves.

## Stop Your Computer from Turning Off the Monitor

Windows has a power management setting that will shut off your monitor after a specified amount of time. If you don't want it to shut off your monitor, you can change it by following the instructions below.

- From the **Start** menu, click **Control Panel**, and then click **Hardware and Sound**. Next, click Power Options, and select "Choose When to Turn Off Display."

- Look for the **Turn off the display** box. Click the down arrow to select the amount of time you want the computer to wait before shutting off the monitor. If you never want it to shut off at all, select that option.

- After you finish those steps, your monitor will stay turned on until you want it to be off or until you shut it off yourself.

## Customize Which Commands Appear on the Status Bar

The status bar is the bar that appears across the bottom of the screen in many programs and provides information about the active file. For example, the status bar in Microsoft Word shows the active page number, number of pages in the document, and word count.

In several Microsoft Office programs, including Word, Excel, PowerPoint, and Access, you can customize what appears on the status bar.

To do this, right-click the status bar, and then click to show or hide the options you want.

## SHORTCUTS AND OTHER "TRICKS"

We all love shortcuts, whether it's a faster way to get somewhere or just a quicker way to get a project done, yet we don't customize our computers. To be efficient, you need to use shortcuts and other tricks.

## Put Shortcuts on the Desktop

There are two possible methods to create a shortcut on the desktop. The steps below are also shown in Figures 12.8 through 12.12.

### CREATING A SHORTCUT TO A PROGRAM OR FILE

- Right-click an open area on the desktop, click **New**, and then click **Shortcut**.

- Click **Browse**.

- Locate the program or file to which you want to create a shortcut, click it, click **Open**, and then click **Next**.

- Type a name for the shortcut. If a **Finish** button appears at the bottom of the dialog box, click it. If a **Next** button appears at the bottom of the dialog box, click it, click the icon you want to use for the shortcut, and then click the **Finish** button.

**Figure 12.8**   Accessing the Shortcut Feature

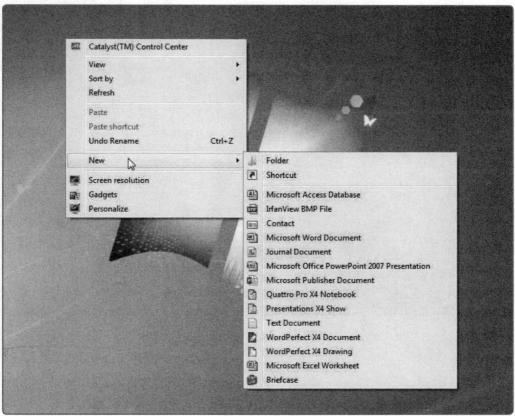

**Figure 12.9**   Browse

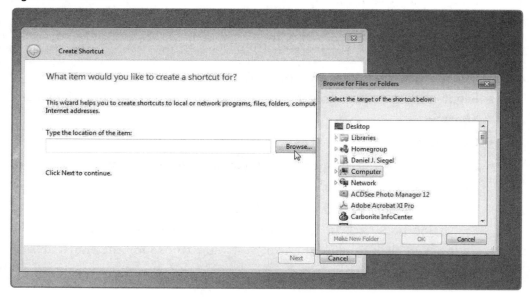

**Figure 12.10**   Locating the File for a Shortcut

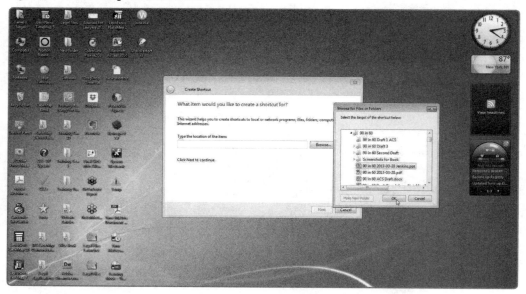

**Figure 12.11**   Location of the File or Program for Shortcut

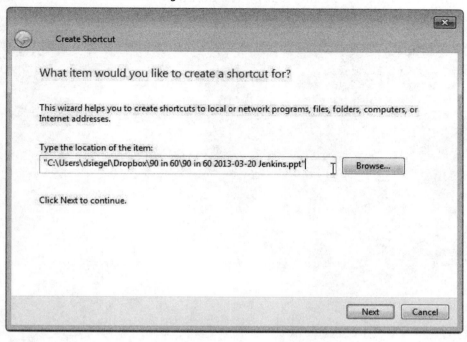

**Figure 12.12**   Naming the Shortcut

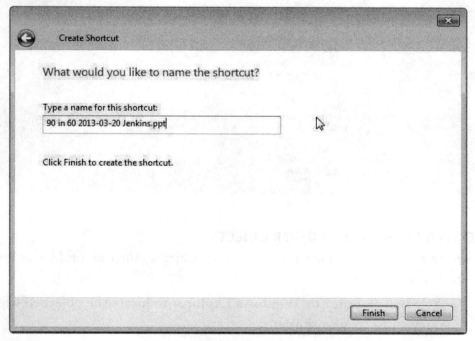

Figure 12.13 shows the shortcut on the desktop.

**Figure 12.13** Shortcut on Desktop

## CREATING SHORTCUTS TO OTHER OBJECTS

To create a shortcut on the desktop to other objects (such as a folder or computer), follow these steps:

- Use **My Computer** or **Windows Explorer** to locate the object to which you want to create a shortcut.
- Right-click the object, and then click *Create Shortcut*.
- Drag the new shortcut to an open area on the desktop.

## Helpful Tips

To modify settings for a shortcut, right-click the shortcut and then click **Properties**. Settings that can be modified include the key combination used to start the shortcut and whether the program starts minimized, maximized, or normally.

To delete a shortcut, right-click the shortcut and then click **Delete**. You can also drag the shortcut to the **Recycle Bin**. When you delete a shortcut to an object, the original object is not deleted.

After you create a shortcut to a printer, you can print documents by dragging the documents to the printer shortcut. The program used to print the document will open briefly and then close.

## Use Built-In Keyboard Shortcuts

Keyboard shortcuts are combinations of two or more keys that, when pressed, can be used to perform a task that would typically require a mouse or other pointing device. Keyboard shortcuts can make it easier to interact with your computer, saving you time and effort as you work with Windows and other programs. Most programs also provide accelerator keys that can make it easier to work with menus and other commands. Check the menus of programs for accelerator keys. If a letter is underlined in a menu, it usually means that pressing the **Alt** key in combination with the underlined key will have the same effect as clicking that menu item. Pressing the **Alt** key in some programs, such as Paint and WordPad, shows commands that are labeled with additional keys that you can press to use them.

### SPECIAL CHARACTERS

A special character is a character, like the section (§) or paragraph (❡) symbol, that is not located on your keyboard. You can insert special characters by using **Character Map** or by pressing a combination of keys on your keyboard.

### USING CHARACTER MAP

Character Map lets you view the characters that are available in a selected font. Using Character Map, you can copy individual characters or a group of characters to the Clipboard and paste them into any program that can display them.

- Open Character Map by clicking the **Start** button and typing "Character Map" in the search box. In the list of results, click **Character Map**.
- Click the **Font** list, and then select the font you want to use.

- Click the special character you want to insert into the document.
- Click *Select*, and then click *Copy*.
- Open your document and click the location in the document where you want the special character to appear.
- Click the *Edit* menu, and then click *Paste* (or Ctrl+P).

### USING KEYBOARD SHORTCUTS

You can also create special characters, such as paragraph symbols and other items, by typing a series of keys in conjunction with the **Alt** key or using your computer's internal character map.

To locate and insert the special characters without knowing their key codes, do the following:

- Open Character Map by clicking the *Start* menu.
- In the search box, type "Character Map," and then, in the list of results, click *Character Map*.
- Click the *Font* list, and then click the font you want to use.
- Click the special character you want to insert into the document.
- Click *Select*, and then click *Copy*.
- Open your document and click the location in the document where you want the special character to appear.
- Click the *Edit* menu, and then click *Paste*.

To locate and insert the special characters using their keyboard combination codes, you will need a character map. The one mentioned above lists the keystrokes for each character. Alternatively, various websites list them. One very good one is http://www.forlang.wsu.edu/help/keyboards.asp. Here's how to insert the character using the special characters codes:

- Ensure that the *Num Lock* key has been pressed to activate the numeric key section of the keyboard.
- Press the *Alt* key and hold it down.
- While the *Alt* key is pressed, type the sequence of numbers (on the numeric keypad) from the Alt code in the table in the appendix that corresponds to the character you want to type.
- Release the *Alt* key, and the character will appear.

There are some gaps in the numerical sequence of Alt codes because either those elements do not exist or they are duplicates of elements listed elsewhere.

Some word processing programs will not recognize all of these Alt functions.

## WINDOWS SYSTEM KEY COMBINATIONS

- **Ctrl+Shift+Esc**: Opens Task Manager
- **Ctrl+Esc**: Open **Start** menu
- **Alt+Tab**: Switch between open programs
- **Alt+F4**: Quit program
- **Shift+Delete**: Delete item permanently
- **Windows Logo+L**: Lock the computer (without using Ctrl+Alt+Delete)

## WINDOWS PROGRAM KEY COMBINATIONS

- **Ctrl+C**: Copy
- **Ctrl+X**: Cut
- **Ctrl+V**: Paste
- **Ctrl+Z**: Undo
- **Ctrl+B**: Bold
- **Ctrl+U**: Underline
- **Ctrl+I**: Italic

## GENERAL KEYBOARD-ONLY COMMANDS

- **F1**: Start Windows Help
- **F10**: Activate menu bar options
- **Shift+F10**: Open a shortcut menu for the selected item (this is the same as right-clicking an object)
- **Ctrl+Esc**: Open the Start menu (use the arrow keys to select an item)
- **Ctrl+Esc or Esc**: Select the Start button (press the **Tab** key to select the task bar; press Shift+F10 for a context menu)
- **Ctrl+Shift+Esc**: Open Windows Task Manager
- **Alt+down arrow**: Open a drop-down list box
- **Alt+Tab**: Switch to another running program (hold down the *Alt* key and then press the *Tab* key to view the task-switching window)
- **Shift**: Press and hold down the *Shift* key while you insert a CD-ROM to bypass the automatic-run feature

- **Alt+underlined letter in menu**: Open the menu
- **Alt+F4**: Close the current window
- **Ctrl+F4**: Close the current MDI window
- **Alt+F6**: Switch between multiple windows in the same program (for example, when the Notepad Find dialog box is displayed, Alt+F6 switches between the Find dialog box and the main Notepad window)

### TO COPY A FILE
- Press and hold down the *Ctrl* key while you drag a file to another folder.
- **Ctrl+C** (or Ctrl+Insert)

### TO CREATE A SHORTCUT
Press and hold down the *Ctrl* and *Shift* keys while you drag a file to the desktop or a folder.

### GENERAL FOLDER/SHORTCUT CONTROL

| Keystroke | Action |
| --- | --- |
| F4 | Select the Go to a Different Folder box and move down the entries in the box (if the toolbar is active in Windows Explorer) |
| F5 | Refresh the current window |
| F6 | Move among panes in Windows Explorer |
| Ctrl+G | Open the Go to Folder tool (in Windows 95 Windows Explorer only) |
| Ctrl+Z | Undo the last command |
| Ctrl+A | Select all the items in the current window |
| Backspace | Switch to the parent folder |
| Shift+Click the **Close** button | For folders, close the current folder plus all parent folders |

## CUSTOMIZE YOUR PROGRAMS AND TOOLBARS

Many people don't realize you can customize most program toolbars. For example, you can add or remove tools and commands on any toolbar in Microsoft Windows.

## Customizing in Pre-ribbon Versions of Office

### ADD A TOOL OR COMMAND TO A TOOLBAR

- Select *View > Toolbars > Customize*. The Customize dialog box appears.
- Click the *Command* tab. The Commands panel is displayed. This panel contains a list of tool and command categories as well as all tools and commands in each category.
- Click and hold on a tool or command name in the list of tools and commands.
- Drag the tool or command name to the desired position on the toolbar. An insertion cursor should appear.
- Release the mouse button to place the tool or command on the toolbar.

### REMOVE A TOOL OR COMMAND FROM A TOOLBAR

- Select *View > Toolbars > Customize*. The Customize dialog box appears.
- Click and hold on a tool or command name in the toolbar.
- Drag the tool or command name anywhere outside of the toolbar.
- Release the mouse button to remove the tool or command from the toolbar.

### MOVE A TOOL OR COMMAND ON A TOOLBAR

- Select the *View > Toolbars > Customize*. The Customize dialog box appears.
- Click and hold on a tool or command name in the toolbar.
- Drag the tool or command name to the desired position on the toolbar. An insertion cursor should appear.
- Release the mouse button to reposition the tool or command on the toolbar.

## Customizing in Ribbon Versions of Office (Using the Quick Access Toolbar)

The Quick Access Toolbar is a customizable toolbar in the Office Suite that permits you to go directly to saved commands regardless of which tab is displayed. You can place the Quick Access Toolbar either above or below the Ribbon, and you can add buttons for popular commands to the Quick Access Toolbar.

### ADD A COMMAND TO THE QUICK ACCESS TOOLBAR

You can add a command to the **Quick Access** toolbar directly from commands that are displayed on the ribbon.

- Click the appropriate tab or group to display the command that you want to add to the Quick Access toolbar.
- Right-click the command, and then click *Add to Quick Access Toolbar* on the drop-down menu.

### ADD A COMMAND TO THE QUICK ACCESS TOOLBAR THAT ISN'T ON THE RIBBON

- Right-click on the *Quick Access* toolbar, or right-click on the down arrow on the right end of the toolbar.
- Click *Customize Quick Access Toolbar*, which opens a dialog box.
- In the dialog box, click the down arrow on the "Choose commands from" box, and click *Commands Not in the Ribbon*.
- Find the command in the list, and then click *Add*.

## Remove a Command from the Quick Access Toolbar

- Right-click the command you want to remove from the Quick Access toolbar.
- Click *Remove from Quick Access Toolbar* on the drop-down menu.

### CHANGE THE ORDER OF THE COMMANDS ON THE QUICK ACCESS TOOLBAR

- Right-click the *Quick Access* toolbar.
- Click *Customize Quick Access Toolbar* on the drop-down menu, which opens a dialog box.
- In the dialog box, under *Customize Quick Access Toolbar* (on the right), click the command you want to move.
- Click the arrow buttons to move up or down.

### CUSTOMIZE THE QUICK ACCESS TOOLBAR BY USING THE OPTIONS COMMAND

You can add, remove, and change the order of the commands on the Quick Access toolbar by using the Options command.

- Click the *File* tab.
- Click *Options*.
- Click *Quick Access Toolbar*.
- Make the changes you want.

## EXPLORE YOUR COMPUTER

Windows Explorer is the tool used to view files on a Windows computer. Just click on the Computer icon on your desktop and it will open the file tree that allows you to navigate to another folder or location. Once you have the file tree open, you have many options for viewing the files:

### Icons

- extra large
- large
- medium
- small

The icons view places the emphasis on icons, although file titles are also shown. The tiles view is similar, but in addition to icons and titles, this view shows the file type and size as well. The content view shows the icon, title, author, date modified, and size of the file.

### List

The list view shows the title of the file accompanied by a very small icon. Dan finds this view the most helpful because it allows you to view more files in a window than any other way, so you see more and scroll less.

### Details

The details view shows you the icon, the title, and the date the file was last modified, as well as the type and size of the file. Allison finds this view to be the most effective for her; it has the information she needs but is still small enough to fit many items on one screen.

### Tiles

The tiles view displays icons, sorted alphabetically into vertical columns, with information about the file next to each icon.

### Content

The content view displays medium icons in a vertical column with information about the date files were modified.

Once you've chosen your preferred view, right-click to sort files (for example, by name or date) to view them more quickly and efficiently.

# Conclusion

Lawyers contend with numerous competing priorities on a daily basis, and, as such, productivity will continue to be a challenge into the foreseeable future. In this book, we've given you strategies for defining your most important tasks and projects so you can focus your efforts on the clients and activities that will bring you the highest return and hopefully the most satisfaction in your practice.

We've provided you with tips on setting goals and planning the tasks required to reach those goals. We've talked about ways to eliminate (or at least limit) distractions and interruptions. We've helped you clear out obstacles to your success, whether those obstacles are in the form of paper or electronic clutter or bad clients who keep you from doing your best work for those who appreciate (and pay for) it. We've shown you how to get more done by delegating effectively, conducting more valuable meetings, using your calendar as a tool to complete important tasks, and creating systems for repetitive tasks or activities to create a more consistent client experience.

In Part II of this book, we walked you through many of the most popular technology platforms and software programs used by lawyers today and gave you some "insider tips" and little-known tricks to help you accomplish your daily work more efficiently, without sacrificing quality or effectiveness.

Although you'll never be 100 percent productive or eliminate distractions completely (lawyers *are* human, after all), we are confident that the strategies, tips, and tricks you've learned in this book can help you get much more work done in much less time, provide better service to your clients, and even improve your profitability.

# Index

Page numbers followed by "*f*" refer to figures. Page numbers followed by "n" refer to footnotes.